T0356796

ALASKA

OFF THE BEATEN PATH® SERIES

SEVENTH EDITION

ALASKA

OFF THE BEATEN PATH®

LISA MALONEY

Globe
Pequot

ESSEX, CONNECTICUT

All the information in this guidebook is subject to change. We recommend that you call ahead to obtain current information before traveling.

Globe Pequot

An imprint of The Globe Pequot Publishing Group, Inc.
64 South Main Street
Essex, CT 06426
www.globepequot.com

Distributed by NATIONAL BOOK NETWORK

Copyright © 2025 by The Globe Pequot Publishing Group, Inc.

All rights reserved. No part of this book may be reproduced in any form or by any electronic or mechanical means, including information storage and retrieval systems, without written permission from the publisher, except by a reviewer who may quote passages in a review.

British Library Cataloguing in Publication Information available

Library of Congress Cataloging-in-Publication Data Available

ISBN 978-1-4930-8727-3 (paper)
ISBN 978-1-4930-8728-0 (electronic)

∞™ The paper used in this publication meets the minimum requirements of American National Standard for Information Sciences—Permanence of Paper for Printed Library Materials, ANSI/NISO Z39.48-1992.

To everyone who's shown me ways of doing, and being, better. I hope to continue learning and growing.
—Lisa Maloney

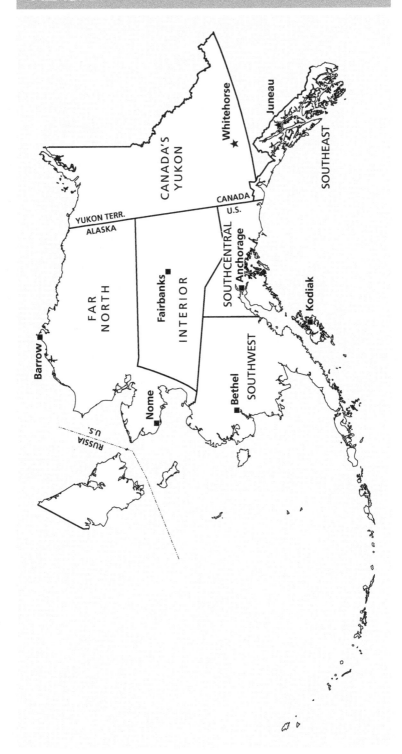

Contents

About the Author

Lisa's parents dragged her to Alaska at a young age, (figuratively) kicking and screaming because she didn't know what an "Alaska" was and was sure she wouldn't like it. In a way, that early sentiment was correct: She didn't like Alaska. She loved it, and is still here more than 35 years later.

Sometime around 2005, Lisa got her start as an outdoors columnist and reporter with local newspapers. She went on to serve as senior editor for *Alaska Magazine;* to pen *Moon Alaska, Day Hiking Southcentral Alaska,* and *50 Hikes Around Anchorage;* and write for *National Geographic, Condé Nast Traveler,* the *New Zealand Herald, Fodor's Travel, Frommer's,* and many more.

When Lisa's not busy writing you'll probably find her reading, hiking, kayaking, dancing, or playing traditional Irish music—one of many passions that tend to lure her off the beaten path—on the button accordion and fiddle.

Introduction

Chances are, if you stay here long enough, someone's going to ask you: "So, what brought you to Alaska?"

In my case, my parents dragged me here. My father was in the Air Force, and our previous duty station was overseas in what was, at the time, West Germany. Alaska also counted as an overseas assignment, and if you took two overseas assignments in a row you got to choose your next duty station. So, much to my 8- or 9-year-old chagrin (nobody remembers exactly how old I was when we got here), off to Alaska we went.

I had no idea what an "Alaska" was, and when I asked my mother about it she explained that there would be a lot of mountains and snow. My young mind really had no way of conceptualizing what she described so, somehow, I decided Alaska must be one long ridgeline of mountain peaks, all perpetually covered in snow.

"But Mom," I wailed with all the fervor my young, horse-obsessed body could muster, "There won't be any horses!"

She assured me that not only were there horses in Alaska, they wore special shoes to help them deal with the ice and snow.

"But they'll be all crooked from walking around the mountains," I declared, picturing the horses trudging stolid, one-way laps around that long mountain ridge. Surely they'd end up with their "uphill" legs being shorter, to cope with the slant of the mountains.

Mom continued to reassure me that Alaskan horses did have four legs of all the same length, but I'm pretty sure I remained stubbornly skeptical until we landed in Alaska and I discovered that the people, moose, and dogs weren't built crooked, either.

The ironic part is that, as much as I protested our initial arrival in Alaska, I'm the family member who chose to stay here. My Alaska odometer recently ticked over to 35 years in-state and, while I'm conscious that I am and will forever be a transplant, I've put down enough roots here that it feels like home.

I happen to live in Alaska's biggest city, Anchorage, which hovers a little under 300,000 people—about 40 percent of the state's entire population. Anchorage isn't perfect, and it's definitely not off the beaten path. But it made a fine base camp for my youthful adventures, especially once I had my driver's license and discovered that, with enough blankets, mattress pads, and creativity, I could turn almost any vehicle into a budget RV.

The rest of my family wasn't particularly outdoorsy, so they watched in perplexity as my young self first begged to be allowed to play in the greenbelt behind the house (my older sibling grudgingly going along to stand watch for moose and, I suppose, any signs of stranger danger), then started hiking once I hit my late teens. Sometimes I hit the trail with friends, but often I went on my own, in cheerful and knowing defiance of the common-sense dictate for hiking in groups. I so dearly loved sitting on isolated mountaintops watching "cloud TV" as puffs of water vapor scudded across the sky or sometimes, if the peak was high enough and the clouds low enough, boiled along the mountain slopes below me. I also loved "bird TV" and "moose TV," which usually involved me sitting in the bushes or in a tree at a respectful distance, just watching the wildlife go on about their lives.

I think what I'm trying to express is that although it took me a little while to grow from that protesting child into the adult I am now, thoroughly struck by the same fascination and enthrallment that draws millions of visitors to Alaska every year, once that fascination finally hit me it never went away. As preoccupied as I can get with everyday responsibilities like work schedules and bills, all I have to do is lift my head, catch sight of the Chugach Mountains that ring the city on two sides, and at least some of those preoccupations wash away. I still stop to watch moose TV, fox TV, bird TV, creek TV, and whatever other "nature TV" is available from a safe distance—enjoying all the ways nature and her wild unpredictability can grasp my attention and smooth the bunched-up wrinkles of stress and hurry out of it.

I also love Alaska's ever-rotating kaleidoscope of seasons. Although in some years it can feel genuinely difficult to say farewell to summer, there is always something interesting going on: Whether it's trees and tundra plants changing color, berries ripening, leaves falling, lakes and rivers freezing over, snow falling, ice melting, the first green buds of spring leafing out, migratory birds coming back to their summer home . . . here we exist in a glorious tumble of seasons, and if the season you most love is on its way out, you can trust that it will come back around before long.

You do need to keep that seasonality in mind when planning your visit: For example, you'll pretty much never be able to see the northern lights during the height of summer (even when they shine, the night skies up here are just too bright to see them) and you can't go bear-watching during the winter because, hey, the bears are asleep for the season. But if you pick one season or another to visit in, you can enjoy an almost never-ending parade of ways to experience Alaska. (Except in spring: Try to avoid spring if you can, at least in Southcentral and Interior Alaska, because it tends to be the muddy, dusty season of snowmelt and bare trees that haven't yet leafed out for the summer. If you want to visit in the spring I suggest heading to Southeast Alaska, where that season always feels more lush and youthful. Fall, on the other hand, can be absolutely spectacular in Southcentral and Interior Alaska.)

Lastly, if you've heard the enduring joke that Anchorage (being such a big city) is "just 30 minutes from the real Alaska," it's not entirely wrong: We do have such a profusion of urban amenities here that the city itself doesn't always feel that remote. But growing up here has shown me that in some ways, you don't have to try that hard to get off the beaten path. It just happens, whether you're in the city or out of it, almost like slipping in and out of alternate dimensions: Maybe one moment you're walking a paved trail in the city, and the next you're face to face with a moose or a bear. Or one moment you're driving on a normal enough highway and the next you're on a boat, watching humpback whales breach and calving glaciers dump tons of ice into the sea.

All of which means that Alaska is the perfect place for nudging yourself out of your comfort zone to whatever degree you desire—or bringing your comfort zone with you as you explore a place unlike any other. When you plan a visit here you are quite literally choosing your own adventures, and only you can say how close you want to get to the edge of wildness that, I think, fascinates us all to some degree or another.

Maybe you want to see glaciers from the comfort of a plush motorcoach, or gaze out the window of a train's full-service dining room. Maybe you have a tent, a camp stove, and plans to hike and camp your way across the state—or you're willing to watch bears from the relative safety of a lodge, but don't really want to camp in a tent surrounded by bear-resistant electric fencing.

However you decide to visit Alaska, whichever paths (beaten or not) you choose to start your explorations, you can trust that it will be breathtaking. Bears, moose, and sometimes even wolves might ramble across the road while sea lions moan and growl from the water, or orcas—killer whales, the wolves of the sea—may surge through the water as humpbacks leap and splash like bus-sized kindergarteners. Glaciers might stand still and silent—or dump tons of ice onto land or sea. And mountain vistas will fill more than your camera lens can capture.

No matter what, as long as you're ready to get up and leave your hotel room (or cabin, or tent), you won't be disappointed.

A Very Small Sketch of a Very Big State

All of Alaska, of course, is located north and west of what geographers call "the contiguous states" of the United States. The Canadian provinces of British Columbia and the Yukon Territory sit in between. Consider this: If Alaska were laid atop a map of the contiguous United States, its size would be one-fifth of the country. It is larger than the three other largest states in the country combined, and it boasts some of the tallest mountains and longest rivers in the world.

In fact, when traveling from one end of the state to the other, you'll encounter varying climates and vastly different landscapes. It's as if Alaska is several countries within itself.

That's why it's best to break Alaska into five generally categorized geographic regions. The southernmost of Alaska's five regions, and closest to the Lower 48, as Alaskans call these sister states, is **Southeast Alaska.** It's a place of thousands of forested islands plus a long sliver of mainland abutting northern British Columbia. **Southcentral Alaska** forms an arch around the top of the Gulf of Alaska and extends inland roughly to the Alaska Range of mountains, a towering wall of peaks and masses that separates Southcentral from **Interior Alaska.** Interior Alaska, in turn, forms the huge middle of the state, with Canada's Yukon Territory to the east of it. The Interior's westerly border stops just short of the Bering Sea. Farther north, in fact as far north as you can get and still be in North America, lies **Far North Alaska.** Finally, **Southwest Alaska** takes in the westernmost approaches of the Alaska mainland, the Alaska Peninsula, Kodiak Island, the long, long string of Aleutian Islands that extends almost to Japan, plus the Pribilof Islands and others of the Bering Sea.

In this book I include a sixth region, **Canada's Yukon Territory,** because—since it is adjacent both to Southeast and Interior Alaska—you cannot drive from the Alaska panhandle to the main body of Alaska without going through this friendly, fascinating portion of Canada.

Some Notes and Cautions

First, a bit about the Alaska lifestyle and dress. Because we are off the beaten path, things are pretty informal all over the state. Friendly is a way of life up here, and you never have to worry about asking an Alaskan for help, or directions, or for the answer to what you think may be a dumb question. "Comfortably casual" is the dress code of the day, every day, even in big city hotels and restaurants. Ladies can certainly wear a cocktail dress or dressy pantsuit in the evening, and their escorts can likewise wear a coat and tie if they'd like, but it really isn't necessary.

For outdoor wear, comfortable walking shoes (or broken-in boots if you're a hiker) are a must. The weather can vary wildly all over the state, so plan to do what Alaskans do: Dress in layers that start with light shirts and/or undershirts then graduate to heavier shirts, sweaters, and outerwear that repels wind and water. A puffy jacket, which has either down or synthetic insulation inside it, can be especially useful for keeping warm without adding a lot of weight or bulk to your luggage. Layering allows you to add protection or to peel off excess clothing as the weather dictates. *Very important:* A lightweight combination windbreaker/raincoat should always be at the top of your pack or suitcase.

Now about money: Truth to tell, the cost of living is higher in Alaska than in most other states. Depending on where you are (in a large, easily accessible city or a remote bush community), costs for lodging and food could be the same as you're accustomed to paying, or only a few percentage points higher—or they could be a great deal more. I have tried to show prices for most admissions, meals, overnights, and other costs. At the time of this writing, all the prices (plus telephone numbers, addresses, emails, websites, and other such data) were current. But things can change; hotel and meal prices, in particular, may well be higher when you make your trip. When a hotel or B&B price is quoted here, it's usually for a double. Singles may (or may not) be less; extra guests in a room usually cost more. There is no statewide sales tax in Alaska, but most municipalities impose one on goods, services, and overnight accommodations. Sales taxes are not included in the prices quoted in this book. Also, keep in mind that many businesses are open only in the summer—either May through September or June through August—and prices quoted here reflect summer rates.

Remember that when you travel in the Yukon, distances are measured in kilometers, not miles; when speed limits are posted at 90 kilometers per hour, that's the same as 55 miles per hour in the United States. Likewise, our Canadian friends pump gasoline in liters, not gallons.

Cell phone service is commonplace in most Alaska communities but ranges from sparse to non-existent in more remote areas, and you will encounter occasional dead spots or gaps in service, even on our highways and other areas that aren't so far from city centers. Cell phone service has vastly improved over the years, but it's still best not to rely exclusively on a cell phone for communications. Also, while cities in Alaska have all the conveniences of Lower 48 places, including 911 service, such emergency response systems are not in place in smaller, rural communities.

Friends from Outside often ask, "When is the best time to visit Alaska?" The answer is, anytime you want to come. Summer obviously ranks as Alaska's most popular season, but the "shoulder" months of May, September, and early October offer the advantages of fewer crowds, often discounted prices, and an unhurried, more relaxed pace of living.

Winter is coming into its own as a visitor season, too, with an active, statewide agenda of downhill and cross-country skiing, sled dog mushing and racing, winter carnivals, and viewing the eerie and spectacular aurora borealis, the northern lights. Obviously, you have to dress for the season (snug base layers, warm sweaters and fleece pants if you need them, and a water- and rain-proof, or at least water- and rain-resistant, outer layer for tours and activities out of doors). But if you use common sense and take the advice of the locals, you can happily and safely experience Alaska during the time of year many Alaskans enjoy their state the most.

Finally, it seems incredible but, more than four decades after becoming the forty-ninth state of the United States, Alaskans still get asked if we use U.S. currency and stamps. The answer, of course, is emphatically yes—though if you arrive here with Canadian dimes, quarters, and other small change in your pocket or purse, merchants will sometimes accept a few of them at face value. Canadian dollars, on the other hand, may (or may not) be accepted according to current value on the international money exchanges. That mostly goes for communities near the border, like Tok: I wouldn't try to pay with Canadian cash when deeper in Alaska, although you might be able to squeak a few Canadian coins into larger transactions.

Now, enough of the technical stuff. Read on. Come. Visit. Enjoy!

—Lisa Maloney

Southeast Alaska

Incredible place, Southeast Alaska. It's a place of islands—
more than 1,000—and a land of lush forests, snowcapped
mountains, cascading waterfalls, steep-walled fjords, and magnificent glaciers. From the glaciers fall tens of thousands of
huge and minuscule icebergs that dot the seascape and glitter
within great bays and inlets. It is a region of proud and skillful
Tlingit, Haida, and Ts'msyen Indigenous peoples, whose totem
poles and other works of art are beginning to receive the rec-
ognition they deserve. It is a land, too, with a colorful, gutsy
gold rush past and a place where today huge salmon, monster
halibut, and bountiful trout await the angler's lure in salt water,
lakes, and streams.

It's an easy place to get to, despite a lack of road access.
Scores of elegant cruise ships embark each week in summer
from West Coast ports en route to the Southeast Alaska panhandle. Stateroom-equipped ferry liners of the Alaska Marine
Highway System likewise ply these waters from Bellingham,
Washington and, when staffing levels and maintenance needs
allow, from Prince Rupert, British Columbia. And, of course,
the jets of Alaska Airlines, plus other carriers in the summer,
depart daily from Seattle and other cities in the Lower 48 states

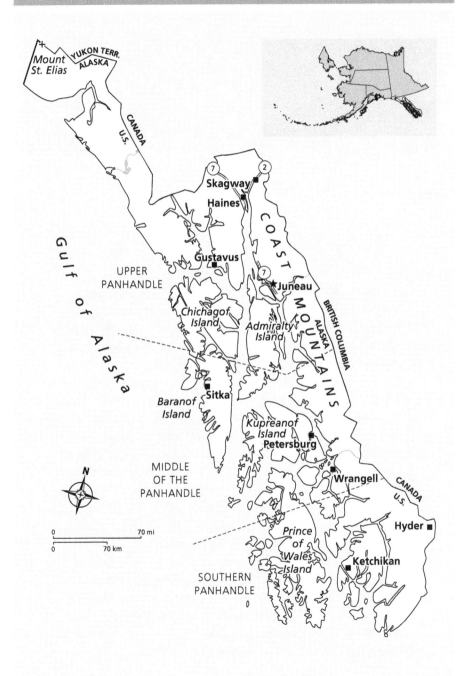

TOP 10 PLACES IN SOUTHEAST ALASKA

Alaska Chilkat Bald Eagle Preserve	Dyea Campground
Alaska Icefield Expeditions	Glacier Bay National Park and Preserve
Alaskan Brewing Company	Laughing Raven Lodge
Alaska's Boardwalk Lodge	Seawolf Adventures
Chilkoot Trail	Sitka National Historical Park

en route to the land that nineteenth-century naturalist John Muir called "one of the most wonderful countries in the world." Here's what Southeast Alaska holds in store for visitors these days.

Southern Southeast

Alaskans call **Ketchikan** their First City because it's the first Alaskan port of call for cruise ships, ferries, yachts, and many airlines en route to the forty-ninth state. Spread out along the shores of **Revillagigedo Island** (the name is Spanish; locals just say "Revilla"), the town is just a few blocks wide, but it's miles long. The hustling, bustling city's economy lies in commercial fishing and tourism. Timber, once a thriving business, has all but halted in the Southeast, but a few people still make their living with small logging projects. Sportfishing for salmon, halibut, and freshwater species can be superb. So is the sightseeing at local totem parks and from the decks of small cruisers that explore nearby islands and waters.

For travelers who seek a cruise-like experience, the small ships of half a dozen companies offer comfortable vessels with staterooms, dining rooms, ample decks, observation lounges, and bars—but not the Vegas-like theaters, ballrooms, casinos, boutiques, and crowds of the big liners. Some of these boats can nose into small bays and inlets for close-up looks at bears, deer, and other wildlife. Also pleasurable are the whales. When they are in the vicinity, the skipper can cut the engine and drift for a half hour or more to watch the water acrobatics of the great beasts. One option is available from **Classic Alaska Charters** (907-225-0608, classicalaskacharters.com), which offers a 40-foot motor yacht for custom trips of 5 days or more. This is the perfect choice for those who want a personalized or flexible itinerary, or for groups or families who want a vessel all to themselves.

For a whole slew of cruise packages aboard smaller vessels, check out **Alaskan Dream Cruises** (888-862-8881; alaskandreamcruises.com). They operate eight ships in Alaskan waters, each carrying no more than ninety travelers. Guests enjoy wildlife viewing from the forward lounges and the generous decks as well as overnight accommodations on board. Try the 5-night North to True Alaska expedition that includes Glacier Bay National Park, or the popular 8-night Alaska's Inside Passage Sojourn option, which takes you into smaller ports like Wrangell and Kasaan in addition to the flagship stops of the larger ships. If you're more interested in wildlife and glaciers, try the Ice of the Inside Passage cruise, an 8-night adventure that showcases seven glaciers and the prolific sea life around them and includes a stop at a remote Alaskan village. All port stops include optional excursions highlighting local culture. Most of the Alaskan Dream Cruises boats set sail from Juneau, with some returning there and others docking in other Southeastern ports.

You'll see more authentic totem poles around Ketchikan than any place else in the world. One of the outstanding collections stands in **Saxman,** 2½ miles south of Ketchikan on the South Tongass Highway. Deeply carved figures represent eagles and ravens, bears and killer whales, and even the figure of a hapless youth caught in the bite of a giant rock oyster as the tide comes in. Elsewhere in the park you'll find a traditional community house and on-site carving center. Four-hour motorcoach tours by **Faces of Ketchikan** (formerly Cape Fox Tours; 907-331-3068; facesofketchikan.com) include a visit to Saxman Village and a feast of Dungeness crab.

The **Totem Heritage Center** (907-225-5900; www.ketchikanmuseums .org), at 601 Deermount Street, a half mile or so from downtown, houses priceless nineteenth-century totem poles rescued from the natural process of decay they would otherwise undergo if left out in nature. They are absolutely majestic. The **Tongass Historical Museum** (907-225-5600; ketchikanmuseums.org), downtown at 629 Dock Street, contains exhibits and artifacts from Ketchikan's Native history and its fishing, mining, and timbering heritage. Both centers are open year-round. Summer hours are 8:00 a.m. to 5:00 p.m. daily, and winter hours may be more limited. Admission to either center is $6, with discounts for seniors and free for those 17 and under, or you can access both with a $9 Museum Pass.

Another good totem-viewing location requires a scenic 15-minute air flight or 1-hour ferry to the Ts'msyen village of **Metlakatla** on Annette Island.

Stories in Wood

Totem poles are erected as "story poles" by Alaska Native people who live in Southeastern Alaska, as well as the northwest coast of the United States and Canada, and are unique to these regions. They are usually carved from yellow or red cedar and can stand for 50 or 60 years. Totem poles can be seen today at several locations, including Totem Bight Park, Saxman Totem Park, and the Totem Heritage Cultural Center near Ketchikan; Klawock Totem Park on Prince of Wales Island; and Sitka National Historical Park.

Among sites to see and explore in Metlakatla is the village founder *Father William Duncan's Cottage,* built in 1891 and now a museum that chronicles the history of Annette Island's original First Nations people and the lay Anglican priest who was involved in founding this community. To really get to know area history, join a local guide from *Metlakatla Tours* (907-886-8687; metlakatla.com/tourism). Tours start from $150 and take in the museum, the church, the community fisheries plant, and the *Tribal Longhouse,* which serves as a Ts'msyen clan house where dancing and ceremonies take place. *Laughing Berry Tours* (907-723-9835; laughingberry.com) also offers tours from a local's perspective as they explore the community's historic buildings and some of its prettiest natural spaces. Laughing Berry also runs a gift shop where you can buy authentic Alaska Native artwork, and they run a small rental car business.

southeast alaska facts

The name Ketchikan is derived from the Tlingit word *Kitschk-Hin,* meaning "the creek of the thundering wings of an eagle."

If you're a hiker, you'll find Ketchikan a great place to roam from, with lots of ocean, forest, lake, and mountain trails. The 3½-mile *Deer Mountain Trail,* which begins practically downtown and runs to the 3,000-foot summit, provides a particularly grand vista of the city below and nearby islands and ocean waters. Ask for directions to the trailhead at the *Ketchikan Visitor Information Center,* downtown at 131 Front Street. Call the visitor center at (907) 225–6166 or (800) 770–3300 or visit the local visitor association website at visit-ketchikan.com.

Earlier, we mentioned the opportunity to explore waters around Ketchikan by small sightseeing cruise. *True Alaskan Tours* (888-289-0081; truealaskantours.com) offers a 5¼-hour excursion from downtown Ketchikan to *Misty Fjords National Monument,* a wondrous 2.2-million-acre national treasure

TOP ANNUAL EVENTS IN SOUTHEAST ALASKA

Little Norway Festival, in Petersburg; held each May to celebrate Norwegian Independence Day. For information call 907-772-4636 or visit petersburg.org.

Juneau Jazz and Classics, a weeklong celebration in May of some of the best jazz around. For further information call 907-463-3378 or go to jazzandclassics.org.

Southeast Alaska State Fair, held each year in Haines. Five fun-filled days every summer, with a parade and entertainment each night. For information call 907-766-2476 or visit seakfair.org.

Alaska Bald Eagle Festival, held each November to celebrate the return of thousands of eagles to the Chilkat Valley to feast on a late salmon run. For information call 907-766-6418 or see visithaines.com.

lined by cliffs towering thousands of feet above the sea and waterfalls cascading into the placid waters. View New Eddystone Rock, a volcanic plug rising 237 feet from the waters of Behm Canal, or keep watch for seals, bald eagles, and seabirds. The cost, including a light meal and beverages, is $275 per person. True Alaskan Tours also offers a shorter, 2-hour *Waterfront & Wildlife* day cruise for $118, which takes in areas where many of Ketchikan's historical events took place. Cruise by Ketchikan Creek—the community's former "Creek Street red-light district"—where salmon may be seen jumping as they begin their upstream migration. From the vessel, view Saxman Totem Park (with its collection of intriguing totem poles) and Pennock Island, where hardy individuals pursue the pioneering lifestyle. Learn about the island's rainforest from the warmth of the cabin or out on deck.

If you want professionals to organize, equip, and guide you on a Misty Fjord kayaking trip, Betsey Burdett and Geoff Gross offer 2 ½-hour to 6-day excursions within Misty Fjords National Monument as well as among the Barrier Islands in the South Prince of Wales Island Wilderness area. Their company, *Southeast Exposure* (37 Potter Road; 907–225–8829; southeastexposure.com), also offers day trips along the Ketchikan waterfront and into semi-wilderness waters nearby. Single fiberglass kayaks rent for $45 per day. Guided 2 ½-hour waterfront tours start at $50. A 6-day Misty Fjords trip is $950 per person.

Perhaps one of the best ways to see what Ketchikan is really about is to take advantage of one of the best travel bargains around: Rent one of a network of *US Forest Service cabins* in the wilderness for as little as $25 per cabin. The Forest Service maintains more than 150 warm and weather-tight cabins beside remote mountain lakes and isolated ocean shores throughout the *Tongass National Forest,* which makes up most of Southeast Alaska.

Another forty such units exist in Southcentral Alaska's *Chugach National Forest.* Cabins may be reserved for up to a week at a time, and reservations can be made up to 180 days in advance using the toll-free number 877-444-6777 or accessing recreation.gov.

Most units have bunks to accommodate up to six and contain either wood- or oil-burning stoves. Don't, however, expect a "Hilton in the wilderness." You bring your own food, sleeping bags, and other supplies. Privies are "down the path," and you might want to bring your own toilet paper, too, just to be safe. Mostly these cabins are fly-in units, though you can reach a few by boat or hiking trail. For bear protection, Alaskans and visitors often carry bear spray and a 30-06 or larger rifle. No permit is required. It's seldom, however, that someone has to use their bear spray, and even more rare that somebody needs to use a firearm.

Virtually every town in both regions has charter air services that specialize in serving fly-in campers. Rates vary with the distance you need to fly.

For information about public use cabins in the Tongass, call 877-444-6777 or visit the *Southeast Alaska Discovery Center* at 50 Main Street in Ketchikan. For similar information concerning the Chugach, contact the *Alaska Public Lands Information Center* in Anchorage at 907-644-3661 or 866-869-6887 or https://www.nps.gov/anch/planyourvisit/visitor-centers-in-alaska .htm.

From Ketchikan, a popular fly-in-only choice is *Patching Lake Cabin,* a woodstove-equipped mountain lake unit with a skiff on site. You'll find trout in the water for fishing plus the possibility of deer and black bear in the woods for viewing. (Don't, however, even think of feeding these critters or observing them too closely.) The local US Forest Service number for information is 907-228-6220. Although the cabin rents for only $60 a night during the peak summer season, a fly-in charter to Patching Lake can cost anywhere from $860 to $1500 or more. Generally for this type of trip you're buying the use of the entire plane. The number of passengers on a small plan can range anywhere from two to ten, depending on the aircraft, and there are strict weight/space limits for both you and your luggage.

While in Ketchikan, don't pass up two boating opportunities offered by *Alaska Travel Adventures.* For $139 and 3 ½ hours of your time, you'll glide across a quiet lake surrounded by forest and mountains. Look closely for bald eagles. A guide will help maneuver the boat while also teaching about the surrounding Tongass rainforest and the plants and animals that flourish there. If you're not keen on paddling, opt for the $189 Rainforest Island Adventure. You'll start with a guided hike, mostly by boardwalk, through old-growth forest and along a beach, learning about the traditionally symbiotic relationship between local Indigenous peoples and the lush forest. After a hearty snack, take a ride in a motorized raft to look for sea lions, porpoises, harbor seals, and bald eagles. For more information call 800-323-5757 or visit alaskatraveladventures.com.

southeast alaska facts

The Tongass National Forest, in Southeast Alaska, is the largest U.S. forest at about sixteen million acres.

A unique venture among Alaska Travel Adventures' outdoor opportunities is their Backcountry Jeep Safari. The company offers Jeep-led tours through remote land, mostly in Southeast Alaska. The Ketchikan-based adventure is one of the company's most popular. It's a 4-hour trip that combines off-road riding in your own colorful Jeep Wrangler as well as paddling in giant canoes. Reach Alaska Travel Adventures at the above numbers and website.

Ketchikan-based **Taquan Air** (907–225–8800; taquanair.com) has been flying visitors and locals alike on air excursions since 1977. For $349 per person, they offer a 1-hour flightseeing excursion over Misty Fjords National Monument and some of the most incredible scenery in Alaska, from 3,000-foot-high walls of granite to lush forests to snowcapped mountains. Look for mountain goats, bears, deer, wolves, and moose, and land at a remote location for some real serenity.

Taquan Air's 3½-hour **Anan Wildlife Observatory** trek is priced at $425 per person and takes you within a stone's throw of some of Alaska's most awesome brown and black bears during the height of the silver-salmon spawning season, July through September. But don't fear: Guides are with you every step of the way, from the plane ride to the observatory to the half-mile hike along a maintained US Forest Service trail that leads to the bears' territory.

One of Taquan's shorter (35 minutes) and more affordable ($139) flights is the Alps, Eagles, and Totems tour, where you can view by air the forested fjord while keeping an eye open for bears, goats, and, of course, eagles. The flight takes you over the rustic community of **Herring Cove** before returning along the coast by Saxman Native village to Ketchikan.

It's not located off the beaten path, but the smallish, moderately priced **Gilmore Hotel,** at 326 Front Street (907-225-9423; wyndhamhotels.com), is sometimes overlooked. It's now part of Wyndham, but still retains much of its early-twentieth-century charm. The hotel

southeast alaska facts

More than a thousand islands make up the 500-mile-long Alexander Archipelago, which extends from Icy Bay, north of Yakutat, to the border between the United States and Canada at the south end of Prince of Wales Island.

offers a commanding view of Ketchikan's frantic waterfront, taking in fishermen preparing their nets, luxury cruise liners in port, freighters heaped with cargo, and a constant stream of floatplanes landing, taking off, or flying down the channel. Built in 1927 of solid concrete, the hotel's forty rooms are modern, clean, and have full baths and color TVs. Summer rates begin at $169 per night. It's on the National Register of Historic Places. *Annabelle's Famous Keg and Chowder House* off the hotel lobby offers room service or restaurant dining on the premises. The gorgeous 20-foot mahogany bar at Annabelle's is well worth a look-see, as are the murals that depict Ketchikan's notorious old Creek Street red-light district, where Annabelle entertained as a favorite lady of the night in the 1920s.

Speaking of *Creek Street* and its entrepreneurs, do give the lane a stroll, off Stedman Street opposite the big harbor downtown called Thomas Basin. A former brothel called *Dolly's House* (open daily in the summer) has been restored as a museum there, as have numerous other "houses," which now contain boutiques, gift shops, and galleries.

Ketchikan On Foot (907-632-7307; ketchikanonfoot.com) should probably be called *Ketchikan On Four Feet,* because it includes the company of huskies (dogs) as assistant tour guides. The company is locally run, so it's a great opportunity to really get to know a town that so many people zip quickly in and out of, either chasing a cruise ship or running away from cruise ship crowds. Prices start from $53 for adults, and $43 for children under 12.

The *Black Bear Inn* (907-617-7567; stayinalaska.com) is far enough out of downtown Ketchikan that it starts to feel like you really have wandered off the beaten path; some guests describe it as a fairy tale. The three suites include fireplaces, free WiFi, and private baths. There's a massive, ten-person hot tub out on the deck, and the property is bordered by spruce and cedar trees that often hold ravens and eagles. Laundry service and a self-serve continental breakfast are included in your stay, which starts from $265.

The Inn at Creek Street offers budget-friendly accommodations with some serious personality. The first time I made reservations there, it took me a little while to figure out that the inn isn't a single building but a collection of various boutique hotels along centered around Ketchikan's Creek Street district, much of it built on pilings over the actual creek. Because you're shopping a collection of different buildings, the amenities and prices can vary. Expect nightly rates to start around $180, and if you're willing to pay a little extra, almost all the buildings have some sort of waterfront view.

It's not quite the biggest island under the American flag (the Big Island of Hawaii and Kodiak Island in Southwest Alaska rank first and second in that category), but *Prince of Wales Island* (POW) is huge nonetheless: 2,231 square miles of forested mountains, deep U-shaped valleys, lakes, streams, and 900 miles of coastal shores, bays, and inlets. You get to Prince of Wales by state ferry from Ketchikan or Wrangell or by plane. POW is not without controversy: Environmentalists say the island has been overlogged; the timber industry says reforestation is coming along very nicely. Regardless of the difference of opinion, there are still plenty of scenic spots to explore, from secluded coves to seaside villages to lush expanses of old-growth forest. One thing logging has done is create lots of roads (some gravel, others asphalt) that you can use for exploring and camping. Kayaking or canoeing is superb at lots of freshwater and saltwater access points.

If your budget allows, at **Alaska's Boardwalk Lodge** you'll enjoy first-class lodging, amenities, and service along with astounding outdoor adventures on Prince of Wales Island. Tucked beside the ocean next to a pristine tidewater pond, this hand-hewn log lodge is the perfect launching point for your favorite activities, from prime saltwater fishing for halibut, salmon, lingcod, and snapper to fly fishing in the area's abundant streams and lakes to adventure treks to the totems of **Kasaan** and the huge **El Capitan Cave.** Between the made-to-order breakfasts, the gourmet meals featuring surf-and-turf selections, the beautifully landscaped grounds, the inviting outdoor hot tub, and a guest-to-staff ratio that's nearly one to one, you'll likely never have felt so pampered. The guides are first-class, and all of the staff is eager to please. High-season rates start at $1,148 per person, per night, for an all-inclusive stay with pro-guided fresh- or saltwater fishing. The lodge also partners with local businesses to offer land-tour options. You'll need to arrange your own transportation to the lodge: You can take the **Inter-Island Ferry** (866-308-4848; interislandferry .com) from Ketchikan to Hollis, or hop on a small **Island Air Express** (888-387-8989; islandairx.com) plane to Klawock. Ferry pricing starts at about $105 round-trip, while a round trip on the plane starts at about $410. In both cases, a $200 pickup/drop-off fee applies for lodge staff to come and get you. For more information call 907-204-8832 or visit boardwalklodge.com.

For do-it-yourselfers the US Forest Service has two campgrounds and more than twenty rental cabins on lakes and inlets throughout the island, starting from just $30 a night. Call 907-826-3271 in Craig or 907-828-3304 at Thorne Bay. For reservations call 877-444-6777 or access recreation.gov. The forest service also offers daily tours of the huge El Capitan Cave at the north end of the island. The **Log Cabin Resort** (907–755–2205; alaskaslogcabin.com) offers beachfront condo units with full kitchens at $195 a night for up to two people, or $1,170 for the week. They also offer charter fishing.

The **Fireweed Lodge** (907–755–2930; alaskafishingkingsalmon.com), also in Klawock, offers nineteen rooms, fishing charters, and access to excellent hiking and canoeing. During the June through August peak season they tend to function as an all-inclusive lodge, starting at $3,500 per person in a group of four, $3,900 per person in a group of three, or $4,400 per person in a group of two (those prices vary because you are, essentially, chartering the entire boat for your group). Nightly room rentals are available from $200 in April, May, and September; you can sometimes snag a stand-alone room at the last minute during the busy season, too, but those bookings only happen at the last minute. À la carte, full-day fishing charters are also available on turnover days, starting from $1,300 for two people, and roughly $200 per extra person up to four. Again, you're chartering the entire boat for the day of fishing.

McFarland's Lodge (541-571-8304; mcfarlandslodge.com) provides beachfront log cabins at Thorne Bay. The $385-per-night units are suited for up to four guests, but six can fit comfortably for an extra $90 per additional person. Owners Jim and Jeannie McFarland also offer guided and nonguided trips around Thorne Bay. You can rent a 15-foot aluminum skiff for $145 if you want to hit the water on your own.

It would be easy to miss *Hyder,* in southernmost Southeast Alaska. In fact, sadly, most travelers do. If you're Alaska-bound, however, and traveling along British Columbia's Yellowhead Highway between Prince George and Prince Rupert, take the 140-mile paved Cassiar Highway north from its junction with the Yellowhead Highway (about 150 miles before Prince Rupert). Then take the access road off the Cassiar to Hyder. This road also leads to Hyder's very close neighbor, *Stewart.* Stewart (population 400 or so) sits in British Columbia, Canada, and Hyder (current population less than 20 people) lies in Alaska. They're separated by 2 miles and the *U.S.–Canada border.*

What's to see in and around Hyder? For one thing, you'll find spectacular glaciers to view, including *Salmon Glacier,* the world's fifth largest, only 20 miles north of town. You'll also find abandoned mine sites, late nineteenth-century buildings to photograph, superb fishing, hiking trails, and—3 miles north of town—a salmon stream and bear observatory where you can see black bears or brown bears. Your first stop in this part of Alaska should be at the *Hyder Community Association* building in town. There you can get information on the area and check out a small collection of museum items that tell the story of Hyder.

The seasonal U.S. Forest Service *bear-viewing area at Fish Creek* attracts up to 40,000 summertime visitors each year, drawn there by the chance to see both brown and black bears gorging themselves on the rich salmon run. You can drive to the bear-viewing area, but during peak viewing season (mid-July to late September) you need a pass ($5 per day) to enter. You can't buy the passes on site; get them in advance on recreation.gov.

In Stewart, the **Stewart Museum** (250-636-2229; stewartbcmuseum.com), at 703 Brightwell, displays wildlife as well as bits and pieces of local history. Also in Stewart, the **Ripley Creek Inn** (205-636-2344; ripleycreekinn.com), just a couple of miles from the U.S.-Canada border, offers rooms in renovated, historic buildings, plus a more modern lodge building. The historic buildings range from prospectors' cabins to old stores and a former brothel, and each of these rooms is truly one of a kind. Rates start from $125 CDN.

The Middle of the Panhandle

Wrangell is a natural for the visitor who wants an out-of-the-way travel experience in a locale that's still a little rough around the edges. It's clean, neat, and easy to get around, but everything isn't laid out for you. You get there either by a daily Alaska Airlines jet from Juneau, Ketchikan, or Seattle or by the ferries of the Alaska Marine Highway System. The tour company movers of masses have seemingly passed Wrangell by, at least for now. The mega-cruise ships rarely call, and even medium or small vessels stop much less frequently than in Ketchikan, Sitka, and Juneau. The result is that it's a made-to-order destination for travelers who enjoy ferreting out backcountry or backyard jewels in the rough (literally and figuratively)—from mysterious petroglyphs to some of the best and most photogenic totem poles in Alaska. Now, for a little background:

Wrangell history goes back possibly 8,000 years, when someone (no one knows who) carved mysterious stick-figure petroglyph etchings in stone along the seashore. More recently, according to Tlingit oral history, the present Native peoples settled the area more than 2,000 years ago, arriving via the Stikine River. Sometime in the 1700s a Tlingit chief named Shakes (the first of several to claim that name) selected the present site of Wrangell as home for his people.

In the early 1800s English, American, and Russian ships came exploring. The Russians established a community called Redoubt St. Dionysius in 1834. The English obtained a lease and occupied the same site, calling it Fort Stikine, in 1840. With the sale of Alaska to the United States in 1867, the community came under American jurisdiction and was called Fort Wrangell. Gold mining, fur trading, fisheries, and commerce have been Wrangell's economic staples since.

Recent years have seen the modest beginnings of tourism, and it's true, there's a lot in and around the community for visitors to experience. A good place to visit early, in order to get oriented, is the **Chamber of Commerce Visitor Information Center** in the **James and Elsie Nolan Center** at 296 Campbell Drive (907-874-3770; wrangell.com). This beautiful, all-in-one building also holds the **Wrangell Museum,** which is well worth a visit. It includes masterfully carved totemic house posts, dating from 1770 to 1790, from the Bear Tribal House on Chief Shakes Island. Also on display are artifacts from the Russian and British occupations and from the gold rush era, petroglyphs, bird and natural history exhibits, minerals, and various other items. Hours during the April to October tourist season are 10:00 a.m. to 5:00 p.m. Monday through Friday and variable hours on weekends, with slightly reduced hours in winter. Museum admission costs $12.

The most notable cultural site in the community is **Chief Shakes Island,** connected to Wrangell by a walking bridge and located in the middle of Wrangell Harbor. The tribal house and totems there are among the best carved and most colorful in Alaska.

You can see some petroglyphs on display at the city museum and library, but most must be sought out at low tide on Wrangell Island's mysterious **Petroglyph Beach State Historic Park** north of town. The etched figures on the rocks, three dozen or more, seem to depict spirit faces, fish, owls, spirals, and other designs, although no one knows what the figures really mean or who created them. To reach them, turn left on Evergreen Avenue from the ferry terminal. Walk north on Evergreen about 0.75

southeast alaska facts

The city of Wrangell, on Wrangell Island in Southeast Alaska, has been ruled by three nations since its founding by fur traders in 1811: Russia, Great Britain, and the United States.

mile to a boardwalk leading to the beach. Walk down the boardwalk and head right toward the big rock outcropping on the northern high-tide limit of the beach. Don't, under any circumstances, attempt to move these rocks. You may, of course, photograph them.

A moderately difficult hike (due to a rapid ascent) over the **Rainbow Falls Trail** can be short or long, depending on whether you extend the distance by also hiking the high country ridges along the 2.7-mile **Institute Creek Trail** that junctions along the way with the Rainbow Falls Trail. The basic route takes you about 0.75 mile from its start at mile 4.6 on the Zimovia Highway to an observation platform and a great view of picturesque Rainbow Falls, then later to a sweeping view of Chichagof Pass. Another popular hiking choice in town is **Mount Dewey,** also called Muir Mountain since John Muir climbed it in 1879 and caused a considerable stir among the locals when he lit a huge bonfire at the top. The trail is primitive in places, but the view from the top is considered well worth the effort.

If that's not enough outdoor recreation for you, you can rent your own sea kayaks and canoes from *Alaska Vistas* (907-874-3006; alaskavistas.com) or rent canoes, e-bikes, and skiffs from *Breakaway Adventures* (907-874-2499; breakawayadventures.com)

Wrangell is known for producing beautiful garnets. Mining—or more accurately, chipping—rights at the famous *Wrangell Garnet Ledge* are reserved for Wrangell's children and their families, but you can buy garnets from the youngsters, who you'll find selling them at the docks to cruise ship and ferry passengers. Local kids sell the garnets for anywhere from $1 to $50, depending on size.

Though you probably didn't travel all the way to Southeast Alaska to play a round of golf, it's worth noting that one of the attractions in Wrangell is the *Muskeg Meadows Golf Course* (907-874-4653; wrangellalaskagolf.com). This regulation nine-hole course features some of the most spectacular scenery a golfer could hope for, from ocean views to snow-studded mountains to lush rainforest. And what other course has a raven rule? If your ball is stolen by a raven, you may replace it without penalty as long as you have a witness. If you happen to be in Wrangell in April, you can take in the annual open tournament, held in conjunction with the Wrangell Stikine River Birding Festival, formerly known as the Wrangell Garnet Festival, which celebrates the arrival of bald eagles at the Stikine River.

For close-to-town overnight accommodations, Wrangell's largest hotel is the *Stikine Inn* (907-874-3388; stikineinn.com), complete with about three dozen rooms, a restaurant, and meeting rooms. Prices vary from about $315 to $390, depending upon the room.

The Sourdough Lodge (907-874-3613; thesourdoughlodge.com) at 1104 Peninsula Avenue started life some years back as a small bunkhouse for loggers. Today the rustic log lodge offers comfortable accommodations, including the Jacuzzi-equipped Harding River suite that sleeps four, as well as standard rooms with bath. Standard room rates start at $220 in season, or $300 for the Harding River suite.

John Verhey operates *Alaska Vistas* (907-874-3006; alaskavistas.com), which he established in 1995 as the first paddle-sports outfitter in Wrangell. He rents kayaks and canoes and offers fully guided paddle trips, rafting trips, bear-viewing tours to Anan Creek Wildlife Observatory, tours to go whale watching or see the LeConte Glacier, fully guided kayak trips, Stikine River raft trips, and jet boat tours. Single kayak rentals are $55 per day, and doubles rent for $65 per day. Fully guided rates include everything you'll need for a safe and comfortable experience, with prices ranging anywhere from $180 for a 2-hour guided paddling tour to $350 for bear viewing. Serious river runners might try the Stikine River raft trip.

southeastalaskafacts

The Stikine River is the fastest-flowing navigable river in North America.

For another option, try *Breakaway Adventures* (907-874-2488; breakawayadventures.com), a jet boat tour operation that's been on the Stikine River for more than 30 years. They offer tours up the Stikine River, to Anan Creek Wildlife Observatory to see bears, and to the LeConte Glacier, the southernmost saltwater glacier in North America. They also rent e-bikes. Tour prices range from $220 to $350, and e-bike rentals start at $25.

Remember those bargain-priced fly-in US Forest Service cabins in the wilderness (starting as low as $25 per night)? Twenty-two of them are located in the Wrangell Ranger District, including one near the Anan Wildlife Observatory that rents for a relatively pricey $75 a night. Call 907-874-2323 for information. For reservations visit recreation.gov or call the park reservation system at 877-444-6777. If you're a hot tub buff, ask for information about the *Chief Shakes Hot Springs* tubs (one sheltered, one not) that the forest service has placed along the Stikine River about 22 miles from Wrangell.

High above the surface, *Sunrise Aviation* (907-874-2319; no website) will take you flightseeing over the Stikine River and several glaciers, ice-clogged LeConte Bay, and various high country lakes in a plane that holds five passengers. Custom flight-sees and drop-offs for wilderness adventures also are available. On the ground, Mark Galla's *Alaska Peak and Seas* (907-470-3200; www.wedoalaska.com) will take you into the backcountry for just about any trip you can imagine.

If you're tired of running with the crowd or dealing with big tour companies that run the show from outside the state, take in all that this part of the state has to offer with *Alaska Charters and Adventures* (907-874-4157; alaskaupclose.com). With a limit of six guests per boat, Alaska Charters promises the kind of intimate experiences with the wilderness that you just can't get when you're part of a big group. Whether it's the Stikine River by jet boat, a trek to Anan Wildlife Observatory or LeConte Glacier, kayaking, canoeing, fishing, or whale watching, you'll be able to arrange it with this locally owned company specializing in custom tours.

Back in 1897, when the rest of the world went crazy over gold in the Klondike, Norwegian-born Peter Buschmann came north, too, but only as far as Mitkof Island in Southeast Alaska. He settled there to fish and eventually built a salmon cannery and sawmill. Other Norwegians, noting the great fisheries of the region, the abundant ice from nearby LeConte Glacier, and the majestic

surroundings, joined Buschmann and his family and named their community
Petersburg.

Today Petersburg thrives as one of the most active fishing ports in the
United States. Fishermen seine, troll, and gillnet for salmon in the summer;
seek halibut into the fall; fish for herring in the spring; go after crab in the
winter; and harvest shrimp year-round. Sport fishing for salmon and halibut is
especially rewarding.

About 3,000 Alaskans call Petersburg home. Most of them fish or work in
the fisheries industry or in businesses that service the fishermen. In the summer one of the most pleasant no-cost "tours" you can take is simply to wander
in Petersburg's three public harbors along 2.5 miles of floats, watching the
1,200 or so commercial fishing vessels that may be in port at any one time.
Tourism is a rapidly growing but not yet dominant industry in Petersburg, and
therein—as in Wrangell—lies much of the community's charm. The town is
"real." And it's clean, neat, well laid out, and noticeably Norwegian, with its
rosemaling floral designs on buildings and homes and its huge, white 1912
Sons of Norway Hall downtown (complete with a **Viking sailing vessel**
ready to put to sea).

The town, no surprise, is nicknamed Little Norway, and its biggest celebration is the **Little Norway Festival,** timed each May to celebrate Norwegian
Independence Day.

A good place to start your visit is the **Petersburg Visitor Information
Center** (907-772-4636; petersburg.org) at First and Fram Streets. Office hours
are 9:00 a.m. to 5:00 p.m. Monday through Saturday during the summer.

The community's biggest visitor attraction is nearby LeConte Glacier, one
of the most active in North America, with a constant succession of icebergs
calving and crashing explosively from its wide face into the frigid waters of
LeConte Bay. Many days the big and little bergs literally carpet bay waters from
shore to shore, and sightseeing boats must gently push the ice aside as they
cruise in front of the glacier.

The waters of North Frederick Sound, also near Petersburg, provide superb
viewing of another major visitor attraction: humpback whales. Large numbers
of these gentle giants feed here in the summer months, to the considerable
delight of visitors as well as locals. Several charter operators offer LeConte
Glacier and whale-watching excursions. One of your best options is **Whale
Song Cruises** (907-518-1912; whalesongcruises.com), which is captained by a
longtime Petersburg resident.

Another fine way to experience Petersburg is by taking part in a **Tongass
Kayak Adventures** (907-518-4440; tongasskayak.com) guided sea-kayaking

trip. A $150, 3-hour tour of Petersburg Creek takes place almost daily through the summer. Or opt for a more challenging $450 LeConte Glacier Bay paddle.

For a bird's-eye view of LeConte Glacier, you can book a flightseeing excursion with **Petersburg Flying Service** (907-518-1957; petersburgfly-ingservice.net). A 50-minute flight costs about $250 per person.

Petersburg now has an excellent website to help you plan your trip. The listings at petersburg.org highlight many points of interest, including **Eagle's Roost Park** off Nordic Drive, just a few minutes' walk from downtown. One or two eagles are almost always in residence to pose for pictures on their craggy perches.

You'll know you've arrived at the **Clausen Memorial Museum** (907-772-3598; clausenmuseum.com), located at Second and Fram Streets, when you see the large bronze sculpture called *Fisk* (Norwegian for "fish"), which displays the many species of fish to be found in these waters. Inside, exhibits vary from an old-time fish-gutting machine (called an *iron chink*) to the re-created office of a pioneer cannery owner. There are also fur farming exhibits; Native artifacts, including a traditional canoe; and early-day community photographs. Don't miss the two huge wall-mounted salmon, one of them the largest king ever caught (126½ pounds) and the other, the world's largest chum (a 36-pounder). Admission costs $5 for adults, free for children 12 and under.

Those who are in the area to fish—and want to do it on their own—should check out **Jensen's Boat Rentals** (907-772-4635; jensensboatrentals.com), which rents fast 18-foot skiffs to reach the best fishing spots. The boats are also nice for obtaining a scenic view of the town from the water or for touring around to see the sites.

The US Forest Service rents numerous cabins in the national forest around Petersburg, including **Ravens Roost,** one of the relatively few forest service shelters you can hike to. It's located on the mountain behind Petersburg Airport, nearly 4 miles by trail or 3 by helicopter. The Raven Trail begins near the orange-and-white tank south of the airport with 1 mile of boardwalk through muskeg (spongy bog) before the trail's ascent begins. The middle section is relatively steep, then flattens along the ridgetop. The easy way to enjoy the experience is to fly in by helicopter, then hike out downhill. The cabin rents for $60 per night per party. For details, visit recreation.gov or call 877-444-6777. **Temsco Helicopters** (907-772-4780; temscoair.com) will drop you off at the cabin, usually for their minimum charge; call for exact pricing.

When Petersburg folk talk of driving "out the road," they're referring to the 34-mile **Mitkof Highway,** along which you can visit the **Falls Creek Fish Ladder** near mile 11 and the **Crystal Lake Fish Hatchery** and **Blind**

Slough Recreation Area at mile 17.5. Birders visiting in the wintertime will especially enjoy the *Trumpeter Swan Observatory* at mile 16.

For the fisherman, *Indigenous Adventure* (907-518-4054; indigenousadventure.com) offers quality saltwater and freshwater fishing trips, with the option for an expedition-style stay at a fish camp. The cabins at fish camp are dry (that is, without running water) but you'll be accompanied by a guide and a cook, so this "roughing it" experience still comes with some real perks. Prices start at $250 per person for a half-day freshwater or saltwater trip, with a two-person minimum.

Magic Man Charters (907-772-9255; magicmansportfishing.com) also offers saltwater salmon or halibut fishing trips starting from $250 per person, with a three-person minimum, plus options for LeConte Bay glacier tours (from $250 per person) and whale watching (from $350 per person). If you're looking for a downtown lodging location, call the *Tides Inn* at First and Dolphin Streets (907-772-4288; tidesinnalaska.net). Ask for a room overlooking the harbor. Owner Gloria Ohmer was born and raised in Petersburg, and she's an absolute fount of knowledge about things to see and do. Rates start from $160 for single occupancy in the summer, plus $10 per additional person, and are a little lower in the winter. Your stay includes a complimentary continental breakfast plus free airport and ferry transfers. Nonsmoking rooms are available.

Nordic House Bed and Breakfast, three blocks north of the ferry terminal (806 South Nordic Drive; 907-518-1926; nordichouse.net), offers a view of the Wrangell Narrows, boats, planes, and sometimes even wildlife. Rates start from $180. They also offer a 24-foot Hewes Craft boat for rent. *Rocky Point Resort,* 11 miles south of town on Wrangell Narrows, offers saltwater fishing for salmon, halibut, trout, crab, and shrimp in protected waters. Package getaways include a cabin, a motorized skiff, meals, fishing gear, and freezing facilities so that you can take your catch home. Call 907-772-4405 or visit rockypointresortak.com for reservations and information.

For really standout seafood, visit *Inga's Galley* (907-772-2090; no website) a humble-looking shack at North Nordic Drive and Gjoa Street. It may not look fancy on the outside, but their dishes are consistently stellar.

Many Alaskans and most visitors rank *Sitka* as the most visually beautiful community in the state. Perched at the base of majestic mountains on Baranof Island, the community looks westerly toward hundreds of big and little, near and distant isles, mountains, and a massive volcano. Native Alaskan and Russian history abounds in this community. It was the hub and headquarters of Russian America and the czars' vast sea otter-pelt gathering and trading empire until the United States purchased Alaska in 1867. Sitka served as Alaska's territorial capital until the early years of the twentieth century.

Be sure to visit the **Sheldon Jackson Museum** (907-747-8981; museums .alaska.gov) at 104 College Drive in Sitka. The octagonal-shaped building itself ranks as something of an artifact, having been constructed in 1895 as the first concrete structure in Alaska. This small museum is named for the nineteenth-century Presbyterian missionary and educator who supplied a large portion of the collection. Though it's often overlooked, most visitors find it well worth a stop. The well-presented collection emphasizes the Native peoples of Alaska: the Tlingit, Haida, and Ts'msyen of the Southeast; Athabascan of the Interior; Aleut and Alutiiq peoples from Southwest Alaska; and Yup'ik and Inupiat of the far north. You'll never get a better, closer look at a Tlingit dugout canoe, an Athabascan birch-bark canoe, an ancient two-passenger Aleut baidarka (kayak), and two Inupiat kayaks. You'll see Alaska Native battle armor as well as exquisite Inupiat fur parkas. The museum operates 9:00 a.m. to 4:30 p.m. Monday through Saturday in summer, with limited hours on Sunday and during the winter. Admission is $9 for adults, $8 for seniors 65 and up, and free for youth 18 and under.

For visitors with RVs or tents, the campgrounds of choice in Sitka are clearly the two **US Forest Service campgrounds at Starrigavan Bay,** nearly 8 miles north of town on Halibut Point Road. Both feature private campsites surrounded by thick, towering trees. Near the entrance to the upper campground you'll also find one of Alaska's easiest walking trails. The **Starrigavan Estuary** wheelchair-accessible trail, a 0.5-mile elevated boardwalk, takes you beside open wetlands and into deep and dark woods of spruce, hemlock, and alder trees.

Another short and gentle hike, this one at the south end of Lincoln Street on the shores of Sitka Sound, lies within **Sitka National Historical Park.** Actually, you can enjoy two trails there—one a 1.5-mile stroll back into Alaska history on the site of the bloodiest battle fought between Tlingit people and

Second to One

When you visit Sitka you visit the largest city, in area, in the Western Hemisphere. It's the second largest in the world. There are 4,710 square miles within the unified city and borough municipal borders. Juneau, at 3,108 square miles, comes in third. Kiruna, Sweden, with 5,458 square miles, ranks as the world's largest city.

nineteenth-century Russians, the other (less frequented by visitors) a 0.75-mile jogging course.

If your tastes run far off the beaten path, you may consider chartering a boat for a drop-off at the sea-level trailhead of the **Mount Edgecumbe National Recreation Trail** on Kruzof Island, about 10 miles west of Sitka. The 6.7-mile trail up the side of this volcanic crater (a look-alike for Japan's Mount Fuji) is steep and usually takes about 8 hours. From the summit, the view of ocean waters and myriad islands is a mind boggler.

If you've never experienced the fun of a kayak trip, here's a good place to start. **Alaska Travel Adventures** (907-789-0052; alaskatraveladventures.com) offers a 3-hour sea-kayaking adventure, led by experienced guides through protected island waterways. The $209, 3-hour tour often includes views of deer, brown bears, seals, and (always) eagles. **Sitka Sound Ocean Adventures** (907-752-0660; kayaksitka.com) offers a 2-hour paddling adventure for $143 per person.

For the local perspective, take a walking tour guided by Sitka residents ("Sitkans") through **Sitka Walking Tours** (916-234-6871; sitkawalkingtours. com). The 1-hour walking tour through historic downtown Sitka (which starts at $39 per person) includes a lofty view of ocean and islands from **Castle Hill** (where "Russian America" officially became "Alaska, U.S.A." in 1867); a re-created **Russian Blockhouse;** historic houses; the **Saint Michael's Russian Orthodox Cathedral;** and the **Russian Bishop's House** (part of Sitka National Historical Park). You can also take a 2-hour guided rainforest hike (from $119).

On days when cruise ships are in port—which is almost every day in the summer—the **Sitka Tribe of Alaska's Tribal Tours/Historical and Cultural Sightseeing Tours** (907-747-7137; sitkatours.com) offers a tour from the perspective of the Tlingit people who lived here before, during, and after the Russians and still live here today. The narrated 2 ½-hour excursion, priced starting at roughly $70 for independent travelers, takes in Sitka National Historical Park, Sheldon Jackson Museum, a narrative drive through Sitka's Native village, and a traditional dance performance.

The US Forest Service lists twenty-four fly-in or boat-in cabins accessible from Sitka. Probably the most exotic in all of Alaska is the **White Sulphur Springs Cabin** (from $60 a night) on nearby Chichagof Island. It features a weather-tight log cabin with large windows facing out from a picturesque rocky beach onto the broad Pacific—plus an adjacent structure containing an oversize hot springs bath (almost a pool) with the same awesome ocean view. (*Note:* Cabin rental does not include exclusive use of the hot springs. Locals, fishermen, and visitors can and do frequent this spot.) Getting to this cabin is costlier than most because you have to helicopter in, but if you can afford the tariff, the trip itself will rank as one of your vacation highlights of a lifetime. The local forest service number in Sitka is 907-747-6671. For reservations call 877-444–6777 or visit recreation.gov.

For a wildlife-viewing excursion geared toward the independent traveler, check out the *Sitka Sea Otter & Wildlife Quest,* a 2-hour cruise ($149 per person) that explores some of the great bays and narrow passages in and around Sitka while looking for sea otters, three species of whales (humpback, killer, and minke), brown bears, sea lions, black-tailed deer, seals, and eagles. Longer tour options are available, too. For more information call 888-289-0081 or visit allenmarinetours.com.

Here's another quality wildlife viewing excursion by water: *Four B Charters* (907-351-7483; whalesinsitka.com) offers 2 ½-hour tours to *St. Lazaria National Wildlife Refuge* for a view that sets birders cackling. *St. Lazaria,* a 65-acre island some 15 miles west of Sitka, contains the nests of an estimated two thousand rhinoceros auklets, five thousand common and thick-billed murres, two thousand tufted puffins (comical little creatures sometimes called sea parrots or flying footballs), 450,000 fork-tailed and Leache's storm petrels,

A Spectacular Series of Splashes

I love riding the Alaska state ferries through Southeast Alaska: Even the shortest "main line" trip is about 4 hours long, and some can last for days as you travel through exactly the same waters cruise ships ply (for a whole lot more money).

One of the most spectacular things I've ever seen took place on a ferry ride from Juneau to Petersburg. I was camped out beneath the heating lamps on the upper-deck solarium, sound asleep, when something, I don't know what, prompted me to sit straight up and open my eyes.

The very first thing I saw was a humpback whale, breaching just off the stern of the ship. Followed by another. And another. I've never seen so many whales that were so active all at once, and all I could do—all I *wanted* to do—was sit there and stare.

I don't remember how long the spectacle went on for. I just remember sitting there on the plastic lounger, still warm inside my sleeping bag, watching as some uncounted number of whales did . . . what, exactly? Even whale experts freely admit they don't know why humpbacks behave like this, especially during a time when they should, by all rights, be focused on packing down as much nutrition as possible before journeying back out to their winter breeding grounds.

But regardless of whether they were playing, communicating with each other, communicating with us, ridding themselves of barnacles or other parasites . . . that day, and the memory of humpback whales leaping like so many bus-sized salmon, will be with me forever.

plus eagles and other winged species. En route there's a good possibility you'll view whales, seals, sea lions, and sea otters. The tour starts at $185 per person, with a two-person minimum.

Duane and Tracie Lambeth's *Dove Island Lodge* (907-747-5660; doveislandlodge.com) is the place to go if you want to experience both saltwater and freshwater fishing in a relaxed setting. From the picturesque Dove Island, you can spend your days fishing and your evenings paddling around in a kayak or relaxing in a spacious hot tub. The Lambeths have boats ranging from 16 to 38 feet and can get you just about anywhere in Sitka Sound and the surrounding area. A new lodge has been added to the already breathtaking resort area, so guests can enjoy new amenities including a spa lined with bricks of Himalayan salt, a wood-fired Finnish sauna, and a fire pit right at water's edge.

The primary goal of the *Alaska Raptor Center,* at 1000 Raptor Way (907-747-8662; alaskaraptor.org), is healing injured birds of prey, especially eagles. But the center has a worthy program for two-legged human types as well. The $16 admission fee allows you to walk through the center's 17-acre campus, which is home to more than two hundred recovering birds each year, including peregrine falcons, bald eagles, golden eagles, and countless owls. A 0.75-mile nature trail offers visitors a chance to see bald eagles close-up in an uncaged natural habitat, as does the bald eagle flight training center. And if you've got extra time, try something really different and volunteer at the center. A training program offers volunteers a mini-lesson in raptor rehabilitation.

If you're into two-wheel tripping, *Tide Rips Adventures* (907-623-8852; tideripsebikes.com) offers e-bike rentals with both pedal assist and thumb throttles. All-terrain fat bikes and cargo bike models are available.

Sitka has a bevy of B&Bs, virtually every one of them more than adequate. Several are outstanding. *Burgess Bauder's Lighthouse* (907-623-8410; sitkalighthouse.com) is, well, different. It's not exactly a B&B, since the host doesn't reside in or near the premises. But it certainly isn't your usual lodge or inn, either. It's a real lighthouse that Bauder constructed and located on an island a few minutes by boat from downtown Sitka. Your arrival and departure water taxi rides are covered as part of your stay, and you have access to a skiff, kayaks, and paddleboards for exploring, though you may not wish to stray far from the tranquil surroundings. Small wooden hot tubs offer relaxing moments in the evening. The lighthouse will sleep six people in two bedrooms that offer commanding views. You do your own cooking. Rates start at roughly $1,500 a night once all fees are included (you're renting the entire lighthouse, so bring some friends to split with).

Another great home-away-from-home option is *Sitka Rock Suites* (218-831-9578; sitkarocksuites.com), offering eleven waterfront and water-view

Castle Hill: A Palace of Conflict

Once a rocky fortress for Sitka's Tlingit people, surrounded on three sides by water, Castle Hill still is the high point between downtown Sitka and the bridge to Japonski Island. Here the Russian governors, beginning with Alexander Baranov, presided over Russian America. Two buildings occupied the site before the "castle" was built. The first was destroyed by fire, the second by earthquake. The castle, or "Baranov's Castle," was built in 1830 and was renowned for its opulence in what was then a remote and wild country.

A light placed at the top of the castle to guide mariners made the building the first lighthouse in Alaska.

After the U.S. purchase of Russian America in 1867, Baranov's Castle fell into disrepair; in 1894, it burned to the ground.

Today Castle Hill is a historic monument where a commanding view of Sitka and the surrounding islands can still be had. Ramps have been constructed to make the former fortress wheelchair accessible.

studios and one-bedroom and two-bedroom suites. You can enjoy gorgeous views and can do some wildlife watching right from your deck. Rates start from $200 per night, and if you're inclined to stay awhile, they also rent by the month in the off-season.

Port Alexander is one of those small, isolated communities that visitors end up raving about. Located at the southern tip of Baranof Island, the town once boasted two thousand residents. Today there are about fifty, among them Peter Mooney, who with his wife, Susan Taylor, operates *Laughing Raven Lodge* (907-568-2266; portalexander.com), a secluded getaway offering wildlife viewing, hiking, kayaking, and fishing. Rooms are located right by the water, so don't be surprised if you're awakened during the night by whales spouting. Four rooms are available, each with its own bath, and skiffs and kayaks are available for exploring the water. Packages include room, board, guided fishing, fish processing, and packaging. All-inclusive package prices average out to about $1,100 per person, per day and include airfare from Juneau, accommodations, gourmet family-style meals, guided fishing, all the gear you need, and fish processing for up to 50 pounds of fish caught.

The Upper Panhandle

Juneau, Alaska's state capital, is arguably the most scenic capital city in the nation. The most populated portion of town sits on the shores of Gastineau

Channel, backed up by awesomely steep Mount Juneau, Mount Roberts, and various other peaks in the 3,000-foot-and-higher class. Within Juneau's 3,108 square miles you'll find big bays, tiny inlets, thickly vegetated islands, and numerous glaciers (including **Mendenhall Glacier,** the second most-visited river of ice in Alaska). The town also contains large portions of the Juneau Icefield—a 1,500-square-mile, high-altitude desert of hardpack ice and snow that extends from behind the city to beyond the Canadian border. It's from the overflow of this ice field that Mendenhall, Taku, and other great glaciers descend. Juneau had its start in 1880 as a miners' camp after a local Native chief, Kowee, led prospectors Joe Juneau and Dick Harris over Snowslide Gulch into Silver Bow Basin. They found, according to Harris's account, gold "in streaks running through the rock and little lumps as large as peas or beans."

You can see exhibits of the community's gold-mining history in the small, often overlooked *Juneau–Douglas City Museum* (907-586-3572; juneau.org /library/museum) at Fourth and Main Streets, open 9:00 a.m. until 6:00 p.m. weekdays, 10:00 a.m. to 4:30 p.m. weekends. Admission is $7.

You can view more history, including displays of Alaska Native artifacts from all over the state and wild animal dioramas, in the *Alaska State Museum* (907-465-2901; museums.alaska.gov/asm/) at 395 Whittier Street, a couple of blocks from downtown. If traveling with young children, don't miss the Discovery Room where kids can climb aboard a child-size copy of Captain James Cook's eighteenth-century vessel *Discovery,* stroke wild animal pelts, and dress in period costumes. Museum admission is $14. Hours are 9:00 a.m. to 4:30 p.m. Tuesday through Sunday and 1:00 p.m. to 4:30 p.m. Monday.

Also often passed by—but for history buffs, well worth the effort of a few blocks' climb to Chicken Ridge from downtown—is *Wickersham House* (907-586-9001; dnr.alaska.gov/parks/units/wickrshm.htm) at 213 Seventh Street, the restored Victorian home of Judge James Wickersham, a pioneer jurist and Alaska territorial (nonvoting) delegate to Congress. You can see the judge's artifact collection and period furniture as well as interpretive displays and a grand hilltop view of the city's business district. Daily informal tours of the century-old house range from a half-hour to several hours, depending upon how much time and interest you have. Sip tea from bone china teacups and learn about Wickersham's fascinating and adventurous life. The house is listed as a state historic site, and tours are held daily in the summer, except Wednesday. Your admission fee of $5 helps keep the place up.

Juneau is blessed with an incredible number of hiking trails, many of them remnants of old mining roads dating from the 1920s or earlier. If you don't have wheels you can easily reach several from downtown Juneau, including the *Mount Roberts Trail* (2.7 miles one way), which begins at the end of

Sixth Street; *Perseverance Trail* (3.5 miles one way), which you access by walking up Gold Street to Basin Road; and the *Mount Juneau Trail* (2 steep miles one way), which begins as a side trail about ½ mile along the Perseverance Trail. The Mount Roberts and Mount Juneau treks meander through thick forests until they break out, finally, above timberline for awesome aerial views of green forests, Gastineau Channel, and Douglas Island, across the water.

You'll need to drive or take a shuttle (readily available near the cruise docks) to reach the popular, mostly easy trails around Mendenhall Glacier, which is about 13 miles north of downtown Juneau. One of the more challenging hikes here is the *West Glacier Trail* (3.5. miles one way), which takes you from the parking lot on the west side of Mendenhall Lake through alder and willow forests for a mostly gradual climb up the side of Mount McGinnis. Your destination is a 1,300-foot vantage point from which you can look down on the rolling white expanse of the glacier and the glittering blue lake in front of it. If you want knowledgeable local expertise while you're trekking in the area, *Gastineau Guiding* (907-586-8231; stepintoalaska.com) offers daily escorted hikes along forest trails to saltwater shores and alongside historic remains and relics of the community's gold-producing heyday. Prices start at $109 for hiking only, but some trips also including whale watching and other adventures.

Beer aficionados take note: *Alaskan Brewing Company's* (907-780-5866; www.alaskanbeer.com) amber beer and pale ale brews have taken gold medals and blue ribbons in tasting competitions across the country. Although legally they can't serve food in the tap room, you can buy something to eat from the excellent food trucks stationed right outside the brewery door, then bring it in to enjoy with your beer.

Speaking of tasting brews, Alaska's best-known saloon, the *Red Dog* (907-463-3658; reddogsaloon.com), is located downtown at 278 South Franklin Street. But don't overlook the saloon in the *Alaskan Hotel and Bar* (907-318-9470; thealaskanhotel .com), at 167 South Franklin. The big, ornate back bar there is worth a look-see whether or not you imbibe. The hotel, incidentally, was built in 1913 and offers refurbished rooms with

southeast alaska facts

The Juneau Icefield, in the Coast Mountains north of Juneau, covers more than 1,200 square miles and is the source of more than thirty glaciers, including the Mendenhall, Taku, Eagle, and Herbert.

private and shared baths. The summer rates start at about $130 for a room with a shared bath and $165 for a private bath.

About dining in Juneau: The opportunities are mouthwateringly wide, from Mexican cuisine downtown at *El Sombrero* (157 South Franklin; 907-586-6770; no website) to arguably Alaska's best Friday clam chowder at the old-fashioned *Douglas Cafe* (916 Third Street; 907-364-3307; no website) across the obvious bridge you can see from downtown Juneau, in the community of Douglas. The cafe is perhaps the only restaurant in Juneau that features amber clams and amber mussels.

Deckhand Dave's (no phone number; deckhanddaves.com) anchors Juneau's nascent food truck court at 139 South Franklin Street. This food truck is so famous it isn't exactly off the beaten path—but it has gotten that famous for a reason: Dave's fish tacos, made of the freshest catch, are sublime.

Dockside in downtown Juneau, you'll find a couple of great eateries with terrific waterfront views. For fine dining and fresh seafood, you can't beat the *Twisted Fish Company* (907-463-5033; twistedfishcompany.com). While you're waiting for your table, you can shop for goodies to take home at the adjoining *Taku Wild Alaska Seafood* store (800-582-5122; takustore.com). This family-owned business provides fresh seafood to many Alaskan restaurants, and they're happy to offer samples of their smoked salmon to visitors. Their seasoned rubs, especially the sugar maple dry rub, are great with salmon, halibut, and even plain old chicken.

The long-standing *Silverbow Inn* (120 Second Street; 907-586-4146; silverbowinn.com) is worth a stop for those who enjoy a history lesson. The inn offers a few rooms for the night, but—although thoroughly modern—shows its late-nineteenth century age. The bagel shop below is a nice place to enjoy breakfast away from the bustle of the main tourist drag on South Franklin.

If you're a Friday visitor, plan to pick up a sack lunch at any of several downtown sidewalk vendors and head for the *State Office Building* —the S.O.B., in local parlance. There in the structure's great atrium, local and visiting organists perform each week on a grand and lusty old Kimball theater pipe organ that dates back to 1928, to the considerable delight of scores of brown-bag lunch consumers perched on benches and ledges. The concerts usually start at noon.

One of the best ways to really appreciate Juneau is by staying in one of those nifty US Forest Service cabins scattered throughout the area. There are five cabins you can hike to straight from Juneau and dozens that are accessible by air or boat. Two of the closer (and therefore less costly to reach by plane) lakeside cabins are the *East Turner Lake* and *West Turner Lake* units up Taku Inlet, south of the city. Trout and char fishing can be productive from either end of the lake, and wildlife watching can include brown bears (from a distance, please!), deer, mountain goats, and waterfowl. The cabins each rent for $45 a night. Make reservations at recreation.gov or by calling 877-444-6777.

Don't overlook the *Alaska State Parks public use cabins.* They are equally nice, and several are accessible by trail. The Juneau Convention and Visitors Bureau, AKA *Travel Juneau* (907-586-2201; traveljuneau.com) at 800 Glacier Avenue can give you more information about everything going on here.

Wild Coast Excursions (775-572-WILD; wildcoastexcursions.com) offers big, "trip of a lifetime" excursions like fly-in bear-viewing to *Pack Creek* on *Admiralty Island* or *Waterfall Creek* on *Chichagof Island.* Both trips start at about $1,000 per person.

In particular, the Pack Creek trip takes you to a place the Tlingit call Xootsnoowú or *kootz-na-hoo,* which translates to something like "Fortress of the Bears." This trip offers an almost unparalleled opportunity to view brown (grizzly) bears in their natural forest habitat from the safety of the US Forest Service's bear-viewing platform.

You can get more information about the Pack Creek bear-viewing area, including a list of approved guiding companies and procedures for getting an unguided permit, from the *Juneau Ranger District of Tongass National Forest* (907-586-8800; fs.usda.gov/detail/tongass/). You can get this information in person at 8510 Mendenhall Loop Road in Juneau, but travelers who wait until they get here usually find the limited number of permits are long gone. The website also lists air charter companies that transport permit holders to Pack Creek.

In Juneau, *Alaska Travel Adventures* (907-789-0052; alaskatravel adventures.com) offers a splashy Mendenhall Glacier Float Trip down almost all white water on the Mendenhall River for $199; a Historic Gold Mining and Panning Adventure in the shadow of the old AJ mine for $99; Glacier View Sea Kayaking through protected waters north of town, priced at $154; and the outdoor *Gold Creek Salmon Bake* (transport from the downtown docks included) for $79. This, incidentally, is Alaska's longest-running salmon bake and many say it's the best in the state. The menu includes not only fresh

Silver Bow and Gold

A Tlingit man named Chief Kowee is the true discoverer of gold in the Juneau area, not Joe Juneau and Dick Harris, the two prospectors often credited. It was Kowee who brought ore samples to entrepreneur Richard Pilz, hoping to bring prosperity to his people. Pilz then outfitted Harris and Juneau and sent them to find the source. When they returned empty-handed, Kowee led them to the source at Gold Creek in Silver Bow Basin in 1880.

king salmon steaks (grilled on an open pit over alder coals and glazed with a brown sugar and butter sauce) but barbecued ribs, baked beans, and lots of other trimmings, plus your choice of complimentary wine, beer, coffee, or soft drink. All this takes place in sheltered surroundings alongside a sparkling stream and waterfall at the site of old mine diggings. And don't forget the live folk music to enhance the entire scene. To avoid a cast of thousands, call ahead to ask when the busloads of cruise ship passengers are expected, then plan your own arrival earlier or later.

If you're like to tackle a kayaking trip on your own, **Alaska Boat & Kayak Rental Shop** (907-209-6088; www.juneaukayak.com) rents single and tandem (double) sea kayaks, along with stand-up paddleboards. The knowledgeable and experienced staff are very helpful, and they also offer a smattering of guided tours. Single kayaks rent for $60 a day, double kayaks rent for $80 per day, and stand-up paddleboards rent for $55 per day, including appropriate safety gear. The rental center is located at 11521 Glacier Highway.

If skiing is your thing and you're in Juneau during the winter months, **Eaglecrest Ski Area** (907-790-2000; skieaglecrest.com), about 20 minutes from downtown off North Douglas Highway, offers slopes (and two double chairlifts) for everyone from beginner to expert.

You'll find numerous ways to see glaciers around Juneau—on motorcoach tours, from boats, during hikes, and looking down from airplanes. Perhaps the most exciting way to see glaciers, short of actually hiking there on your own, is by helicopter. Several companies have filled that niche, including **Coastal Helicopters Inc.** (907-789-5610; coastalhelicopters.com), which is the only ADA-accessible helicopter service in the area, and **Temsco Helicopters** (877-789-9501; temscoair.com). During these flights you not only fly over one or more rivers of ice, you also touch down and disembark from your chopper for 20 minutes or so of frolicking on the hardpack ice. Fares are in the $380 to $690 range. Both companies offer tours that include exciting sled dog rides on the glaciers. Be sure to ask for specials.

One of Southeast's most dramatic sights is **Tracy Arm Fjord,** a long, deep, meandering waterway whose steep walls rise for thousands of feet. Whales, seals, mountain goats, deer, and bears are among the wildlife viewing possibilities. **True Alaskan Tours** (888-289-0081; truealaskantours.com) offers a trip into the fjord aboard a specially built expedition vessel. Your goal is to spend some time with both the north and south Sawyer glaciers, although sometimes drifting ice forces the captain to detour down another beautiful fjord, Endicott Arm, instead. The all-day cruise includes a picnic-style lunch and complimentary hot chocolate, coffee, and tea, and costs $315 per person.

If you're planning to keep both feet on terra firma, there are a couple of land-based options in Juneau. One is a visit to the **Shrine of St. Therese** (shrine ofsainttherese.org) overlooking Lynn Canal at mile 23 of the Glacier Highway. After St. Therese was pronounced patroness of Alaska in 1925, local priest Father William LeVasseur envisioned a retreat center in her honor. Hundreds of volunteers moved thousands of rocks to build the quaint chapel and surrounding buildings. Today the shrine is part of a retreat center that includes gardens, a labyrinth, and cabin rentals. The shrine and grounds are open daily from 8:00 a.m. to 10:00 p.m. during the summer, closing at 8:00 p.m. in the winter. Cabin rentals are modest, with prices starting at $65 per night for the Hermitage Cabin, which has no running water or electricity. The cabins are intended for visitors seeking solitude in an atmosphere of retreat.

The Jorgenson House (907-723-4202; jorgensonhouse.com) provides another unusual option—this one for visitors who'd like to learn how to prepare some of the incredible fresh foods, particularly seafood, that grace Alaskan tables. For $279 you can join a cooking class led by an award-winning chef that culminates with a feast of the delicious dishes you helped prepare. The House is also a bed and breakfast, with luxurious rooms and full-service breakfasts; rates start at a splurge-worthy $645.

You'll find a number of good-value B&B accommodations in and around Juneau. **Auke Lake Bed & Breakfast** (907-957-9263; aukelakebb.com) sits on the shores of Auke Lake, just 5 miles from Juneau's top visitor attraction, Mendenhall Glacier. Some rooms have lake views, there's a Jacuzzi on the back deck, and your stay includes access to gear for kayaking and canoeing.

Beachside Villa Luxury Inn (907-500-7008; beachsidevilla.com), situated just across Gastineau Channel from downtown Juneau, is more of a boutique hotel. They offer private entrances, complimentary WiFi, and complimentary beverages and snacks, starting from $289 for a basic, double-occupancy king room. Their higher-end suites (from $309) have jetted hot tubs and water views.

Exceptional accommodations can also be had at **Alaska's Capital Inn Bed and Breakfast** (907-586-6507; alaskacapitalinn.com). This exquisitely restored 1906 home perched on a downtown hillside overlooking the harbor features several rooms, from the former maid's quarters at $425 per night to the sumptuous Governor's Suite with double whirlpool and private fireplace for $489 per night. Period antiques grace all the rooms, and gourmet breakfasts include specialties like lemon soufflé hotcakes and Dungeness crab eggs Benedict.

The **Juneau International Hostel** (907-586-9559; juneauhostel.net), located at 614 Harris Street, is a particular pleasure for fans of hosteling. It's located in a large, historic, rambling house on the side of a hill called Chicken Ridge. Clean and spacious, it's just a few blocks above downtown Juneau. In spite of its relatively large capacity (forty-eight beds, sitting room with fireplace and library, laundry), it's filled almost all the time in the summer. Reservations are a must. The cost is $30 per adult or $15 per (accompanied) child between 6 and 17 years old, plus one chore per person to help keep the space tidy.

If your plans call for a trip between Juneau and Sitka, one of the most pleasant ways to travel between the two ports is via ferries of the *Alaska Marine Highway System* (800-642-0066; ferryalaska.com). Try to catch whichever ferry happens to be stopping at Hoonah, Tenakee Springs (most trips), and Angoon. Of course, you don't have to be heading to Sitka to visit these small communities. You can, if you like, simply take a round-trip from Juneau to one or all three, then return by ferry or small plane to Juneau.

Located on the northeast shore of Chichagof Island, about 40 miles and 3 ferry hours north of Juneau, lies *Hoonah,* a thriving village of mostly Tlingit people. If you're not laying over, check with your ship's purser and see if you have time to mosey into the village (about a 15-minute walk). If you don't, at least take the time to visit the graveyard right across the highway from the ferry dock. You'll find some graves there that are quite old, others new, some traditional with angel figures, others marked with the distinctive Russian Orthodox Church's cross and its distinctive crossbar pattern, and still others with cast figures from the Tlingit totemic tradition.

In town you'll find two restaurants plus lodging, grocery, gift, and general merchandise establishments. Nearby Icy Strait Point is wildly popular with cruise ship visitors that just sleep on the ship, but there are a few shoreside accommodations for people who arrive by ferry or plane. Check out *Icy Strait Lodge* (907-531-1853; icystraitlodge.com), which also offers car rentals, boat rentals, and a restaurant/bar combo; rooms start at $175 for a room with one queen bed, or $190 for two queen beds. You can also stay at *Port Frederick Lodge* (907-945-3337; portfredericklodge.com), a three-bedroom lodge that sleeps up to seven people and offers laundry facilities, a full kitchen, a firepit and sauna, and the chance of seeing humpback whales right from the lodge on summer days.

Want to see a genuine brown bear while you're in the area? Check out the village garbage dump (honest), about 2 miles from town. But do not walk to the site. Get someone to drive you, or hire a cab. These critters are big and wild.

Between Hoonah and Sitka, the ferry stops occasionally at *Tenakee Springs,* long enough sometimes for passengers to run with towel in hand to the community's hot springs for a quick, relaxing soak. The springs,

Bold and Beautiful Lituya Bay

In 1958 an earthquake rattled the land in Southeast Alaska along the Fairweather fault, and a huge chunk of earth—40 million cubic feet of dirt and rocks—broke off from a piece of mountainside and landed in a picturesque T-shaped body of water known as Lituya Bay. It's hard to say there is a "prettiest" place in Alaska. Snow-tipped mountains, aquamarine glaciers, forested hillsides, and broad sweeping rivers all have a way of capturing the eye. But Lituya Bay, on the passage north from Cross Sound to the community of Yakutat, might just qualify.

On this day, though, July 10 to be exact, you would not have wanted to be in Lituya Bay. As the landslide thundered into the water, it caused a giant wave—called a splash or seiche wave—that surged to the opposite side of the bay at the alarming height of 1,740 feet, taller than the 1,250-foot Empire State Building.

The wave plucked the trees along the bay like a gardener pulling weeds. It scoured the soil down to bedrock. Surely any animals in the wave's path were swept out to sea and gone forever. Later, the unearthed trees floated in the bay like matchsticks, stripped of their bark and branches, and twisted into splinters. Even loggers couldn't salvage the useless debris.

The Lituya Bay seiche wave set a record that has never come close to being broken. The second-highest recorded seiche wave was a mere 230 feet, caused by a landslide in a lake in Norway.

incidentally, provided one of the principal reasons for the community's founding back in 1899. Miners would journey to the site every winter when cold weather shut down their "diggin's" and they'd stay for weeks or months. The tradition continues, sort of. Lots of Juneauites, Sitkans, and other Southeast Alaska residents still come to take in the waters, both winter and summer. Interestingly, there are posted hours for men's bathing and other hours for women. But never the twain meet, at least not in the 5-by-9-foot bathing pool. You'll find several overnight options in Tenakee Springs, including the **Bear Rental Cabin** (907-736-2252; no website) just around the corner from **Tenakee Springs Market** (907-736-2205; tenakeespringsak.com), the town's only grocery, hardware, and liquor store. The cabin has two single beds and rents for $125 a night, with substantial discounts for multi-night or weekly stays. You can sometimes see whales right from the covered deck of **Sea View Cottage** (907-314-3439; no website), which has one queen bed and rents for $100 a night, double occupancy, with a 3-night minimum.

Another option is to book a sportfishing package from **Fishing Bear Charters & Lodge** (907-736-2350; fishingbearcharters.com). They offer guided fishing trips for salmon, halibut, and steelhead when in season. Fishing in the area is first rate; beachcombing and hiking are likewise, and chances are good that you will see sea life in the water—humpback whales, seals, sea lions, and otters. The one-way ferry trip from Juneau to Tenakee Springs starts at $56 for a walk-on (no vehicle) fare.

The Tlingit village of *Angoon* offers yet another offbeat destination from Juneau. Located on the northwest coast of Admiralty Island, the community is accessible by ferry and by air from Juneau, which is 60 air miles away. Two very comfortable lodging possibilities at Angoon—the *Favorite Bay Lodge* (907-788-3344; favoritebay.com) and the *Whalers' Cove Lodge* (800-423-3123; whalerscovelodge.com)—provide all the comforts with easy access to sportfishing, kayaking, canoeing, and simple sightseeing. The islands and waters of Kootznahoo Inlet and Mitchell Bay are prime kayaking locales.

Favorite Bay offers all-inclusive packages starting from $6,110 per person for 2 days and 3 nights, including meals, round-trip float plane transportation from Juneau, guided activities every day, and processing for up to 100 pounds of fish. Whaler's Cove offers similarly all-inclusive packages starting from $5,220 per person plus tax.

Here's one of the most economical day cruises you can experience in Alaska. Twice a month on Sunday mornings, Alaska state ferries depart from Auke Bay terminal (about 14 miles north of Juneau) for the picturesque fishing village of *Pelican,* on the northwest corner of Chichagof Island. The route takes you through Icy Straits, past prime whale-watching waters off Point Adolphus. Along the way you may view sea lions, seals, bears, deer, eagles, and other wildlife. Arrival at Pelican is at midday, and you have an hour and a half to walk along the town boardwalks, stroll around the commercial fishing docks, and watch as commercial fishers unload halibut, salmon, crab, and black cod at the cold storage plant. You can have lunch at the popular *Rose's Bar and Grill* (no phone number; open seasonally). The return ferry departs midafternoon and arrives 7 hours later in Juneau. If that's too much time afloat, you can fly back on *Alaska Seaplanes* (907-789-3331; alaskaseaplanes.com), starting from $219. The ferry trip from Juneau starts from $69 each way (800-642-0066; visit ferryalaska.com). For fully high-end lodging, plan to stay at the *Highliner Lodge* (877-386-0397; highlinerlodge.com). The rooms and suites are comfortable, with all-inclusive stays starting from $5,500 per guest for 3 days and 4 nights. Those prices include round-trip transport from Juneau, meals, full-day guided fishing trips, fish processing, and basics like waterproof rain gear to help you stay comfortable.

The people of *Haines* will tell you, perhaps with some justification, that their community has the best summer weather in Southeast Alaska. The warmer, drier air of the Yukon interior regions, they say, flows over Chilkat Pass into the Chilkat Valley and brings with it more sunshine and less rainfall than other panhandle communities experience. Whatever the reason, Haines and vicinity do offer the visitor a pleasurable place to perch for a day—or a few days.

Sadly, many visitors pass Haines by. They're in such a toot to get off the ferry and rush north to the main body of Alaska, they miss many of Haines's considerable pleasures, like the cultural exhibits at old Fort William Henry Seward. The old fort itself is now a National Historic Landmark, with rows of elegant officers' homes and a military parade ground. You'll also find a fascinating museum of Southeastern Alaska, an excellent museum of natural history, and a state park that many rank among America's most pleasurable.

You get to Haines aboard the ferries of the Alaska Marine Highway System, either from Skagway, an hour's sailing from the north, or from Juneau, about 4 ½ hours from the south. Passengers-only water taxis make several round-trips daily between Haines and Skagway, so it's easy to make day trips from one to the other. Or, if you're already on the Alaska Highway or are starting your trip from the Yukon Territory, you can drive to Haines over the 151-mile Haines Highway, which joins with the Alaska Highway at Haines Junction, Yukon Territory, Canada. You can also fly to Haines with any of several excellent small-plane carriers that provide frequent scheduled flights from Juneau and Skagway. A round-trip on Alaska Seaplanes starts at about $350. Rugged coastlines, thickly forested islands, high-rising mountains, and Davidson and Rainbow Glaciers are only a few of the sights you encounter along the way.

southeast alaska facts

In June 1986, Hubbard Glacier advanced so quickly that it sealed off Russell Fjord, turning the saltwater inlet into a freshwater lake. Concern for the fate of seals and porpoises trapped by the ice led to several unsuccessful rescue attempts. In October of that year, the ice dam broke and the animals escaped. The 80-mile-long glacier, which terminates in Yakutat Bay, has advanced at least ten times since the last ice age.

Once you're in Haines, a good place to stop for advice, a map, and literature is the *visitor information center* (907-766-6418; visithaines.com) on Second Avenue South, about a block from the Haines downtown business district. Only a few minutes' walk from the visitor center is the *Sheldon Museum and Cultural Center* (907-766-2366; sheldonmuseum.org), on the harbor end of Main Street. Steve Sheldon arrived in Haines from his native Ohio in 1911 and met and married a woman from Pennsylvania, also an avid collector. Their family hobby has resulted in what is now the Sheldon Museum, a collection that encompasses Tlingit basketry and totemic art (including a rare, unfinished Chilkat ceremonial blanket), mementos of Fort Seward (later called

Chilkoot Barracks when it housed the only U.S. troops in Alaska), photos of colorful Jack Dalton, plus pack saddles and other gear Dalton used to clear the Dalton Trail toll road to the Klondike. You can also see the shotgun he kept loaded behind the bar of his saloon. The museum is generally open 10:00 a.m. to 5:00 p.m. Tuesday through Saturday, and they open on other days if a cruise ship is in town. Admission is $10 for adults, free for children 12 and under.

Another museum, part of the *American Bald Eagle Foundation* (907-766-3094; baldeagles.org), features a collection of Southeast Alaska natural history. The animals, birds, and fish of the region are displayed in a beautiful diorama of taxidermy. The foundation is a block from the visitor information center, at the intersection of Second Avenue South and the Haines Highway. Admission costs $25 and includes a visit to the raptor center as well.

Haines's premier attraction is unquestionably *Fort William Henry Seward,* established in 1904, renamed Chilkoot Barracks in 1922, and deactivated in 1946. The government sold the entire fort to a group of World War II veterans in 1947, and although their plans to create a business cooperative did not fully work out, the fort's picturesque buildings have been largely preserved. You can, in fact, sleep and dine in any of several grand old officers' quarters, which now serve as hotels, motels, or B&Bs. Other old structures still at the fort include warehouses, the cable office, and barracks. One large building now houses the *Chilkat Center for the Arts.* In still other fort buildings, you can see contemporary Tlingit craftsmen of *Alaska Indian Arts* (AIA) fashion large and small works of traditional art from wood, silver, fabric, and soapstone. Totem poles carved and created by AIA on the fort grounds can be seen all over Alaska and, indeed, the world. You'll see traditional art, too, at the *Totem Village Tribal House,* also on the fort parade grounds.

Adjacent to the fairgrounds at the northern edge of the city (Haines is home to the *Southeast Alaska State Fair* each August), you'll come to some gold rush–era buildings that may seem vaguely familiar. These buildings, now called *Dalton City,* served as the set for the Walt Disney movie *White Fang,* based on Jack London's novel. When the moviemaking ended, the Disney company donated the set to the community. The buildings may be of recent origin, but they present an authentic picture of a gold rush community during the tumultuous time of the Klondike gold stampede. Picture-taking opportunities abound, and the "city" is sometimes used for summer concerts.

A site often overlooked by visitors is *Chilkat State Park,* about 8 miles south of town on Mud Bay Road. You don't have to be a camper to enjoy this forested 6,000-acre wonderland on the Chilkat Peninsula. For visitors seeking just an afternoon outing, there are ample trails, saltwater beach walks, and gorgeous views of Davidson and Rainbow Glaciers. The state charges $20 for camping here, and there's a public use cabin, the **Glacier View Cabin**, that you can rent from $60 a night, if you're willing to hike 1½ miles to this foot-access-only building (for reservations, alaskastateparks.reserveamerica.com; 844-351-9733).

In the late fall and early winter, throngs of eager birders arrive to visit the **Alaska Chilkat Bald Eagle Preserve,** just a few minutes' drive from the city. There, 2,500 to 4,000 American bald eagles gather each year to feast on a late run of Chilkat River salmon. This is the world's largest concentration of bald eagles, and the spectacle is easily seen from turnoffs alongside the highway. Eagles and many other bird species can be viewed there year-round, and other wildlife is frequently spotted, especially during summer float trips down the stream.

Chilkat Guides (907-313-4420; chilkatguides.com) offers daily raft trips through some of the most spectacular portions of the Chilkat River and the preserve. This is a gentle float in spacious 18-foot rubber rafts. Eagles, bears, moose, even wolves, if you're lucky, may be seen during the 4-hour trip. The tour begins with a motorcoach pickup near the old army dock, and includes a 30-mile drive to the preserve. Then comes the float downriver to a haul-out spot near the village of Klukwan. The price starts from $150 for adults.

Chilkat Guides also offers float trips down the magnificent **Alsek and Tatshenshini Rivers,** which flow out of the Canadian interior. These 13- and 10-day trips, respectively, open up some of the world's most awesome mountain/glacier/wild river country. Exciting whitewater, relaxing floats, abundant wildlife, and wild-country treks are only a few of the features of these premier experiences, which begin in Haines and end in Yakutat, for a jet flight back to Juneau. Prices start from $6,300 plus tax for the Alsek River and $5,500 plus tax for the Tatshenshini River.

Another option for shorter sightseeing of the area is with **Alaska Nature Tours** (907-766-2876; alaskanaturetours.net), one of Haines's longest-running tour operators. The company offers guided hikes that range from relatively easy to strenuous all-day affairs. Try the Chilkat Rainforest Nature Hike, which travels through rainforest, coastal meadow, and beach over its 3-mile course.

southeastalaskatrivia

What is believed to be the tallest Sitka spruce in Alaska stands near the Naha River, 35 miles north of Ketchikan. The behemoth is 250 feet tall and measures 71 inches around at its base. If confirmed by state forestry officials, it will top the old record holder, a 185-foot tree at Exchange Cove on Prince of Wales Island.

The hike comes with a picnic lunch and is perfect for those who want to take it easy and enjoy the scenery. The 4-hour, mostly flat trek starts from $90.

Hikers who want more of a challenge could tackle the DIY hike up *Mount Ripinsky,* a local favorite that will take all day to climb. The reward for this strenuous hike is stunning views of ice-capped mountains and vistas from some 3,600 feet above town. There are three different trailheads; visithaines.com is a good source for details.

Here's something different to try while in Haines: You can visit one of the oldest fish cannery sites in all of Southeast Alaska at *Haines Packing Company* (907-766-2883; hainespacking.com). The cannery is located at mile 5.5 of Mud Bay Road. Bring your camera and call ahead to confirm their hours. They also have a store in downtown Haines, where you can buy a variety of Alaska-made goods.

Bicyclists can join other pedalers on day rides or longer tours through *Sockeye Cycle* (907-766-2869; sockeyecycle.com) of both Haines and Skagway. In Haines they're located on Portage Street, uphill from the dock in Fort Seward. Their excursions include a day trip to *Chilkoot Lake,* from $109 per adult or, at the other end of the difficulty spectrum, a 350-mile, 9-day Golden Circle Tour north from Haines up the Haines Highway to Canada's Yukon, east to Whitehorse in the Yukon Territory on the Alaska Highway, then south on the Klondike Highway to Skagway. That trip starts at $3,450 per person, with a single supplement of $600 if you're alone. If you just want to rent a bike and explore on your own, prices start at $34 for 4 hours or $55 for a full day.

For historical accommodations overlooking the Fort Seward parade grounds and also (from some of the rooms) the harbor, check out the *Hotel Halsingland* (907-766-2000; hotelhalsingland.com). Once the quarters for the fort commanders and bachelor officers, this hotel is on the National Register of Historic Places and each of its thirty-five guest rooms is full of individual quirks and personality. The beds are comfortable, and the home-baked goods in the morning are to die for. The hotel used to have some of the best dinners in town, too, but their restaurant has been closed for a number of seasons now. If you happen to find it open during a visit, you must go. Rooms start from $159. Hotel Halsingland is also the site of the local *Avis Car Rental* (907-766-2733; avisalaska.com).

Also on the parade grounds in Officers' Row are *Fort Seward Condos* (907-766-2708; fortsewardcondos.com) originally established by the late Ted and Mimi Gregg, who were among the original purchasers of the fort back in the 1940s. These completely furnished one-, two-, and three-bedroom apartments come with fully equipped kitchens. Rates start at $180 per night with a 2-night minimum.

If you want to stay on the waterfront, check out *A Sheltered Harbor Bed and Breakfast* (907-766-2741; asheltEredharbor.com). There are five rooms with private baths, and breakfasts are a tasty, filling affair. Prices start from $115 single occupancy or $135 double occupancy. The *Beach Roadhouse* (907-314-0571; beachroadhouse.com) isn't actually on the beach, but it's close to the trailhead for *Battery Point*, a popular hike along the coast. Accommodations include cabins, private rooms, and a yurt (starting from $140). *Lynn View Lodge* (907-314-0976; lynnviewlodge.com) is very close to the coast, with beautiful views of *Tanani Bay* and *Lynn Canal*, plus private beach access and a small car rental company. Their accommodations include cabins and a small front room (both from $150), suites from $200, and a self-contained apartment from $240.

For a unique experience, check out *Valley of the Eagles Golf Links* (907-766-2401; hainesgolf.com). Located right next to the ocean on glacial rebound lands that are rising almost an inch a year, the course features spectacular scenery, including trout and salmon streams. It's not uncommon to see tracks where moose or bear have ambled across the artificial turf, which has been installed to protect the area from the effects of harsh chemical fertilizers. Don't expect perfect, manicured greens, but that's all part of the charm.

Haines has developed into a haven for wonderfully eclectic off-road adventures. Just a few of the wonderful options that take you off the asphalt include *Chilkat River Adventures* (907-313-4422; jetboatalaska.com), which offers boat tours into remote parts of the Chilkat Bald Eagle Preserve, where you may also see other wildlife including moose and bears; *Fly Drake* (907-314-0675; flydrake.com) and *Mountain Flying Service* (907-766-3007; mountainflyingservice.com), both of which offer flightseeing tours over Glacier Bay and air-taxi service for backcountry drop-offs; and *Rainbow Glacier Tours* (907-766-3576; tourhaines.com), which offers photography, wildlife, and rafting tours.

Haines Rafting Company (907-314-0340; hainesrafting.com) also offers rafting tours in a small-group, multi-day format, and *SEAK Expeditions* (907-303-0234; seakexpeditions.com) offers sea-kayaking day trips and longer excursions. If you like more independent water excursions, *Alaska River Outfitters* (907-766-3307; alaskariveroutfitters.com) will rent you a raft, pack your food, and drop you at a put-in location on either the Tatshenshini or the Alsek River.

When you're ready to leave town, if you're Skagway bound and don't have a car, consider the *Haines Skagway Fast Ferry* or *HSFF* (hainesskagway fastferry.com), which can ferry you in 45 minutes across the water what would take 6 hours to drive. Their large, comfortable fast ferries make half a dozen crossings per day and have plenty of observation deck space for sightseeing. The cost starts from $102 round-trip or $55 one way.

In the annals of the nineteenth-century American frontier, no town had a more frantic, frenzied, fascinating history than *Skagway.* This city at the northern end of Lynn Canal, some 90 miles north of Juneau, was packed to overflowing during the "Days of '98," when thousands of would-be gold seekers poured into the community to outfit themselves for treks to the Klondike gold fields. It was one of the most lawless towns under the American flag. Jefferson "Soapy" Smith and his gang of toughs and con men controlled the city, prompting the superintendent of the Canadian North West Mounted Police across the border to call it "little better than hell on earth." Much of the town today makes up the *Klondike Gold Rush National Historical Park,* which is amazingly well-preserved, with many structures from the late nineteenth and early twentieth centuries still standing and in use. There's still a lot of violence in this town . . . but it's all make-believe, a nightly reenactment of the July 8, 1898, shootout between "good guy" citizen Frank Reid and "bad guy" desperado Soapy Smith. (Both men died in the encounter.)

There's more to Skagway than gold rush structures and shoot-outs, though. There is, for instance, the *White Pass & Yukon Route* (907-343-7373; wpyr .com). Declared an International Historic Civil Engineering Landmark by the American Society of Civil Engineers—a designation achieved by barely more than a dozen other projects, including the Eiffel Tower in Paris and the Statue of Liberty in New York—the narrow-gauge railway provides one of North America's premier rail experiences. Construction of the line between Skagway and Whitehorse, Yukon, began in 1898, against horrendous grades and incredible natural obstacles. The builders clawed and blasted their way to the 2,885-foot White Pass in 1899 and to Whitehorse the following year. The WP&YR today carries visitors from Skagway, at sea level, to the pass in the incredibly short distance of only 20 miles.

The fully narrated 3-hour tour, called the Summit Excursion, starts from $146 for adults and takes in the most spectacular sights of the cliff-hanging mountain and lush valley. Another option is the 8-hour excursion to *Lake Bennett* and on to Carcross, Yukon Territory, where

southeast*alaska*facts

Early on October 24, 1918, the SS *Princess Sophia,* a passenger vessel carrying 350 people, went aground on Vanderbilt Reef in Lynn Canal. Forced off the reef the following evening by storm and high tides, the *Princess Sophia* sank and all aboard perished.

some 20,000 stampeders camped during the winter of 1898 after climbing and crossing the Chilkoot Pass. (They then proceeded by boat and raft through additional lakes, rapids, and riverways to the Klondike.) Prices for that excursion start from $265 per person.

Speaking of the railroad, the headquarters and information center of the Klondike Gold Rush National Historical Park is located in the restored old **WP&YR Depot,** at Second Avenue and Broadway. You'll find historical photos, artifacts, and film showings there plus visitor information about the town and current conditions on the **Chilkoot Trail.** Walks through the downtown historic district guided by park service rangers leave from the center several times daily. The National Park Service, at substantial effort, has restored a number of Skagway's most historic buildings, including the **Mascot Saloon,** Third Avenue and Broadway, built in 1898, and the **Trail Inn and Pack Train Saloon,** Fourth Avenue and Broadway, constructed in 1908. **Captain Benjamin Moore's cabin,** a half block west of Broadway between Fifth and Sixth Avenues, dates from 1887; the good captain was there, waiting for the gold rush to start, when the first stampeders clambered ashore a decade later. Call 907-983-9200 for information about free walking tours.

The city also has a free self-guided walking tour that takes in downtown businesses and some of the Victorian-style homes in the community. Maps are available at the visitor center. For further information call 907-983-2854.

Other worthwhile stops in Skagway include the **Corrington Museum of Alaska History** (907-983-3939; alaskasbestshopping.com), at Fifth Avenue and Broadway, with exhibits from prehistory to modern-day Alaska, and **Gold Rush Cemetery,** about 1½ miles north from downtown, where Frank Reid and Soapy Smith lie buried.

The **Arctic Brotherhood Hall,** at Second Avenue and Broadway, is worth a look-see if for no other reason than an interesting photo opportunity. It's old, having been built in 1899 to house "Camp Skagway Number 1" of a once-thriving Alaska-Yukon fraternal organization of gold seekers. And its curious, false-fronted facade is covered with more than twenty thousand (count 'em, twenty thousand) big and little rounded pieces of driftwood.

During the Klondike Gold Rush, Skagway was the jumping-off place for the White Pass Trail of '98 horse and wagon route to the Yukon. For stampeders who couldn't afford either pack horses or wagons, the nearby community of **Dyea** (pronounced Dy-EE) was the starting point for the famous Chilkoot Trail to the gold fields. The trail today is part of the Klondike Gold Rush National Historical Park and, like trekkers of old, you, too, can hike from Dyea (accessible by gravel road, 9 miles north of Skagway) to Lake Bennett. It's a 3- to 6-day walk, with some shelters along the way. For details from the National Park office, call 907-983-9200.

Although the Chilkoot Trail is the best-known trail in the area, the hiker with limited time can enjoy several other hiking options, including the easy, woodsy *Lower Dewey Trail,* which is less than a mile long. You'll find the *Skyline Trail and A.B. Mountain* longer (more than 3 miles to the summit), more strenuous, but greatly rewarding. ("A.B.," incidentally, stands for Arctic Brotherhood, a Gold Rush fraternal organization.)

A Chilkoot Trail map and maps of area hiking destinations are available at the city and park service visitor centers.

For the truly adventurous, try Alaska's all-time favorite winter sport in the middle of the summer. *Alaska Icefield Expeditions* (907-983-2886; alaska icefieldexpeditions.com) has teamed up with several local helicopter companies to offer spectacular glacier flightseeing by helicopter combined with a glacier landing and sled dog rides. Meet professional mushers and their four-legged teammates and go for a sled dog ride on the Herbert Glacier, starting at $659 per person.

Another dry-land option is horseback riding with *M&M Tours* (907-983-3900; skagwayalaskatours.com). This 3 ½-hour tour includes round-trip transportation, a snack, and good odds of seeing wildlife as you ride through the rainforest for views of the Dyea tidal flats. Tours start from $180.

While in Skagway, don't pass up the chance to see a true piece of history on Seventh Avenue and Spring Street. Built in 1900, the McCabe Building is the first granite building in the state of Alaska, and it was originally intended to be a women's college. The building now houses the *Skagway City Hall* and *Skagway Museum and Archives* (907-983-2420; skagway.org/museum). The collection includes "good guy" Frank Reid's will, the tie "bad guy" Soapy Smith was wearing during the shootout, and examples of traditional Alaska Native watercraft, including a kayak and a canoe. Admission is $2.

Also in Skagway is *At the White House Bed and Breakfast* (907-983-9000; atthewhitehouse.com), a beautifully renovated Victorian-style home that was almost destroyed by fire in the late '70s. Owners Jan and John Tronrud have done an excellent job decorating the home, which has nine guest rooms. Rates start at $179.

The *Historic Skagway Inn* (907-531-7630; skagwayinn.com), at Seventh and Broadway, traces its origins to 1897 and its days as a brothel providing "services" for lonely gold stampeders. Today the inn contains ten rooms restored to Victorian charm. Some rooms share a bath. Innkeepers Karl Klupar and Rosemary Libert offer full breakfasts, home-baked muffins, fresh-ground coffee, piping-hot tea, courtesy van service (including transportation for hikers to the start of the Chilkoot Trail), and Alaskan expertise. Rates start at $219 for two twin beds. In the evening, incidentally, you can purchase dinner at the restaurant there called *Olivia's at the Skagway Inn.* This is probably Skagway's most expensive restaurant, but expect it to be worth the tariff. It is a fine dining experience.

Skagway Bungalows (907-983-2986; skagwaybungalows.com) offers one of Skagway's most peaceful-feeling experiences, even though it's just 1.5 miles from the airport and ferry terminal. There are two cabins, one with a king-size bed and the other with a queen bed and a double futon. The cabins are basic but comfortable, each with a writing table and chairs, microwave, refrigerator, an electric kettle with complimentary tea, coffee, and cocoa, and—maybe most exciting in this kind of accommodation—a private bathroom with running water. A cabin is $140 per night, double occupancy; additional guests are $20 each.

Perhaps the strangest "cabin" in the US Forest Service wilderness cabin network is the retired White Pass & Yukon Route *Denver Caboose,* located 5½ miles north of Skagway. The view, a stunner, takes in the Skagway River and the Sawtooth Mountains. Visitors may rent this unit for $45 a night, just like most others in the system, but instead of flying, hiking, or boating in you reach the caboose by—you guessed it—taking the train! For information call 877-444-6777 or go to www.recreation.gov.

For a truly off-the-beaten-path camping experience, travel 9 miles down the road to the *Dyea Campground.* There are many things about this hidden treasure that make it so special. First, it only costs $10 per night to camp. Second, it is located among lush green trees, which make the air feel particularly clean and clear. And third, if you're like me and enjoy a closer-to-nature experience, there are only the basics—pit toilets, water from a simple pump, and lots of space to spread a tent and enjoy the surroundings. No humming generators here! For further information on the campground, call the park service at 907-983-9200.

For bicyclists, *Sockeye Cycle* (907-983-2851; sockeyecycle.com) of Skagway and Haines, offers a 10-day Canol Road Tour, which explores the sparsely populated Northeast Yukon Territory via an old World War II dirt road. The tour includes special mountain bikes and gear as well as lodging and three meals a day. You can also rent a bike and explore on your own (from $34 for 4 hours, or $55 for a full day) or book a day trip like the 3-hour Rainforest Bicycle Tour (from $99).

Skagway is the southern terminus of the *Klondike Highway,* which extends into British Columbia and Canada's Yukon Territory. Each fall, on a designated weekend in September, the highway becomes less a highway and more a race course as hundreds of running teams from all over the United States and Canada arrive to race in stages all the way to Whitehorse, 110 miles away. For dates and information about the ***Klondike International Road Relay,*** check out klondikeroadrelay.com or call Sport Yukon at 867-668-4236.

Glacier Bay National Park and the Community of Gustavus

No question about it, ***Glacier Bay National Park and Preserve*** is one of the extraordinary parks of the nation. Home to sixteen massive, glistening saltwater glaciers and the site of hundreds of valley and mountaintop ice masses, Glacier Bay National Park is all about the power of ice in shaping a land. It's a place where the relentless grinding force of glaciers has carved deep, steep-walled saltwater fjords and U-shaped mountain valleys, and it's a place of stark, barren, rocky expanses where glaciers have only recently receded. It's also a land of mature, lush spruce and hemlock forests, where the ice receded decades ago. It's a place where the word *awesome* comes frequently to mind.

Glacier Bay National Park lies some 60 miles west of Juneau, accessible by cruise ship, yacht, jet, or light aircraft. Visits can be as short as a day trip out of Juneau or as long as a week or more. The community of ***Gustavus,*** easily reached by air, abuts the park and provides a rich variety of guiding, fishing, lodging, and supply services.

If you want lodging within the park boundaries, your only choice (though highly pleasurable) is ***Glacier Bay Lodge*** (888-229-8687; visitglacierbay.com) on the shores of ***Bartlett Cove.*** The lodge is a fifty-six-room resort located 10 miles from the community of Gustavus. It contains fully modern guest rooms, dining room, cocktail lounge, small gift shop, and the ***National Park Service Glacier Bay Visitor Center.*** Rooms begin at $280 per person per night. Ask about rooms with a view of the cove and about packages that include meals, the Glacier Bay Day Tour, and transfers from Gustavus.

A high-speed catamaran departs Bartlett Cove daily for a full-day cruise; the aptly named ***Glacier Bay Day Tour*** (888-229-8687; visitglacierbay.com) is the only scheduled tour actually permitted inside Glacier Bay National Park & Preserve. Your outing includes close-up looks at glaciers, thousands of birds, and good prospects of viewing brown bears and mountain goats on land plus whales, porpoises, and seals in the water. Although nobody can guarantee the glaciers will calve while your boat is there, it happens very frequently, and Park Service naturalists accompany each sailing. The fare, including lunch onboard, starts from $272 per person. The lodge (and most other accommodations in this area) would also be happy to help you arrange package tours that include whale watching, kayaking, flightseeing, and fishing.

The Grass Is Always Greener

During a visit to Gustavus—the gateway to Glacier Bay National Park—a few years ago, one of the young staff members in the lodge expressed how much she admired my willingness to travel alone in remote places. We had a nice conversation about solo travel, but I've always regretted not thinking—until it was too late—to mention how adventurous I thought she was, too, for working in such a remote place.

I was just passing through for a few days, taking full advantage of the amenities available to me. Meanwhile she was living there for the summer, thousands of miles from home, juggling all the social dynamics of existing within a small community as an outsider, not to mention the surely challenging dynamics of working closely with a small team on a grueling schedule. If she needed to get away for a while, where was she supposed to go?

That conversation, and what I wish I'd added to it, has stuck in my head as an example of two things: First, never be shy, as I was in that moment, about letting someone else know you admire their fortitude. You never know how much good a simple, sincere compliment can do, and I regret missing that opportunity to let that young woman know I admired her.

Second, the grass really is almost always greener, or perhaps more adventurous-looking, on the other side. I didn't feel I was doing anything unusual by being there on my own, and I imagine she might have said the same about herself working there. But that encounter was a fine illustration of how one person's "easy" can be another's "hard" and vice versa.

Now, about Gustavus, next door to the park. Funny place, this little city. Except it wasn't a proper city, much less a town, until 2004. Until then, the six-hundred-some strong-willed, individualistic citizens who live there voted repeatedly not to become any sort of official city with trappings like mayors or government. But Gustavus has always been a definable community because these same people—as friendly and sharing and helpful as they are fiercely independent—manage to provide everything that they need to happily reside there. They're equally prepared to provide travelers with everything they need to visit for a few days or a season.

The setting is awesome, bounded on three sides by the snowcapped peaks of the Chilkat Range and the Fairweather Mountains and on the fourth by smooth, sandy, saltwater beaches. The community spreads itself sparsely over miles of flat countryside and includes boundless opportunities for berry picking, hiking, bicycle riding, kayaking, golfing, whale watching, freshwater and saltwater angling, beachcombing, birding, and just gawking.

For such a small community, Gustavus has no shortage of fine lodging. The first place that comes to mind is the handcrafted **Bear Track Inn** (907-697-3017; beartrackinn.com), a comfortable, inviting log lodge with 30-foot ceilings, fourteen spacious rooms, and superb food. Nightly rates start at $520 for a meadow view room or $570 for a water view room and include meals and ground transportation; tours like sea kayaking, saltwater and freshwater fishing, and visiting a nearby hot springs all cost extra and can be booked through the inn (and any other lodgings here).

The Bear Track Inn sits on the east side of Gustavus. To the west, the **Glacier Bay Country Inn** (480-725-3446; glacierbayalaska.com) also offers a high-quality experience in a setting of verdant forests and majestic mountains. Here, too—in a distinctive structure with multiangled roofs, dormers, decks, and log-beamed ceilings—informally gracious living and fine dining are trademarks. Lodge rooms start at $329 per person, based on double occupancy; this includes three full meals and ground transportation. Cabins are also available, starting at $449 per person per night. You can book tours through the lodge à la carte, or save a little money with their all-inclusive packages that include daily tours, too.

If you really want to explore Gustavus and Glacier Bay National Park independently, head a short distance down the road from the Glacier Bay Country Inn, also on the west side of Gustavus, to the **Annie Mae Lodge** (907-697-2346; anniemae.com). They rent stand-alone rooms, each with a private bath, refrigerator/freezer, microwave, and coffee machine. No meals or ground transfers are included, nor is there a host on site, so you'll have to handle everything yourself, à la carte.

Glacier Bay, with its protected arms and inlets, provides ideal kayaking waters for sightseeing at sea level. **Glacier Bay Sea Kayaks** (907-697-2257; glacierbayseakayaks.com), operated by longtime Alaskans Bonnie Kaden and Kara Berg, has been renting these crafts to visitors for many years, by the half-day or full day; they also offer guided kayaking in the park, including all gear and equipment. Prices start as low as $60 a day for a single kayak.

Another option is to cruise Glacier Bay aboard the *Seawolf,* a 97-foot ocean yacht with six cabins, a twelve-passenger capacity, and activity areas for all to enjoy. The *Seawolf* crew promises a maximum of 5 hours of travel each day, leaving plenty of time for exploring by water or land. Try guided kayaking with their sturdy double boats and quiet paddles, or go for a nature hike along the shore. Watch the whales, touch a glacier, or pick berries by the handful in season. It's all part of the **Seawolf Adventures** (907-957-1438; seawolfadventures.net) philosophy of making nature more than just a spectator sport. The 6-day Glacier Bay Adventure starts at $6,000 per person. The folks at Seawolf can also help you create a customized adventure. Try to contact them during the off-season, as communications are spotty once they're aboard the vessel.

Spirit Walker Expeditions (800-KAYAKER; seakayakalaska.com) offerings range from kayak day tours to nearby (and aptly named) Pleasant Island to their 6- to 7-day expedition among the (also aptly named) *Myriad Islands,* where hundreds of tiny isles make up a miniature Inside Passage. Prices for these trips range from $220 per person, for a day trip to nearby Pleasant Island, to a $3359 per person for a weeklong Myriad Island adventure.

If you're excited about fishing in this pristine section of Southeast Alaska, you might want to stay with *Alaskan Anglers Inn* (866-510-2800; alaskananglersinn.com). Their all-inclusive 5-day package starts at $4,590 per person, and includes your lodging, meals, ground transportation, fish processing, rain gear, bike rentals, access to guided and self-guided fishing . . . and hot tubs!

Jim Kearns's *Fairweather Adventures* (907-723-3065; fairweather adventures.net) offers lodging and marine wildlife tours at the mouth of Glacier Bay, on the banks of the Salmon River. Kayak trips, sportfishing, beach excursions, and exploring are all available. Lodging and breakfast are included, plus a sack lunch if you go on one of their excursions; you arrange dinner yourself at local restaurants.

When you're ready to leave Gustavus, call *Air Excursions* (907-789-3331; airexcursions.com), which is the primary airplane carrier for the community. Fares start from about $260 one way to Juneau. During the summer, you can also book a 737 flight with *Alaska Airlines* (800-252-7522; alaskaair.com)

For more information in general on the community of Gustavus, contact the *Gustavus Visitor Association* (gustavusak.com) via their online form. They are a big help in trip planning, and especially with location resources such as taxi services that tend to be seasonal, variable, and sometimes only part-time in communities of this size.

True and Unexpected

Justice Creek in Glacier Bay National Park and Preserve was named by the National Park Service after a story by Jack London titled "The Unexpected," in which justice was provided by two prospectors who, in the absence of a court, tried and executed a third person for murder. The story was based on actual events that happened in the vicinity of the creek. On October 6, 1899, one M. S. Severts calmly shared dinner with hosts Hannah and Hans Nelson and two other guests, Fragnallia Stefano and Sam Christianson. When he'd finished eating, Severts got up, went outside, and returned with a Colt .45 revolver. He fired two shots, killing Stefano and wounding Christianson, before turning the gun on Hannah. Hans leaped to her rescue. The couple hired Native people to guard the killer for several weeks while they tried to flag down passing ships. Having no success, they tried Stefano themselves, procured a signed confession, and hung him.

Places to Stay in Southeast Alaska

GUSTAVUS

Annie Mae Lodge
907-697-2346;
anniemae.com.
Essentially a DIY self-catering accommodation.

Bear Track Inn
907-697-3017;
beartrackinn.com.
A comfortable, inviting lodge with spacious rooms and superb food.

Glacier Bay Country Inn
480-725-3446;
glacierbayalaska.com.
A distinctive inn with comfortable rooms and excellent food.

Glacier Bay Lodge
888-229-8687;
www.glacierbaytours.com.
A fifty-six-room resort on the shores of Bartlett Cove.

HAINES

The Beach Roadhouse
731 Beach Road;
907-314-0571;
beachroadhouse.com.
Not quite on the beach, but close.

Fort Seward Condos
4 Fort Seward Drive;
907-766-2708;
fortsewardcondos.com.
Rental condos overlooking Fort Seward's historic parade grounds.

Hotel Halsingland
907-766–2000;
hotelhalsingland.com
Former officers' quarters, now thirty-five guest rooms full of quirks and personality.

Lynn View Lodge
1299 Lutak Road;
907-314-0976;
lynnviewlodge.com.
Beautiful views and private beach access.

A Sheltered Harbor Bed and Breakfast
907-766-2741;
asheltaredharbor.com.
On the waterfront.

HOONAH

Icy Strait Lodge
435 Airport Road;
907-531-1853;
icystraitlodge.com.
An all-in-one lodge for your adventuring needs. Car rentals, too.

Port Frederick Lodge
129 Cedar Drive;
907-945-3337;
portfredericklodge.com.
A three-bedroom lodge; you might see a whale right from the deck.

HYDER/STEWART

Ripley Creek Inn
306 Fifth Avenue;
205-636-2344;
ripleycreekinn.com.
Renovated historic buildings full of personality, plus a modern lodge.

JUNEAU

Alaska's Capital Inn Bed & Breakfast
113 West Fifth Street;
907-586-6507;

alaskacapitalinn.com.
An exquisitely restored 1906 home overlooking downtown Juneau.

Auke Lake Bed & Breakfast
11595 Mendenhall Loop Road;
907-957-9263;
aukelakebb.com.
Lakeside accommodations close to Mendenhall Glacier.

Beachside Villa Luxury Inn
3120 Douglas Highway;
907-500-7008;
beachsidevilla.com.
Boutique hotel just across Gastineau Channel from downtown Juneau.

Driftwood Hotel
435 Willoughby Avenue;
907-586-2280;
dhalaska.com.
Popular lodging for lawmakers in the state capital for the legislative session.

Juneau International Hostel
614 Harris Street;
907-586–9559;
juneauhostel.net.
Clean, spacious and friendly, in a rambling historical house.

Silverbow Inn.
120 Second Street;
907-586-4146;
silverbowinn.com.
Historic downtown boutique hotel with modern accommodations.

Westmark Baranof Hotel
127 North Franklin Street;
907-586-2660;

westmarkhotels.com.
In historic downtown
Juneau.

KETCHIKAN

Black Bear Inn
5528 North Tongass
Highway;
907-617-7567;
stayinalaska.com.
Three fairy-tale suites with
fireplaces and private
bathrooms.

Gilmore Hotel
326 Front Street;
907-225-9423;
wyndhamhotels.com.
Has a commanding view of
Ketchikan's busy waterfront.

**The Inn at
Creek Street**
133 Stedman Street;
907-225-0246;
creekstreet.com.
Budget-friendly
accommodations with
serious personality.

PELICAN

Highliner Lodge
877-386-0397;
highlinerlodge.com.
Comfortable rooms and
suites with all-inclusive
prices.

PETERSBURG

**Nordic House Bed
and Breakfast**
806 South Nordic Drive;
907-518-1926;
nordichouse.net.
Two cozy suites and a boat
for rent; very convenient to
the ferry.

Rocky Point Resort
11 miles south of town on
Wrangell Narrows;
907-772-4405;
rockypointresortak.com.

Rustic cabin suites with
bathrooms and terrific
Norwegian pastries.

Tides Inn
First and Dolphin Streets;
907-772-4288;
tidesinnalaska.net.
Forty-five modern
motel-style rooms with
kitchenettes.

PORT ALEXANDER

**Laughing Raven
Lodge**
907-568-2266;
portalexander.com.
A secluded getaway for
wildlife viewing, hiking,
kayaking, and fishing.

SITKA

**Burgess Bauder's
Lighthouse**
907-623-8410;
sitkalighthouse.com.
Located on an island a
few minutes by boat from
downtown Sitka; use of skiff
included.

Dove Island Lodge
907-747-5660;
doveislandlodge.com.
Fresh- and saltwater fishing
and an amazing spa.

Sitka Rock Suites
218-831-9578;
sitkarocksuites.com.
Studios, one- and two-
bedroom suites on the
water.

SKAGWAY

**At the White House
Bed and Breakfast**
907-983-9000;
atthewhitehouse.com.
Beautifully renovated
Victorian-style home. Two
blocks from downtown.

**Historic
Skagway Inn**
907-531-7630;
skagwayinn.com.
A former brothel, now home
to one of the city's best
restaurants.

**Skagway
Bungalows**
907-983-2986;
skagwaybungalows.com.
One of Skagway's most
peaceful-feeling options.

WRANGELL

**Grand View Bed
& Breakfast**
907-874-3225;
grandviewbnb.com.
Situated right on the water's
edge.

Sourdough Lodge
104 Peninsula Street;
907-874-3613;
thesourdoughlodge.com.
Rustic lodge
with comfortable
accommodations.

Stikine Inn
907-874–3388;
stikineinn.com.
Wrangell's largest hotel,
with thirty-three rooms,
restaurant, and meeting
rooms. One block from ferry
terminal.

Places to Eat in Southeast Alaska

GUSTAVUS

**Fireweed Gallery,
Coffee and
Tea House**
Four Corners;
907-697-3013;

fireweedcoffee.com.
A long-standing favorite
with coffee, tea, light food,
and art.

Mama Bear Kitchen
Four Corners.
Great pizza! Look for their
updates in the Gustavus
Alaska local businesses
Facebook group.

HAINES

**Bamboo Room
Restaurant and
Pioneer Bar**
Near corner of Second and
Main;
907-766-2800;
bamboopioneer.net.
Breakfast, lunch, dinner, and
full bar.

JUNEAU

Deckhand Dave's
139 South Franklin Street;
no phone number;
deckhanddaves.com.

Douglas Cafe
916 Third Street;
907-364-3307;
no website.
Perhaps the only restaurant
in Juneau that features
amber clams and amber
mussels (and, arguably,

Alaska's best clam
chowder).

El Sombrero
157 South Franklin;
907-586-6700;
no website.
Great Mexican cuisine, right
in downtown.

**Gold Creek
Salmon Bake**
907-789-0052;
alaskatraveladventures.com.
All-you-can-eat salmon
buffet, including transport
from the cruise ship docks.

**Twisted Fish
Company**
550 South Franklin Street;
907-463–5033;
twistedfishcompany.com.
Fresh seafood on the
waterfront.

**Westmark
Baranof Hotel**
127 North Franklin Street;
907-586-2660;
westmarkhotels.com.
Fine dining in historic
downtown Juneau.

KETCHIKAN

**Annabelle's
Famous Keg and
Chowder House**
326 Front Street;
907-225-9423.

Famous chowder house
with a gorgeous mahogany
bar.

PETERSBURG

Inga's Galley
North Nordic Drive and Gjoa
Street;
907-772-2090;
no website, but they're on
Facebook.
Fresh, sensational seafood
served out of a modest
building.

SKAGWAY

**Olivia's at the
Skagway Inn**
655 Broadway;
907-531-7630;
olivias-bistro.com.
A fine dining experience.
Pricey but worth it.

WRANGELL

Hungry Beaver
640 Shakes Street;
907-874-3005.
Locally famous pizza;
restaurant and lounge.

Stikine Inn
107 Stikine Avenue;
907-874-3399;
stikineinn.com.
A full-service restaurant with
a sampling of everything,
plus a small cafe.

Canada's Yukon

So, you may be asking, what is a chapter about part of Canada doing in an Alaska guidebook? Actually, there are a couple of reasons.

First, if you're driving from Southeast Alaska to Alaska's interior, you have to go through a small sliver of Canada's British Columbia and a big hunk of Canada's Yukon. From Haines or Skagway at the northern end of the Southeast Alaska ferry system, you can drive the 152-mile Haines Highway or 98 miles of the Klondike Highway to junctions with the Alaska Highway. From there your route lies northwesterly through Canada's Yukon Territory to the rest of Alaska.

Second, from the traveler's point of view, visiting Canada's Yukon is really part of the North Country experience. Aside from a few artificial differences, like Canada's metric road signs, or gasoline pumped in liters instead of gallons, you'll notice few distinctions between the Yukon and Alaska's interior region. Both are lands of rolling hills, majestic mountains, fish-filled lakes, and vast, untrammeled wilderness areas teeming with moose, caribou, bears, and wolves.

In both Interior Alaska and the Yukon, you'll marvel at a sun that nearly doesn't set during the summertime, and in both

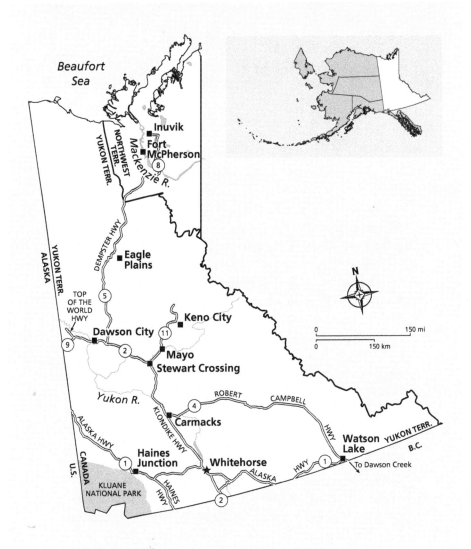

Beaufort Sea

Inuvik

Fort McPherson

NORTHWEST TERR.

YUKON TERR.

Mackenzie R.

8

DEMPSTER HWY

Eagle Plains

YUKON TERR.

ALASKA

TOP OF THE WORLD HWY

5

Dawson City

11

Keno City

9

2

Mayo

Stewart Crossing

Yukon R.

ROBERT

CAMPBELL

4

KLONDIKE HWY

Carmacks

HWY

Watson Lake

YUKON TERR.

B.C.

ALASKA HWY

Haines Junction

1

Whitehorse

ALASKA

HWY

1

To Dawson Creek

CANADA

U.S.

KLUANE NATIONAL PARK

HAINES HWY

2

N

0   150 mi

0   150 km

TOP 10 PLACES IN CANADA'S YUKON

Carcross	Kluane Lake
Discovery Claim	Midnight Dome
Herschel Island	Sign Post Forest
Inn on the Lake Bed and Breakfast	SS *Klondike*
Jack London's cabin	Takhini Hot Springs

you'll find friendly, helpful, outgoing folk who revel in their Native heritage, their gold rush past, and their present-day frontier lifestyle.

The main arterial road of the Yukon Territory is the Alaska Highway, also referred to by many as the Alcan, although some would say that's rather like calling San Francisco "Frisco." The fabled road begins at Dawson Creek in British Columbia, meanders through the Yukon Territory to the Alaska border, and ends at Delta Junction, Alaska—a total journey of 1,422 miles.

The two largest cities of the Yukon are Whitehorse, present-day capital of the territory, and Dawson City (not to be confused with Dawson Creek, B.C.). It was near the present site of Dawson City, in 1896, that the discovery of gold on a tributary of the Klondike River set off one of the world's wildest stampedes.

In both Alaska and the Yukon, you'll see numbers on frequent mileposts or kilometer posts beside the highways. These numbers represent miles or kilometers from a highway's beginning. Home and business addresses and even cities are often referenced in miles or kilometers. Whitehorse, for instance, is shown in a Yukon government guidebook as being located at kilometer 1,455.3 on the Alaska Highway. In this Canadian section of this book, we'll identify most sites by their kilometer-post markings, although in discussing short drives and distances, we'll frequently refer to miles, since most U.S. residents have a better feel for mileage measurements. When, in the next chapter, we're back in Alaska, U.S.A., highway references will be in miles.

Here's a word of explanation about the layout of this chapter. It assumes you'll be traveling northerly through the Yukon to Interior Alaska either from Skagway (over the southern half of the Klondike Highway), Haines (over the Haines Highway), or Dawson Creek (at the start of the Alaska Highway). So, to start with, the chapter discusses sights and options along each of these three northbound approaches to Whitehorse. After a discussion of things to see and do in Whitehorse, the chapter describes the northern portion of the Klondike Highway from near Whitehorse to Dawson City. After suggesting a round-trip on the Dempster Highway from Dawson City to Inuvik in Canada's Northwest

Territories, it deals—still Alaska-bound—with the Top of the World Highway north and west from Dawson City to the point where it crosses the border and meets Alaska's Taylor Highway. The Taylor, in turn, is described from northernmost Eagle to Tetlin Junction on the Alaska Highway, 80 miles northwest of the Alaska border.

Finally, the chapter backtracks to Whitehorse and lists your Alaska Highway options between that city and the point where you cross into Interior Alaska and the United States again. Of course, if you're departing Interior Alaska and heading southerly to Southeast Alaska or Dawson Creek, British Columbia, follow the listings in reverse.

Remember that as of 2025, you need certain types of identification to reenter the United States, even when traveling by road. These include your U.S. passport, passport card, Trusted Traveler program cards like NEXUS or SENTRI if they apply to you, and an enhanced driver's license or Tribal card. Remember to check restrictions on bringing firearms, alcohol, and certain fresh foods across the U.S. and Canadian borders, and be aware that Canada has different rules for entry if you've committed certain criminal offenses, such as driving under the influence. For current information, visit travel.state.gov.

Customs stations may be a few miles on either side of the actual border, with several miles separating the U.S. and Canadian customs stops in some locations. Usually, you only need to stop at the border-crossing station for whichever country you're *entering;* you're not required to stop when you're exiting. And be sure to check customs operating hours when planning your trip. Some stations are open 24 hours, but others, such as the U.S. border crossing on the Top of the World Highway, are open only about 12 hours per day. If the customs checkpoint is closed, the road will be gated and you'll have to wait at the border until it reopens.

The Klondike Highway: Skagway to Whitehorse

Don't let the start of the **Klondike Highway** out of Skagway scare you. The first 10 or 11 miles climb at a pretty steep grade, from sea level to 3,000-feet plus, but after that the going's relatively level and certainly no worse than other mountain roads in the Lower 48 and elsewhere. The road is two lanes wide and asphalt paved for its 98-mile (159-kilometer) length, and it roughly parallels the historic Trail of '98 from Skagway to the Klondike gold fields. It rises from lush, thickly vegetated low country to high rocky mountain and lake terrain with picture-postcard views and cascading waterfalls.

ANNUAL EVENTS IN CANADA'S YUKON

Fireweed Community Market:
867-333-2255;
fireweedmarket.ca.

About 70 vendors attend this outdoor market in Whitehorse, held early May through mid-September.

Yukon Rendezvous Festival
867-667-2148.
yukonrendezvous.com

Held in late February in Whitehorse, this weird and wacky festival is designed to "combat cabin fever."

Yukon Gold Panning Championship:
Call the Klondike Visitors Association at
867-993-5584;
dawsoncity.ca.

Held in July in Dawson City as part of Canada Day festivities.

Yukon Quest Sled Dog Race
1109 Front Street, Whitehorse, Yukon;
867-336-4711;
yukonquest.com

Canadian headquarters for the famous long-distance sled dog race.

At kilometer 43, take the turnout to the east for a spectacular view of *Tormented Valley,* with its little lakes, stunted trees, and rocky landscape of big and little boulders. The historic remains of an ore-crushing mill for the *Venus Mine* can be seen and photographed at kilometer 84. Twelve kilometers farther there's a spectacular view of *Bove Island* and a portion of the Yukon's southern lakes system.

The community of *Carcross,* on the shores of Lake Bennett, lies at kilometer 106. Stop by the visitor reception center in the old *White Pass & Yukon Train Depot* (867-821-4431), where you can get tourist information. Among the off-the-beaten-path stops in this historic gold rush community are the *Matthew Watson General Store* (no number, yukongeneralstore.com) and the *Barracks,* where you can soak up the atmosphere while you shop. If you've got postcards to mail, stop by the *Carcross Post Office* which first opened in 1902, where they used to stamp your passport with your choice of several commemorative postmark stamps. Unofficial passport stamps can cause problems when visiting some countries, so nowadays they'll just stamp your mail. Several prominent figures from the Klondike Gold Rush are buried in Carcross, including Kate Carmacks and Skookum Jim, but due to vandalism, the cemetery has been closed to the public.

If fishing is part of your goal, give *Boreal Kennels* (867-334-6250; borealkennels.com) a call or email. I know, it might seem weird to email a sled dog kennel about a fishing trip, but in this part of the world it's common for businesses to handle a little bit of everything—and to do it well. A guided day fishing trip starts at $395 CDN, and 3- or 5-day overnight adventures are available.

Of course, if you happen to be here during the winter you can contact Boreal Kennels about dog sledding, too. They offer half-day trips, overnight trips, and multi-day expeditions from December to April, starting at $240 CDN per person for a half-day dog-sledding tour.

If time permits, turn right at kilometer 107 and head northeast on the paved 34-mile Tagish Road to *Tagish,* Yukon Territory, then head south on the good but mostly gravel 60-mile Atlin Road to *Atlin,* British Columbia. The drive takes a little more than 2 hours. Atlin is a favorite getaway for Southeast Alaskans, many of whom have summer cottages there. *Atlin Lake* is a huge, meandering, spectacular body of water with lots of recreational opportunities. In the community itself, you can visit the *Atlin Historical Museum* (250-651-7522; atlinshistoricalsocietybc.com) at the corner of Third and Trainor in the town's original one-room schoolhouse. Admission is $5 CDN, and the museum is generally open on Thursday through Sunday from Victoria Day weekend (in mid-May) through Labor Day weekend, from 10:00 a.m. to noon and 1:00 p.m. to 5:00 p.m., although it's always a good idea to call or email ahead and confirm hours for a small institution like this. (Or just find them on Facebook.)

While there, for a small donation you can tour the *MV* **Tarahne,** which once carried freight and passengers across Atlin Lake to Scotia Bay. Tours of the drydocked vessel are available during summer. Also worth noting in town is the cold, bubbly water at the mineral springs under the gazebo at the north end of town. You can rent motorbikes or houseboats, take flightseeing excursions around the area, or engage a guide for excellent lake and stream fishing.

The community has a hotel plus several B&Bs and inns, including the quaint, summers-only, log-style *Spirit Lake Motel* (867-821-4282; spiritlakemotel.com). The *Cabins Over Crag Lake* (867-335-3610; cabinsovercraglake.com) are just a short distance out of town but make a great base camp as long as you have a car. You can enjoy spectacular lake, mountain, and glacier views from their cabins (from $219 CDN for up to two adults and two children, $25 CDN for each additional person) and $250 CDN for the yurt.

yukontrivia

Work on the White Pass and Yukon Route railway began in 1898. By July 6, 1899, the rails topped the summit and reached Lake Bennett. The narrow-gauge railway connected Carcross and Whitehorse in June 1900, and on July 29, 1900, the golden spike was driven at Carcross, marking completion of the entire line.

When you leave, you can avoid duplicating about a third of your route back to Carcross by joining the Alaska Highway at *Jake's Corner* (about 60 miles north of Atlin).

Back on the Klondike Highway, a few minutes' drive beyond Carcross lies *Wild Adventure Yukon* (867-821-4055; wildadventureyukon.ca), formerly known as Caribou Crossing, a 6-acre theme park with live Dall sheep, Stone sheep, bighorn sheep, lynx, an old-time trapper's cabin, the only mounted saber-toothed tiger in existence, plus a cafe and gift shop. On the same property but in a separate building, is the *Wildlife Gallery,* a privately owned collection of mounted Yukon wildlife in authentic dioramas, including the world's largest mounted polar bear at 11 feet 8 inches from nose to tail. Admission is $15 CDN to visit both attractions, and they offer 15- and 30-minute dog mushing experiences (from $45–$60 CDN).

Here's a Yukon superlative for you—a "smallest," not a "biggest." At kilometer 111 you pass the *Carcross Desert,* which at 260 hectares (640 acres) is the smallest desert in the world. Glaciers and a large glacial lake originally covered the area, and when the glaciers retreated, they left sand deposits on the former lake bottoms. The well-named *Emerald Lake,* nestled in the hills farther along at kilometer 120, is the subject of thousands of photo exposures each year.

At kilometer 157 (98 miles beyond its starting point at Skagway), this portion of the Klondike Highway junctions with the Alaska Highway. You're just a few minutes' drive south of Whitehorse. The northern portion of the Klondike Highway, which extends all the way to Dawson City, recommences just north of Whitehorse.

The Haines Highway: Haines to Haines Junction

The Haines Highway (which several Canadian publications call the *Haines Road)* runs 152 miles (246 kilometers) from the water's edge in Haines, Alaska, to *Haines Junction* on the Alaska Highway, west of Whitehorse. They're spectacular miles, sometimes paralleling the path of the old Dalton Trail to the Klondike. In the process, they traverse thick green forests in the Chilkat Valley at lower elevations and high, barren, mystical plains once you've climbed over Chilkat Pass. Your travel log will record frequent views of piercing sawtooth mountains plus lakes that contain monster-size trout. The road is two lanes, asphalt, and open year-round.

yukontrivia

The Yukon Territory comprises 193,380 square miles.
The population of the Yukon Territory is approximately 45,600.
Herschel is the Yukon Territory's only island.

About 9 miles from Haines, you enter the Alaska Chilkat Bald Eagle Preserve where, in winter, thousands of bald eagles gather to feast on the still-abundant salmon of the Chilkat River. If you want to stop, use pullouts and viewing areas about 10 miles farther down the road.

At mile 40 you'll arrive at U.S. Customs, but if you're Canada-bound you normally don't have to stop until you cross the U.S.-Canada border and come to **Canada Customs and Immigration Station** a couple of minutes farther on. (Remember, kilometer posts now replace mileposts in metric-minded Canada.)

You'll cross Chilkat Pass (elevation 1,065 meters; 3,493 feet) at kilometer 102 and come to **Million Dollar Falls Campground** at kilometer 167. There's pleasant camping and fishing here plus a boardwalk leading to views of the almost 200-foot waterfall, and it's an excellent picnicking choice, even if you don't want to spend the night.

Approaching kilometer 188, you come to the **St. Elias Lake Trail,** a novice- and intermediate-friendly hiking trail through subalpine meadows. It's a 6.4-kilometer (4-mile-plus) trek that offers a good chance to spot mountain goats beyond the lake.

You have another camping and fishing opportunity at big, long **Dezadeash Lake** (pronounced DEZ-dee-ash), home to lake trout, northern pike, and grayling, at kilometer 195.

At kilometer 202, you can hike **Rock Glacier Trail** in **Kluane National Park,** a half-hour walk to the rocky residue of a former glacier and a panoramic view. Rock glaciers are a unique landform created when glacial ice and frost-shattered rock mix and flow downhill.

Haines Junction, Yukon Territory, lies at Haines Highway kilometer 246, nearly 153 miles from the road's start in Haines, Alaska. Whitehorse lies about 100 Alaska Highway miles east.

The Alaska Highway: Watson Lake to Whitehorse

Amazingly, the 2,288-kilometer (1,422-mile) Alaska Highway was constructed and connected in just 8 months and 12 days as a military road during World War II. Construction started March 8, 1942, and ended October 24; it was one of the most remarkable road-building feats in modern history. The road, then and now, commences in **Dawson Creek, British Columbia,** originating at the huge, picture-worthy **Milepost 0 Monument** on Tenth Street in downtown Dawson Creek. It ends at Delta Junction, Alaska. Nowadays it's an asphalt road all the way, though the quality of the pavement varies; you'll likely encounter gravel detours from time to time as road crews strive to improve the highway and your vacation experience.

The first major Yukon Territory (Y.T.) community you'll come to (and, therefore, our starting point in this section) is *Watson Lake,* at kilometer 1,021. The *Watson Lake Visitor Information Centre* (867-536-7469; yukon .ca), at the junction of the Alaska and Campbell Highways, is a good place to pick up the latest data on road conditions and visitor attractions in the area. One of them, the mind-blowing *Sign Post Forest,* started in this way: Back in 1942, the American soldier Carl K. Lindley of Danville, Illinois, one of thousands of U.S. servicemen constructing the Alaska Highway, got homesick and erected a sign indicating the mileage back to his hometown. Others did the same, and a tradition took hold. Later, after the war, civilian motorists started driving along the road from the Lower 48 states to Alaska, and they erected signs, too, more than 80,000 signs to date. Among them you'll find one license plate from Virginia that reads AAW–7191, placed there by one of the previous authors of this book.

Just beyond kilometer 1,162, you cross the Continental Divide, separating lands that drain into the Pacific Ocean from those that drain into the Arctic Ocean. Just off the highway at kilometer 1,294, you arrive in the mostly Native community of *Teslin,* originally a summer home for Tlingit people from Southeast Alaska and British Columbia. The *George Johnston Museum* (867-390-2550; heritageyukon.ca) open from 9:00 a.m. to 5:00 p.m. in summer, houses the largest Tlingit artifact collection in the Yukon. You'll see dioramas, rare historical photographs, George Johnston's 1928 Chevrolet, and many post-European and early Yukon exhibits. The museum honors Johnston,

yukon trivia

Whitehorse, the capital of the Yukon Territory, was named for the nearby rapids of the Yukon River, where the frothing water looked like the manes of white horses. The name has been used since 1887.

a Tlingit man who was born in 1884 and died in 1972. An expert photographer, Johnston brought the car, a first in these parts, to Teslin. Admission is $8 CAD for adults, and $6 for seniors 60 and over.

Jake's Corner and access to the Atlin Road lie beyond kilometer 1,392; you come to Whitehorse city limits at kilometer 1,455, about 40 miles later.

Whitehorse is the Yukon Territory's "big city," a modern community of 23,400. It's home to about two-thirds of all the Y.T.'s residents and serves as its hub and transportation center. The town's origins lie in the construction of the White Pass & Yukon Route railway from the ocean port of Skagway early in the twentieth century. Its economy today relies on government, trade, and tourism plus minerals and mining activity.

If you're driving, make the *Yukon Visitor Reception Centre* (867-667-3084; travelyukon.com), at 100 Hanson Street or Second Avenue and Hanson, your first stop in the Whitehorse area. It's operated by the local Department of Tourism and Culture and contains lots of good information, especially about Yukon national parks and historic sites. It's also one of your best sources for up-to-date highway data; pick up on of their free travelogue-style pamphlets of local campgrounds and other attractions, or their larger, magazine-style guide to the area. Located near the center at 30 Electra Crescent is the *Yukon Transportation Museum* (867-668-4792; goytm.ca), which features North Country transport, from dogsleds and stagecoaches to a WP&YR railcar replica and vintage aircraft. Admission is $10 CAD. Another source of visitor information, particularly for sites in and around Whitehorse, is the *Whitehorse Chamber of Commerce Information Centre* (867-667-7545; whitehorsechamber.ca) at 302 Steele Street. If you enjoy historical sites, the information center is a great place to pick up walking tour brochures for many Yukon communities.

Not to be missed is the *MacBride Museum* (1124 Front Street; 867-667-2709; macbridemuseum.com), which has a fascinating 5,000 square feet of artifacts, historic photographs, maps, and exhibits that cover the Yukon from ancient prehistory to the present. The real Sam McGee's cabin (of Robert Service fame) can be seen here, as well as horse wagons and steam engines. Admission is $12 CAD. The museum is open Monday through Saturday during the summer, from 9:30 a.m. until 5:00 p.m., with limited hours in the winter, too.

It seems like everybody who travels through these parts takes a tour of the *SS Klondike,* the largest stern-wheeler to ply the Yukon River, and you should, too. It's located on the shores of the Yukon River, near the Robert Campbell bridge. The 210-foot ship was built in 1929, sank seven years later, but was refloated and rebuilt in 1937. It continued in service until the fifties. Now designated a Parks Canada National Historic Site (see parks.canada.ca), it's been restored to reflect one of the North Country's prime methods of travel during the late 1930s. Admission is $4.50 CAD. Call 867-677-4511 during the summer for more information, or 867-667-3910 during the winter.

You'll probably never have a better chance to see Yukon wildlife than during a drive-through tour of the *Yukon Wildlife Preserve* (867-456-7300; yukonwildlife.ca). In 750 acres of forests, meadows, and marshlands, you can view caribou, elk, bison, moose, mountain goats, sheep, musk ox, mule deer, snowy owls, and rare peregrine falcons. General admission for a self-guided walking tour is $19 CAD, or you can hop on a guided bus tour for $30 CAD. The *Yukon Conservation Society* (867-668-5678; yukonconservation.ca) sponsors free guided hikes around the Whitehorse area during the summer,

The Bishop Who Ate His Boots

The well-known gold rush story "The Bishop Who Ate His Boots" was the inspiration for the famous scene in Charlie Chaplin's movie *The Gold Rush*. Lost at 40 below and out of provisions, Bishop Stringer decided to boil his and his companion's sealskin-and-walrus-sole boots for 7 hours, then drink the broth. According to the bishop, it was "tough and stringy, but palatable and fairly satisfying." Bishop Stringer lost 50 pounds during the ordeal, but eventually found his way to a Native village, where he was nursed back to health.

providing an opportunity to learn about the unique northern flora and fauna as well as the natural history and geology of the land.

An interesting dining experience can be had at a local favorite: **Klondike Rib and Salmon BBQ** (klondikerib.com) at Second Avenue and Steele Street downtown. Here you can sample Alaska salmon and halibut, Texas-style barbecue ribs, English-style fish and chips, plus their specialties—arctic char, caribou, and musk ox. They don't have a phone number, but you can message them on Facebook—just not to make a reservation. Meals are first-come, first-served.

For the traveler in search of art, the **Yukon Arts Centre** (867-667-8574; yukonartscentre.com) at Yukon Place on College Drive offers the territory's largest art gallery, a theater, and an outdoor amphitheater plus a spectacular view. There is no charge, but donations are accepted. Summer hours are Monday through Friday, 10:00 a.m. to 5:00 p.m. Hours during the rest of the year vary slightly. A **Yukon Permanent Art Collection**—showing northern landscapes and lifestyles as portrayed by prominent Canadian artists—is displayed in the foyer of the Yukon Government Administration Building on Second Street. Open weekdays only, 8:30 a.m. to 5:00 p.m.

The government of Yukon has published some great materials for self-guided walking and driving tours, including the mobile apps "Yukon Walking Tours" and "Yukon Sights and Sites." Through the government of Yukon website (yukon.ca/en/historic-sites-tours), you can access self-guided walking tour information for a number of communities, including Carcross, Haines Junction, and Beaver Creek (on the Alaska Highway, just before the Canada/Alaska border).

You don't have to be Anglican (Episcopal) to visit the **Old Log Church Museum** (867–668–2555; oldlogchurchmuseum.ca) located a block off Main Street on Elliott Street and Third Avenue. The sanctuary building, constructed in 1900 for the Church of England, and the log rectory next door are rich in Yukon's history. Exhibits, artifacts, and relics tell the story of the Yukon's history from pre-contact life among aboriginal peoples to early exploration and beyond. Admission is $8 CAD. Open hours are 12:30 p.m. to 4:00 p.m. during the summer, open only by appointment during the winter.

Eclipse Nordic Hot Springs (867-456-8000; eclipsenordichotsprings .ca), formerly the site of Takhini Hot Springs, is still home to the famous hair-freezing contest in winter: When the weather is cold enough you're invited to dunk your head under the water, then resurface and let the air freeze your hair. People vote on the resulting photos, and winners in each category can win up to $2,000 CAD.

The hot springs is considerably less rustic than it used to be. But it's still a don't-miss-it destination just 20–30 minutes from downtown Whitehorse. There are three pools (one of them wheelchair accessible) and eight Japanese-made clay hot tubs, plus, of course, changing rooms, sauna and steam and relaxation rooms, yoga and meditation classes, and a cafe on site. Admission to the hot springs is $60 CAD.

Another option not far outside town is *Inn on the Lake* (867-660-5253; innonthelake.ca). This bed and breakfast has a Jacuzzi suite and personal steam rooms, and, to top it all off, the food is great. Prices range from $249 CAD for a room with a bath to $299 CAD for the deluxe penthouse suite with an in-room Jacuzzi and private balcony. From here, you can make use of local tour companies and outfitters to go mountain biking, kayaking, or canoeing, or take advantage of complimentary golf passes offered by the inn.

In town there are many other accommodations, among them *Historical House Bed and Breakfast* (5128 Fifth Avenue; 867-668-3907; historicalguest-house.com), originally built for none other than Sam McGee. The place features priceless antique furniture, which is perfect for the setting. While there, be sure to converse with the proprietors, Bernie and Pam Phillips. Bernie will be glad to entertain you on his caribou horns—just ask. Rooms are $125 CAD for a single or $140 CAD for a double in the summer.

Bluejay Suites B&B (56 Almond Place; 867-333-9456; bluejay-suites. com) is perfectly situated in a quiet neighborhood with easy access to hiking trails and a large greenbelt, while still only a few minutes' drive from central Whitehorse and major attractions. This B&B is small, with just two rooms, so you can enjoy a certain level of privacy along with the self-serve continental breakfast, en suite baths, and a lovely common area with a wood-burning fireplace and massage chair. The smaller of the two rooms starts at $184 CAD, while the larger of the two rooms starts at $214 CAD; both rooms have a two-night minimum.

If getting on the Yukon River is your goal, stroll down to the waterfront, across from the MacBride Museum, and take your pick of *Yukon Riverboat Tours.* Prices and times vary, but several operators make the decision easy.

From Whitehorse, if you're driving, you have two choices for travel north and west to the main body of Alaska. You can continue on up the Alaska Highway, driving west and then northwest to Haines Junction, Kluane National Park, Beaver Creek, and the U.S. border, or you can drive northerly on the Klondike Highway to Carmacks, Minto, Stewart Crossing, and Dawson City, where you can connect with the Top of the World Highway to the Alaska border.

The Klondike Highway: Whitehorse to Dawson City

The northern portion of the Skagway to Dawson City Klondike Highway starts at kilometer 1,487 on the Alaska Highway, about 9 miles beyond Whitehorse. The first major stop along the way is **Carmacks,** at kilometer 357. (Remember, kilometer posts show the distance from Skagway.) The community is historically important as a stern-wheeler steamboat stop on the Yukon River route between Whitehorse and Dawson City.

Whitehorse-based **Up North Adventures** (867-667-7035; upnorthadventures.com) offers some fine canoeing that passes through the Carmacks area if you want to start a trip from Whitehorse. Enjoy a half-day, full-day, or multi-day self-guided trip along the Yukon River, with prices starting at $90 CAD. Longer, guided trips range from 4 to 15 days and start at $1,2650 CAD. If you like what you see at Up North, check out their other adventures, including guided and self-guided kayak trips, motorboat tours, bicycle tours, and guided ATV tours. They'll shuttle you to and from destinations through the Yukon and into Alaska as part of your self-guided adventure.

At kilometer 380.5, you can see the **Five Finger Rapids** from an observation deck built as part of the Five Finger Rapids Day Use Area of trails and picnic sites. If you have an hour and don't mind the 219 stairs, you can hike down for a closer look at these treacherous rapids.

For campers or picnickers, the Yukon government's **Tatchun Creek Campground** is at kilometer 382.4 of the Klondike Highway, with twelve sites and fishing for grayling and salmon in season. And if you don't mind driving 8 kilometers off the road, there's also great camping at nearby **Tatchun Lake,** with twenty sites. Overnight camping fees start at $18 CAD. For either campground, visit yukon.ca or call 867-667-5648 for more information.

At kilometer 537, you come to **Stewart Crossing,** where you have the opportunity to take a side excursion (about 150 miles round-trip) over the **Silver Trail** through scenic woods and water country to the mining communities of **Mayo, Elsa,** and **Keno City.** If you plan to overnight here, the Yukon government **Five Mile Lake Campground,** just east of Mayo, offers generous campsites, kitchen shelters, launch sites, a swimming beach, and an obstacle course where kids can work off energy. Again, camping fees start at $18 CAD per night.

Keno City, at the far end of the Silver Trail, has a year-round population of only about twenty people—so it's really impressive that they have lodgings of any sort. You might be able to stay in the **Silvermoon Bunkhouse.** Find them on Facebook or call 867-334-4206, but make sure you call and talk to them directly before counting on this as part of your plans. Sometimes the bunkhouse gets rented out for the entire season by reality TV film crews.

The **Mining Museum** (867-995-3103; heritageyukon.ca) at Keno City is a particular delight, with displays that vary from old-time mining equipment to baseball uniforms the local teams wore. Admission costs $5, with discounts for seniors and youth, and children under 12 get in for free. The museum is open daily from late May to early September, and off-season visits can be arranged if you call in advance. If the museum piques your prospecting interests, drive down Duncan Creek Road south of Keno City and cue up your Yukon Sights and Sites mobile app—if you downloaded it—for information about the Duncan Creek gold rush.

yukontrivia

Dawson City's world-famous gambling hall is named for Diamond Tooth Gertie, a bona fide Yukon dance hall queen. Gertie Lovejoy's nickname came from the sparkling diamond she had wedged between her two front teeth. Just as the miners made their fortunes mining gold from the earth, she made hers mining nuggets from the pokes of lonely miners.

Back on the highway toward Dawson, the high point (literally) of a Dawson City visit comes when you drive the Dome Road from its junction at Klondike Highway's kilometer 717 to the top of **Midnight Dome** for a panoramic view of the city, the Yukon and Klondike Rivers, the Bonanza gold fields, and the Ogilvie Mountains. Simply awesome.

Dawson City, of course, is where it all began—the frenzied, frantic, fabled stampede for North Country gold. It started in 1896 when George Carmack, Skookum Jim, and Tagish Charlie found "color"—lots of it—in a Klondike River tributary called Rabbit Creek, later renamed Bonanza Creek. The rush catapulted into international prominence when the vessel *Portland* steamed into Seattle on July 17, 1897, and the *Seattle Post-Intelligencer* screamed "Gold! Gold! Gold!" in its banner headline. A "ton of gold" was proclaimed in the story that followed. The rush was on.

Tens of thousands of gold seekers (most of them ill-prepared and without the slightest concept of the rigors they would face) crowded aboard almost any boat that would float out of West Coast ports and headed for Skagway and the White Pass, Dyea and the Chilkoot Pass, or St. Michael on the Yukon River. Their common goal was Dawson City and the rich gold country around it. It's said that 100,000 gold seekers set out for the Klondike. Some 30,000 made it there.

Today the rush to the Klondike continues, but it's a vastly more comfortable odyssey. Travelers come not to extract riches but to see the place where all the excitement happened. Thanks to eleventh-hour rescue restorations by the national and territorial governments, Dawson City looks remarkably as it did more than a century ago, when it sprang up on the Yukon River shores. Old buildings and landmarks were saved from certain rot and destruction, including the magnificently refurbished 1899 *Palace Grand Theatre*, which you can tour with staff from Parks Canada. At *Diamond Tooth Gertie's Gambling Hall* (867–993–5575; diamondtoothgerties.ca) at the corner of Fourth and Queen, you can take in a can-can show or legally gamble away your "poke" at real gaming tables (as many a prospector did in '98) for an admission charge of $20 CAD, which is good for entry all season long. At the historic old 1901 *post office,* at Third Avenue and King Street (open 9:00 a.m. to 5:00 p.m. Monday through Friday and 11:30 a.m. to 2:30 p.m. Saturday), your first-class letters and postcards will be canceled the old-fashioned way—by hand. Collectors can purchase commemorative stamps.

Before beginning a foray to any of these sites, it's probably wise to get oriented at Tourism Yukon's *Dawson Visitor Reception Centre,* at Front and King Streets (867-993-5566 from May to September; 867-993-5575 from October to April; dawsoncity.ca). While you're there, ask about the *Dawson City walking tours*, ranging from $11 to $14.50 CAD, that originate at the site several times daily. If you plan to extend your trip to Inuvik and Canada's Northwest Territories via the Dempster Highway, cross the street from the Dawson reception center and get highway and other information from the *Northwest Territories Dempster Highway Visitor Information Centre* (1123 Front Street; 867-993-6167; spectacularnwt.com).

At *Jack London's cabin* (867-993-5575; jacklondonmuseum.ca) near Grant Street and Eighth Avenue, you can take part in interpretive tours, daily in the summer, that showcase London's cabin that was discovered in the Yukon wilderness. The structure was carefully disassembled, and half the logs were used to re-create the writer's cabin at its present site in Dawson City. The other half went into the construction of an identical cabin at Jack London Square in Oakland, California. Curator Dick North is one of the premier experts on Jack London as well as author of several books, including one on the famous "Mad Trapper." Admission is $5 CAD. The museum is open seven days a week, 10:00

The Rush Is On

George Washington Carmack is credited with discovering gold at Bonanza Creek, setting off the great rush north for Klondike gold.

It was in 1896 that Carmack and two brothers, Tagish Charlie and Skookum Jim, went looking for gold in the Klondike region. Another prospector, Robert Henderson, reported good color on Gold Bottom Creek but said he didn't want any "Siwashes" (Jim and Charlie were Alaska Native) on Gold Bottom.

So the three partners went looking for their own creek and staked Rabbit Creek, soon to be known as Bonanza Creek. Their strike was the richest in North America and made them wealthy men. They shared their bounty without dispute. They didn't tell Henderson of their discovery, and he did not share in the riches.

a.m. to 4:00 p.m., from mid-May to early September. At Eighth Avenue and Hanson, you'll find the **Robert Service cabin,** where poetry is recited daily in the summer. Inquire at the visitor center about recital times. A guided tour is available for $11 CAD.

For a really in-depth look at Dawson's history, visit the old 1901 **Territorial Administration Building,** where the **Dawson City Museum and Historical Society** (595 Fifth Avenue; 867-993-5291; dawsonmuseum.ca) houses its collection of gold rush–era artifacts, paleontological remains, cultural exhibits of the Han Native people, even a collection of narrow-gauge steam locomotives. There are also vintage film showings and lectures. Admission is $10 CAD, and the museum is open 9:00 a.m. to 5:00 p.m.

Another interesting stop in Dawson is the **Dänojà Zho** (meaning "long time ago house") **Cultural Centre,** where you'll learn about the traditional peoples of the Klondike region. In addition to viewing the exhibits, you can join guided tours and watch live performances. The admission charge starts from $7.35 CAD, and is valid for two days. For more information call 867-993-7100 or visit danojazho.ca.

yukontrivia

The Yukon Territory's Mount Logan, at 5,959 meters (19,551 feet), is Canada's highest mountain.

The Yukon Territory's official flower is fireweed.

There are about 250 active mines in the Dawson gold fields.

If you want to get out into the surrounding wilderness, check with **Ruby Range Adventures** (867-322-8600; rubyrange.com). They offer guided canoe and river expeditions as well as fishing safaris. Tours run from 7 to 22 days.

Another attraction is not far off the beaten path (in fact, it sits on Front Street and First Avenue, on the banks of the Yukon between King and Queen Streets), but it's a must-see if you value restored historical artifacts. We're referring to the **Steamer Keno,** built in 1922 in Whitehorse for service between Stewart City and Mayo Landing, and now located in place of pride on Dawson City's Front Street. It's typical of the breed of shallow-draft riverboats that served the North Country from early gold rush times until well into the twentieth century, and for $15.50 CAD you can climb aboard to explore it. Get your tickets in the nearby visitor center.

The largest wooden-hull, bucket-line gold dredge in North America—old **Gold Dredge Number 4,** two-thirds the size of a football field long and eight whopping stories high—can be seen south of town near the spot where it ceased operations in 1960. The site is beside Bonanza Creek off Bonanza Creek Road, 7.8 miles south of the Klondike Highway. About 2½ miles farther south you'll find **Discovery Claim** (and a monument to mark the spot) on Bonanza Creek, where George Carmack, Skookum Jim, and Tagish Charlie made their history-making discovery.

Another ⁹⁄₁₀-mile to the south is **Free Claim #6** (867-993-5575; dawsoncity .ca/listing/free-claim-6/), which is owned by the Klondike Visitors Association and open for anyone to pan, as long as you use only shovels and gold pans. You can borrow a gold pan at the Visitor Information Center in Dawson City, but if you want a shovel you'll need to supply your own. Shovels are available for purchase from the **Dawson Trading Post** (867-993-5316; https:// dawsoncity.ca/listing/dawson-trading-post/) and **Dawson Hardware** (1083 Second Avenue; 867-993-5433; homehardware.ca)

At the **Dawson City Guesthouse** (867-993-3322; dawsoncityguesthouse .com) at 451 Craig Street, you're situated in a quiet, beautiful setting overlooking both the Klondike and Yukon Rivers. The owners will pick you up at the airport, bus, or waterfront if you don't have your own wheels. Rates start from $195 CAD per night, and each room comes with a dedicated sitting room with a mini fridge, private bathroom, WiFi, hypoallergenic down duvets, and blackout curtains. **Juliette's Manor Bed and Brunch** (867-993-2566; juliettesmanor.com) is within walking distance of most Dawson City attractions. Look for the pink house at Seventh Avenue and Harper Street. Rooms start at $179 and include full breakfasts, use of kitchen facilities for other meals, hot tub, barbecue, and picnic area. Other amenities include WiFi and cable TV, on-site coin-operated laundry, a large deck, a hot tub and sauna, and loaner gold-panning equipment.

Another longtime lodging favorite is **The Downtown** (867–993–5346; coasthotels.com), located 1 block from Diamond Tooth Gertie's and 1 block from the Grand Palace Theatre. And if you want to prove that you're a real sourdough, have a Sourtoe Cocktail in the hotel's *Sourdough Saloon*. Yes, that's a real (preserved) human toe at the bottom of your glass. More than two dozen toes have been donated to the cause over the years, all provided by people who were parted from their piggies for one reason or another—including frostbite, diabetes, and gout—to facilitate this gruesome play on the word "sourdough." Or spend the night in a restored brothel, *Bombay Peggy's* (867-993-6969; www.bombaypeggys.com). For meals and another great lodging option in the center of town, try *Klondike Kate's* (302-737-6100; klondikekates.com) at 1102 Third Avenue, with patio dining and a nice selection of entrees.

A pleasant day trip from Dawson City is the *Fishwheel Charters* (867-993-6237; fishwheeltoursyukon.com) 2-hour tour of the Yukon River. The operators are licensed First Nations river pilots, and they will take you approximately 6 miles downriver to the historic site of Fort Reliance. There you can enjoy tea and bannock and learn about the river's history—past, present, and future. Incidentally, this company also rents wilderness cabins (from $75 CAD)—you bring your own food, they provide the cabin, water, firewood, and transportation—and, in the wintertime, offers snowmachine tours.

When you're ready to leave Dawson City, you have three driving choices. You can retrace the Klondike Highway south to the place just outside of Whitehorse where it meets the Alaska Highway, then continue north on the Alaska Highway to the main body of Alaska. Or you can take the *Top of the World Highway* to the place at the Alaska border where it meets the *Taylor Highway*, which, in turn, also connects with the Alaska Highway in Alaska. Or you

Dredge Number 4

Huge, earth-devouring machines once chewed their way up and down the creek beds of the Yukon River valley, gobbling up everything in their paths, right down to bedrock, processing it all in their complex innards, and spitting out mounds of rubble behind them. Their trails can be traced across the valley floors like giant worm tracks 50 feet high.

The dredges are all gone save one. This 3,000-ton monster produced roughly 300,000 ounces of gold in its lifetime—about 9 tons—and chewed through 65 million cubic yards of gravel. It sank in 1960 and was neglected for 32 years.

In 1992 it was resurrected, and today you can tour its rusting interior. There were seventy-two buckets, each weighing 2 ½ tons, in a continuous chain that pulled material up from the creek bed and dumped it into the dredge's internal gold-sluicing works. Those who remember when it was in operation say that the vibration of the dredge in action was so great that it could be heard more than 10 miles away, and the vibrations physically felt at almost the same distance.

can keep going north and east via the **Dempster Highway** to **Inuvik,** in the Mackenzie Delta, not many miles from the shores of the Arctic Ocean. When you've made it to Inuvik, you have to turn around and drive back the way you came; the Dempster doesn't meet or loop with any other highway.

The Dempster Highway: Dawson City to Inuvik

The third choice, the Dempster Highway, definitely deserves consideration. It stretches 741 kilometers (460 miles) from its starting place about 41 kilometers (25 miles) south of Dawson City on the Klondike Highway. It ends in Inuvik, Northwest Territories, surely one of the most literally colorful communities in North America, with almost every hue of the rainbow represented on homes and buildings.

Along the highway, you pass sometimes through valleys bounded by great granite mountains, at other times over high flat plains, with rolling hills in the distance. Sometimes your route is the legendary trail of the North West Mounted Police, who patrolled the region by dogsled in the days before the highway was built.

Accommodations and service stations are rare along most of the route, so top off your tank every chance you get. Halfway to Inuvik, you come at kilometer 371 to **Eagle Plains** and the **Eagle Plains Hotel and Restaurant** (867-993-2453; eagleplainshotel.ca) which offers thirty-two comfortable rooms, groceries, vehicle services, gas, and a restaurant that serves the tastiest, most satisfying sourdough pancakes this side of the Canadian border. Take the time to examine the display of historic photos on the walls of the restaurant. They tell the tragic story of the Mounties' "Lost Patrol" in 1910 and of Inspector W.J.D. Dempster's finding and retrieval of their frozen bodies. Other pictures relate the murderous exploits of the Mad Trapper of Rat River and the manhunt organized against him in 1932. The Mounties, as always, got their man. Rooms start from $200 CAD.

At kilometer 402, you cross the **Arctic Circle** (take pictures of the monument), and at kilometer 471 you leave the Yukon Territory and enter the Northwest Territories. From now on, kilometer posts show the distance from this point. At kilometer 86, turn off the highway to visit the nearby community of **Fort McPherson.** You can fill up on gasoline and visit the church graveyard where the hapless Lost Patrol members lie buried. Also, if you're in the market for a backpack, duffel bag, or an attaché case, visit the **Fort McPherson Tent and Canvas Factory** (867-952-2179; fortmcphersontent.com). The workmanship is first rate, and almost certainly no one in your hiking club back home will have one with the company's distinctive emblem.

At kilometer 269 and the community of Inuvik, don't fail to visit the igloo-shaped *Our Lady of Victory Church.* Igloo-shaped? It sounds hokey, but the effect when you see it is breathtaking, and the paintings inside, created by Inuvialuit painter Mona Thrasher, are more than inspirational. Take time to see, as well, the *Ingamo Hall Friendship Centre,* an important focus of cultural and community activities whose great hall has the feel of a baronial mansion.

yukon trivia

The lowest temperature ever recorded in North America was in the Yukon Territory. The mercury plummeted to 81.4 degrees below zero in February 1947.

If you'd enjoy an Arctic country setting for your overnight accommodations, consider the *Arctic Chalet* (867-777-3535; arcticchalet.com), a B&B lakeside home and cabins. Olav and Judi Falsnes offer simple but nutritious breakfasts and complimentary canoes. (*Note:* Saturday check-ins must be prearranged.) Rates begin at $200 CAD for a standard cabin, single occupancy; add $25 for each individual person. For a cabin with a full kitchenette, rates start at $250 CAD for the first person. Sled dog rides are available in the winter, starting at $180 CAD for an hour of fun, plus a $25 single supplement if you're the only one in the group. If you're camping, go to the *Jàk Territorial Park* (888-822-2647; nwtparks.ca/explore/dempster-highway/jàk), about 2 miles from town on the Airport Road. Its hilltop location presents a worthwhile view of the Mackenzie Delta, its breezes tend to discourage mosquitoes, and the surrounding land is rich in cranberries, blueberries, and cloudberries. (In the local Indigenous language, Gwich'in, Jàk means "berry.") Rates start from $29 for a primitive campsite and $34 with electric hookup.

The Top of the World Highway: Dawson City to the Alaska Border

Back to Dawson City and the second choice mentioned earlier, driving on the Top of the World Highway to the Taylor Highway. Yes, that's the official name of the road. It begins with a free car-ferry ride over the Yukon River and heads west toward the Alaska border and Alaska's Taylor Highway for 127 kilometers (79 miles). The road, you'll find, really lives up to its name. Much of the time you're on ridgetops looking down on deep valleys. Lots of good scenic photo opportunities here. It's a good gravel road, but slippery in heavy rains. About 105 kilometers (66 miles) beyond Dawson City, you'll cross the *U.S.-Canada border.*

The Taylor Highway: Jack Wade Junction to Eagle and Tetlin Junction

We're now going to talk about part of Alaska again, even though this chapter deals largely with the Canadian Yukon. Travel on the Taylor Highway is so logically connected with the Top of the World Highway from Dawson City, it just doesn't make sense to have you jump pages into other sections of the book.

At *Jack Wade Junction,* where the Taylor and the Top of the World Highways meet, turn north on the Taylor Highway and drive 65 miles to visit *Eagle,* a small but historically important community in the Alaska scheme of things. Still standing is the **Wickersham Courthouse,** where Judge James Wickersham dispensed frontier justice during Eagle's gold rush days early in the twentieth century. Still intact as well are the old Waterfront Customs House, a military mule barn, water wagon shed, NCO (noncommissioned officers) quarters, and other structures that were part of old Fort Egbert. The federal Bureau of Land Management (BLM) has renovated and restored portions of the old fort where, incidentally, Captain Billy Mitchell once served a tour of duty. BLM also maintains a campground just beyond Fort Egbert. You can visit the *Eagle Visitor Center* for the *Yukon–Charley Rivers National Preserve* (907-547-2233; nps.gov/yuch) on the banks of the Yukon near Fort Egbert. Staffers will show you a video about the national preserve and answer any questions.

After your Eagle visit, backtrack south on the Taylor Highway to Jack Wade Junction. The distance from Jack Wade Junction to Tetlin Junction, and the Alaska Highway, is about 96 miles. When you've gone about 30 of those miles, around mile 66, slow down and look for *Chicken.* No, this isn't a joke; it's a town . . . sort of. It's said the community got its name because the miners back in the gold rush days couldn't spell *ptarmigan,* which some called an Alaska chicken anyway. The original mining camp is now abandoned private property and is closed to general traffic. If you turn off the Taylor Highway at the Airport Road, you'll come to the *Chicken Creek Cafe* (no number; chickenalaska.com), known for its pies and baked goods and the gathering place from which tours depart daily for old Chicken. Nearby you'll find the *Chicken Saloon* and *Chicken Mercantile Emporium,* where you can buy a Chicken hat, a Chicken pin, and, naturally, a Chicken T-shirt.

Located right off the Taylor Highway, *The Goldpanner* (907-505-0231; townofchicken.com) is a good opportunity to fill up your gas tank (they have both regular gas and diesel). But, in true Alaska style, they offer you a smorgasbord of almost anything else a traveler can wish for: a gift shop, coffee and a few limited food options including fudge, walking tours, free gold-panning on their claim, WiFi, hotel rooms (from $249), dry cabins (from $219), RV parking (from $30, 20-amp power is an option), tent camping (from $18), showers . . . and the only flush toilets in town.

The Taylor Highway ends (or begins, depending on which way you're traveling) at Tetlin Junction, mile 1,302 on the Alaska Highway, where there's lodging, food, and gas if you've perilously coasted in without buying fuel on the Taylor Highway.

yukontrivia

The Yukon River and its tributaries drain almost one-third of Alaska.

The Alaska Highway: Whitehorse to the Alaska Border

Back in Canada's Yukon and beyond Whitehorse about 90 miles lies Haines Junction, at the junction of the Haines Highway from Haines, Alaska, and the Alaska Highway at kilometer 809. The community calls itself the Gateway to **Kluane.** Kluane (pronounced clue-AW-nee) is the Yukon's biggest lake. Its namesake, **Kluane National Park and Reserve,** is one of the preeminent wilderness national parks of North America.

yukontrivia

About 3 percent of the Yukon Territory is covered by wetlands, a much lower percentage than for the rest of the country. The Yukon's inland waters comprise 1,792 square miles (4,481 square kilometers).

Especially for the hiker, mountain climber, canoe enthusiast, kayaker, and river runner, Kluane National Park is a place to spend days, not hours. To get oriented, visit the **Kluane National Park and Reserve Visitor Centre** (867-634-5248; parks.canada.ca), which is located in the Da Kų Cultural Centre in the small town of Haines Junction. Both centers are on the east side of the Alaska Highway, just north of its junction with the Haines Highway. There, you'll see an international award-winning multimedia presentation about the park, and you'll be able to pick up information about hiking trails and canoe/kayak routes, both long and short. The park itself stretches across a broad swath of land to the west of the Alaska Highway. Summer hours at the visitor center are 9:00 a.m. to 6:00 p.m. daily from mid-May to mid-September.

To see Kluane from the air, arrange a flightseeing trip with providers like **Rocking Star Adventures** (867-334-8675; rockingstar.ca), which offers fixed-wing flights out of Haines Junction ranging from 45 minutes to 2 hours; prices start at $230 CAD per person for the 45-minute tour to see surging glaciers, which "gallop" forward surprisingly fast every 15 years or so. **Icefield**

Discovery (867-841-4204; icefielddiscovery.com) also offers fixed-wing flights. Glacier landings at the Icefield Discovery Camp in Kluane National Park are an option (from $445 CAD), but be aware that their headquarters are about 62 km or 39 miles north of Haines Junction along the Alaska Highway.

For a double treat, stay at **Dalton Trail Lodge** (867-634-2099; daltontrail .com), at Dezadeash Lake bordering the park. The rooms are luxurious, and the double treat comes at dinnertime with scrumptious Swiss cuisine. Meals and accommodations start at $270 CAD with double occupancy, or $320 CAD for a single. One-week packages start at $3,750 CAD per person for a trip focused on hiking, with daily transport to the trailheads; or $4,850 for a fishing-focused trip. All meals, accommodation, and rentals from the lodge are included in the price, with a guide there to help you on one day out of the week.

If you just need a quick place to camp, the **Kathleen Lake Campground** (867-634-7207; parks.canada.ca) in Kluane National Park is a great choice if you get in. Aside from the stunning mountain and lake scenery all around you, it also offers great opportunities for hiking and boating. Camping fees start from $27 per night. Also excellent is **Lake Creek Campground** (no number; yukon. ca). Your stay starts from $20, which includes firewood. Both campgrounds are seasonal, open only from mid-May to mid- or late September.

For straightforward lodging in Haines Junction, consider the **Kluane Park Inn** (867-634-2261; kluaneparkinn.ca) which offers simple, clean rooms with private bathrooms and WiFi, a laundromat, an in-house restaurant, an RV park, and a small camping area. Rooms start from about $149 CAD for a single, $164 CAD for a double, and $179 CAD for three people. Laundry, showers, and even a car wash are all available.

Another lodging option in Haines Junction is the **Raven's Rest Inn** (867-634-2500, ravensrestinn.ca; mile 181 Alaska Highway), which has gorgeous views of the St. Elias Mountains. The inn caters particularly to hikers, and offers lots of adventure gear for rent, from canoes, kayaks, and stand-up paddleboards to bicycles, cross-country skis, hiking gear, fishing gear, and camping gear. Each room has a private bath, and prices start from $215 CAD.

At the **Sheep Mountain Visitor Centre,** kilometer 1,706.8, you can frequently spot a herd of Dall sheep on the nearby slopes. An interpretive trail leads to Soldier's Summit, which was the site of the opening ceremony for the Alaska Highway on November 20, 1942.

At the village of **Burwash Landing,** kilometer 1,061.5, the **Kluane Museum of Natural History** (867-841-5561; kluanemuseum.ca) contains natural history exhibits featuring wildlife of the region as well as Indigenous artifacts, and dioramas. Admission costs $10.

Here's another North Country travel superlative: ***Beaver Creek,*** at kilometer 1,934, is Canada's westernmost community. The roadways around Beaver Creek, on both sides of the border, tend to be riddled with potholes. So, for the sake of your tires and rims, it's better not to rush this section of road. Once you reach the town, ***Tourism Yukon's visitor reception center*** features a special display of wildflowers and dispenses tons of visitor information, especially for visitors entering Canada from Alaska.

If you can get a table—there are only four—***Buckshot Betty's*** (867-862-7111, buckshotbettys.ca) in Beaver Creek offers great home cooking and fresh baked goods, plus tiny cabins that start from just $99 CAD per night. If you're tired, another good place to stay is the ***1202 Motor Inn*** (867-862-7600; 1202motorinn.ca), which offers rooms starting from $85 CAD for single occupancy or $155 CAD double occupancy, some with kitchenettes. They also have RV parking, grassy tent sites, showers, gasoline and diesel fuel, WiFi, and a small convenience store. At kilometer 1,967.5 you arrive at the U.S.-Canada border. Set your clocks back an hour (from Pacific to Alaska time), and start thinking in miles and gallons again.

Places to Stay in Canada's Yukon

ATLIN

Cabins Over Crag Lake
Near kilometer 42 of Tagish Road #8;
867-335-3610;
cabinsovercraglake.com.
Spectacular views. Great base camp if you have a car.

Spirit Lake Motel
Kilometer 72.3, South Klondike Highway;
867-821-4282;
spiritlakemotel.com.
Quaint, log-style lodgings. Summers only.

DAWSON City

Aurora Inn
Fifth Avenue and Harper Street;
867-993-6860;
aurorainn.ca.
Twenty nonsmoking rooms and free WiFi.

Bombay Peggy's
Second Avenue and Princess Street;
867-993-6969;
bombaypeggys.com.
A restored brothel.

Dawson City Guesthouse
451 Craig Street;
867-993-3322;
dawsoncityguesthouse.com.

Nice and quiet, with overlooks of the Klondike and Yukon Rivers.

Downtown Hotel
Second Avenue and Queen Street;
867-993-5346;
coasthotels.com.
Great location—and home of the famous Sour Toe Cocktail.

Juliette's Manor Bed and Brunch
Seventh Avenue and Harper Street;
867-993-2566;
juliettesmanor.com.
Self-catering in a great location.

Klondike Kate's
1102 Third Avenue;
302-737-6100;

klondikekates.com.
Lodgings and nice meals,
too.

EAGLE PLAINS

**Eagle Plains Hotel
and Restaurant**
Kilometer 364, Dempster
Highway;
867-993-2453;
eagleplainshotel.ca.
Comfortable rooms,
vital services, and good
pancakes.

HAINES JUNCTION

Dalton Trail Lodge
867-634-2099;
daltontrail.com;
Borders Kluane National
Park.

Kluane Park Inn
996 Alaska Highway;
867-634-2261;
kluaneparkinn.ca.
Simple, clean rooms with
WiFi and private bathrooms.

Raven's Rest Inn
181 Alaska Highway;
867-634-2500;
ravensrestinn.ca.
Spacious, clean and friendly,
right on the doorstep of
Kluane National Park.

INUVIK

Arctic Chalet
25 Carn Street;
867-777-3535;
arcticchalet.com.
Lakeside B&B home and
cabins within walking
distance of downtown.

KENO

**Silvermoon
Bunkhouse**
867-334-4206;
No website, but they're on
Facebook.
Call and verify availability
first; sometimes the whole
place gets booked.

WHITEHORSE

Bluejay Suites B&B
56 Almond Place;
867-333-9456;
bluejay-suites.com.
Small B&B for those who
appreciate quiet and
privacy.

**Historical House
Bed and Breakfast**
5128 Fifth Avenue;
867-668-3907;
historicalguesthouse.com.
Originally built for the one
and only Sam McGee.

**Inn on the Lake
Bed and Breakfast**
20 miles outside
Whitehorse;
867-660-5253;
innonthelake.ca.
Bed & breakfast with lots of
amenities and activities.

Places to Eat in
Canada's Yukon

CHICKEN

Chicken Creek Cafe
Airport Road (around mile
66 Taylor Highway);

no number;
chickenalaska.com.
Known for pies and baked
goods.

DAWSON CITY

Klondike Kate's
1102 Third Avenue;
302-737-6100;
klondikekates.com.
Casual dining and cabin
rentals in the heart of
historic Dawson.

EAGLE PLAINS

**Eagle Plains Hotel
and Restaurant**
Kilometer 364, Dempster
Highway;
867-993–2453;
eagleplainshotel.ca.
Halfway to Inuvik from
Dawson City. Great
pancakes!

HAINES JUNCTION

Raven's Rest Inn
181 Alaska Highway;
867-634–2500;
ravensrestinn.ca.
Fine European-style dining
with a view.

WHITEHORSE

**Klondike Rib and
Salmon BBQ**
Second Avenue and Steele
Street;
no number, but find them on
Facebook.
Alaska salmon and halibut,
Texas-style barbecue ribs,
English-style fish and chips,
and arctic char, caribou,
and musk ox.

Southcentral Alaska

More than half the population of Alaska lives, works, and plays in Southcentral Alaska, a region of magnificent glaciers, big lakes, forests, fertile river valleys, and many of the tallest mountains in North America. Brown (grizzly) bears, moose, Dall sheep, mountain goats, and wolves thrive hereabouts, and, happily, you'll find no small number of hiking trails and vehicular back roads that offer access for viewing these creatures in their native terrain.

Fact is, there are more miles of asphalt highways, marine highways, byways, airways, and railways in Southcentral than in any other portion of the state. In square miles the region occupies perhaps a fifth of the mainland mass of Alaska. In shape, Southcentral Alaska is a roughly 250-mile-deep arc of land and waters bordered on the south by the Gulf of Alaska, on the north and west by the curving arc of the Alaska mountain range, and on the east by the Canadian border—except at the very bottom, where the Southeast Alaska panhandle comes up to join the main body of Alaska.

Before the arrival of Europeans in the eighteenth century, this region and Alaska's interior were mostly the domain of the Athabascan nation, a tough, resourceful people who lived by

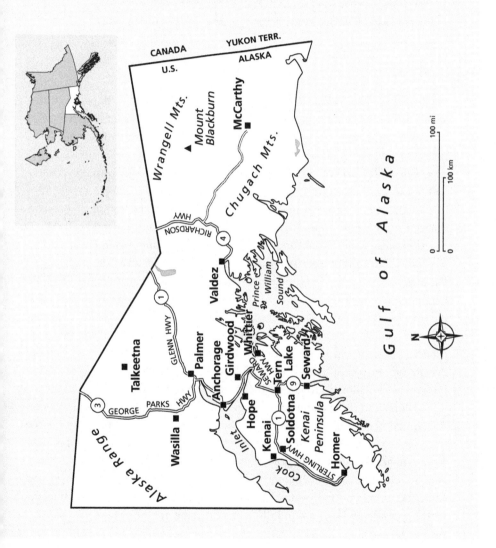

hunting moose, caribou, and bears as well as lesser game and birds. They harvested fish from saltwater shores and freshwater streams. Among their many skills was working in leather, sometimes richly adorned with beads fashioned from hollow porcupine quills and other natural materials. Those skills survive today, especially in the form of colorful decorative beadwork—greatly prized by visitors and residents alike—sewn onto moccasins, vests, and other leather goods.

Southcentral's modern history began in 1741 with the arrival of Russians sailing for the czars (Vitus Bering and Alexei Chirikov), followed by the English (Captains James Cook and George Vancouver) and other Europeans in the 1800s. After the Alaska Purchase of 1867, Americans came sporadically to the region seeking gold and other resources. But it was not until 1915 and the beginning of construction of the Alaska Railroad from Seward to Fairbanks that the area began to come into its own. Anchorage—a city created as construction and managing headquarters for the line—came into being. It later boomed, especially during and after World War II, when military installations swelled the population. In recent years, the development of Alaska's petroleum resources has created additional growth in Anchorage and other communities.

Visitors find the weather surprisingly mild in this region of Alaska. Around Anchorage, for instance, summertime temperatures range in the comfortable mid-60s and 70s. Thanks to the sheltering heights of the Alaska Range, wintertime temperatures usually hover between 10 and 25 degrees—above zero—although they occasionally plunge to 20 or more degrees below. Whenever you come, be prepared for an extraordinary vacation in this part of Alaska. It teems with opportunities both on and off its major roadways.

Anchorage

Since **Anchorage** is the transportation hub of Southcentral Alaska, this chapter treats it as the hub for planning trips in the region. After first detailing the city and its immediate environs, the chapter describes the water world and marine highway routes of Prince William Sound to the southeast, the more southerly highways (including the Seward and the Sterling) of the Kenai Peninsula, then the highways (Parks, Glenn, and Richardson) that head northerly toward Denali National Park and Preserve and other points in Interior Alaska.

Anchorage is Alaska's "Big Apple," a (for Alaska) large and cosmopolitan community of oil executives, college professors and students, business and transportation managers, tradespersons, artists, and no small number of working folks who keep the wheels of all this commerce turning.

southcentral alaska trivia

The first hint of Alaska's rich gold reserves was uncovered by Russian mining engineer Peter Doroshin, who found gold on the Kenai Peninsula in 1850.

Anchorage is also the transportation hub of Alaska. At Ted Stevens Anchorage International Airport, jet flights depart to and arrive from every region in Alaska, other states, Asia, and Europe. The state-owned Alaska Railroad headquarters here and extends southerly to Seward, on Resurrection Bay, and Whittier, in Prince William Sound, and north to Denali National Park and Fairbanks. Three major state highways begin in or near Anchorage: the Seward Highway to the Kenai Peninsula, the Glenn Highway to Tok and the Canadian border, and the Parks Highway to Denali National Park and Fairbanks. Off these arterials you'll find lesser roads that lead to remote villages, near-ghost towns, backwoods lodges, and lots of wilderness terrain for exploring, fishing, photography, and other fun.

First, within Anchorage itself: The number-one stop on any offbeat traveler's itinerary should be the **Alaska Public Lands Information Center,** at Fourth Avenue and F Street downtown (907-644-3661; nps.gov/anch/index .htm). Housed in the old Anchorage Federal Building, circa 1939, the center contains scores of really helpful state and federal exhibits, videos, wildlife mounts, transportation displays, and even a trip-planning computer to assist in organizing your travels. Once you have finished there, head diagonally across the street to the **Visit Anchorage Log Cabin Visitor Information Center** (907-257-2363). Within the cabin's main room, as well as in the adjacent downtown center, you'll find friendly local volunteers and tons of printed material to assist you in planning your stay in the city. Visit the website at www.anchorage.net.

By all means, ask for the excellent free visitor's guide, which contains more than 100 pages of tourist information, including a better-than-average walking

TOP ANNUAL EVENTS IN SOUTHCENTRAL ALASKA

Anchorage Fur Rendezvous

This yearly February winter event in Anchorage gets winter-weary Alaskans out and about. It features sled dog races, carnival rides (yup, even in the winter), and canning, cooking, baking, brewing, and arts-and-crafts competitions (907-274-1177; www.furrondy.net).

Iditarod Trail Sled Dog Race

As Alaska's state sport, dog mushing is celebrated with the premier sled dog race, the Iditarod, the first weekend of every March. The ceremonial start to this 1,049-mile-plus race begins in Anchorage (907-376-5155; www.iditarod.com). You can also visit Iditarod headquarters year-round at 2100 S. Knik-Goose Bay Road, although you need a car to get there.

Kachemak Bay Shorebird Festival

This early May festival celebrates varied and beautiful migratory shorebirds and the people who love them. Bird-watching events take place across the community (907-226-4631; kachemakshorebird.org).

Mount Marathon Race

Spend July Fourth in Seward watching the best of the best race to the top of Seward's backdrop, Mount Marathon, then back down again in this grueling, tough-as-nails event. Accompanied by festival booths, food, and fireworks (907-224-8051; www.seward.com).

Kachemak Bay Wooden Boat Festival

This beloved festival celebrated all things related to traditional boats and boat-building skills, including regular appearances from Alaska's one and only pirate pub band, the Rogues and Wenches. The festival was put on hold during the pandemic, but there is hope that it may return in the years to come (kbwbs.org).

Alaska State Fair

The state's largest fair in the heart of farm country, Palmer, in the Matanuska Valley. From late August to Labor Day, the fair includes carnival rides, arts-and-crafts booths, animal exhibits, giant vegetables, and quilting and canning competitions (907-745-4827; www.alaskastatefair.org).

tour of the downtown vicinity. Among more than two dozen sites noted are the *Alaska Railroad Depot* and old locomotive *Engine Number 1,* built in the early 1900s and used in constructing the Panama Canal as well as the Alaska Railroad; *Elderberry Park* and the *Oscar Anderson House,* the city's first (1915) wood-frame home, open for viewing; and *Oomingmak Musk Ox Producer's Co-op,* where you can see and purchase garments made from Arctic musk ox qiviut (pronounced KEE-vee-ute), the softest yet warmest wool-like material on earth.

Anchorage is a great place to be if you're an aviation buff. At 4721 Aircraft Drive, near the Ted Stevens Anchorage International Airport, is the *Alaska Aviation Heritage Museum* (907-248-5325; alaskaairmuseum.org), which includes twenty-five rare, historical bush planes and dozens of photographs and exhibits. While there, you can watch aircraft being restored, view a bush-plane pioneer film, and check out bush pilot memorabilia. This also is an excellent place to watch Anchorage's many seaplane pilots come and go from the largest floatplane base in the world, *Lake Hood*. Admission is $18 for adults, $15 for seniors, and $11 for children.

The *Tony Knowles Coastal Trail* (named after the former Anchorage mayor and Alaska governor) merits special mention. This wide asphalt trail starts at the west end of Second Avenue and follows the meandering shore of Cook Inlet for 11 scenic miles to *Kincaid Park*. Best of all, the coastal trail connects along the way with other segments of Anchorage's outstanding 120-mile network of bike and pedestrian paths. Ask for a trail system map at the visitor center.

Although downtown Anchorage is brimming with shops touting the best buys and most unique pieces in Alaska Native arts, the best places to find truly artistic works of art are the gift shops in the *Alaska Native Medical Center* (907-729-1122; anmc.org/patients-visitors/craft-shop/), off the corner of Tudor Road and Bragaw Street, and the Alaska Native Heritage Center at 8800 Heritage Center Drive. Neither is within walking distance of downtown, but a trip there will be worth the time and effort. At the medical center, native artists sell their wares from 11:00 a.m. to 2:00 p.m. Monday through Friday. The medical center itself is a work of art; peruse the hallways for a free art tour. The heritage center is even more impressive, with interpretive displays, life-size recreations of traditional dwellings, a small theater, and numerous cultural offerings including traditional music and dance.

The *Anchorage Museum of History and Art* (907-929-9200; anchoragemuseum.org) at Seventh Avenue and A Street also has a small shop with tasteful, authentic art objects for sale. The gift shop number is 907-929-9262. The museum is one of Anchorage's showcases, so it's not very off the beaten path, but a visit to the city isn't complete without a look-see. The museum's exhibits on Alaska history, flora, and fauna, as well as its art exhibits, rival those of metropolitan areas. Admission is $25 for adults.

Another very Alaskan shopping opportunity exists in the open-air downtown *Anchorage Market,* staged each weekend in summer at the Lower Bowl parking lot at the corner of Third Avenue and E Street. You can pick up made-in-Alaska arts and crafts, antiques, fresh produce, fish, and garage sale items. Hours run approximately 10:00 a.m. to 6:00 p.m. on Saturday and 11:00 a.m. to 5:00 p.m. on Sunday. No charge for admission.

One of the best things the Alaska legislature ever did was to set aside *Chugach State Park,* nearly half a million acres of wild and wondrous mountain valleys and alpine country, right smack-dab next to Anchorage. From numerous gateways along city roads and state highways, you'll find access to gentle and tough trails to hike, lakes to fish, rivers to kayak or canoe, and wildlife to see and photograph. Among the latter are moose, Dall sheep, mountain goats, plus brown (grizzly) and black bears. For trail information, visit dnr.alaska.gov/parks/index.htm and select the Chugach region, or call 907-345-5014.

You'll find Anchorage one of the most pleasant communities in Alaska to be hungry in. For dinner it's almost impossible to beat *Jens' Restaurant* (907-561-5367; jensrestaurant.com), located in midtown Anchorage at 701 West 36th Avenue. It can be pricey (entrees range from $30 to above $50), but where else will you find the likes of plaintain-crusted rockfish and grilled Kodiak scallops on citrus and pistachio quinoa? If your taste buds run to Italian cuisine, try the *Ristorante Orso,* downtown at Fifth Avenue and G Street (907-222-3232; orso-alaska.com). You can devour great hamburgers at the *Arctic Roadrunner* (907-561-1245; no website) at 5300 Old Seward Highway. For chicken done fast and right, the *Lucky Wishbone,* at 1033 East Fifth Avenue (907–272–3454; luckywishbonealaska.com), is one of Anchorage's oldest restaurants and a long-standing favorite among locals.

You absolutely, positively, cannot miss the best pizza this side of the Mississippi at Anchorage's *Moose's Tooth Pub & Pizzeria* (907-258-2537; moosestooth.net), named after one of Denali's more treacherous-looking ridges. You can order everything from a halibut pie to a Popeye (a spinach-laden special) to a traditional meat-lover's favorite. The Caesar salad is especially delicious, the pizza's fresh, the beer is homebrewed, and the atmosphere is kid friendly yet adult oriented. This is a favorite among locals, and it's usually crowded at peak times, so come early if you can. The restaurant is in a tricky location, at 3300 Old Seward Highway, but it's worth the trip.

Gwennie's Old Alaska Restaurant (4333 Spenard Road, 907-243-2090; gwenniesoldalaska.shop) is kitschy, but it, too, is a favorite among locals for breakfast, lunch, and dinner. The big, rambling structure displays lots of

---

About 287,000 people, or 40 percent of Alaska's entire population, lives in Anchorage.

Some of the largest tidal ranges in the world, 38.9 feet (11.9 meters), take place in Upper Cook Inlet near Anchorage.

Anchorage is the state's largest city, but Southeast Alaska's Juneau is the state capital.

The strongest earthquake ever recorded in North America struck Alaska, causing heavy damage to Anchorage, on March 27, 1964. It was given a magnitude of 9.2 on the Richter scale.

historical photos and relics on the walls, and its menu features Alaskan reindeer omelets, smoked salmon, and king crab. Prices are moderate.

Visitors often feel intimidated by **Chilkoot Charlie's** (2435 Spenard Road, 907-272-1010; koots.com) and pass it by, but if you want to rub elbows (literally) with Alaskans in a frontier saloon setting, drop by Anchorage's best-known watering hole. Called Koot's by the locals, it's located at 2435 Spenard Road. Just come out, and they'll shoehorn you in somehow.

For tours, taking the train, and bike rentals, there's no beating the convenience of staying in a downtown hotel or B&B. But if you'd rather stay in a different part of town, the **Dimond Center Hotel** (907-770-5000; dimondcenterhotel.com) in South Anchorage offers comparable rates to most other hotels in town, starting from $399 a night. The hotel is located adjacent to one of the state's biggest malls, although visitors from big cities will probably not be too impressed by our shopping options. To me, this has always felt like a low-key business hotel that isn't quite ready to say it's a business hotel. It's best if you have a car, but the mall does have a small transit center that can connect you to Anchorage's sparse but slowly improving bus service.

southcentralalaskatrivia

Anchorage's Lake Hood is the busiest seaplane base in the world. During summer as many as 800 takeoffs and landings can occur in a single day.

Pop singer Jewel grew up on her family's homestead near Homer, on Kachemak Bay.

It's no secret that lodging prices in Anchorage have zoomed skyward in recent years. If you have a car, **Camai Bed and Breakfast** (907-333-2219; camaibnb.com), located near the center of town, remains one of the best deals going. Each of their three rooms has a private bathroom, with prices starting from $150 double occupancy—practically unheard of, nowadays, during the summer high season. The fee for additional people is $20 each.

Considering its location, **Susitna Place** (907-274-3344; susitnaplace.com) is even more of a steal. They offer two suites with jetted tubs (from $225) and, if you can get by without the jetted tub, three rooms with private bathrooms (from $180). But it's the downtown location, located within easy walking distance of the Tony Knowles Coastal Trail and Westchester Lagoon—two favorite outdoor landmarks that also give you access to Anchorage's great trail system—that really make this B&B stand out.

Parkside Guest House (907-683-2290; parksideguesthouse.com) is a little more expensive. But its central downtown location, just off the miles-long swath of grass called Delaney Park, or the Park Strip for locals, makes it even better for exploring Anchorage's most urban attractions on foot. This guest-house is still conveniently close to the Tony Knowles Coastal Trail, too. Prices start from $315 double occupancy and include WiFi, a continental breakfast on your preferred schedule, luggage storage, and access to laundry facilities.

Base Camp Anchorage Hostel (907-274-1252; basecampanchorage. com), located in the quirky Spenard neighborhood at 1037 West 26th Avenue, is the only truly high-rated hostel in Anchorage. It's seasonal, open only from May through September, and especially caters to an outdoorsy clientele, although all travelers are welcome. The hostel isn't very big, so reservations are recommended. You can book all-female and mixed dorms, or one private room. Amenities include free DIY breakfast, a fully equipped kitchen, in-room lockers, secure storage, bear spray and gear rentals, a wood-burning sauna, community garden, and even a sensory deprivation float tank.

If you're looking for an exceptional fly-out experience in Southcentral Alaska, check out the *Within the Wild Adventure Company* (907-274-2710; withinthewild.com). Karl and Kirsten Dixon have created remote experiences for guests from all over the world at their handcrafted Tutke Bay Lodge. Bear viewing, hiking, canoeing, and fishing are among myriad activities that await. Or you can simply sit back on the porch, revel in the view, and marvel at the gracious simplicity of life out here. Kirsten's gourmet cooking classes using home-grown foods are an unexpected delight, as are the elegant but hearty meals she and her chefs prepare.

Remember the Tony Knowles Coastal Trail that was mentioned earlier? One of the best ways to see the trail is by bicycle, and one of the best places to rent a bicycle is right downtown, only 5 blocks from the trail. *Downtown Bicycle Rental* (907-279-3334; alaska-bike-rentals.com) offers hybrid, moun-tain, touring, and children's bikes at hourly and day rates, depending upon the bike. You'll get a free lock, helmet, and map of Anchorage's extensive trail system. The shop is at Fourth Avenue between C and D Streets.

Here's another quality bike tour, this one offered by *Alaskan Bicycle Adventures* (907-245-2175; alaskabike.com). They call it Bicycle Alaska, and it is a 7-day, 7-night adventure through some of Alaska's most beautiful country. There are 6 days of cycling, with an average of 70 miles per day, and the trip is topped off with a cruise in the glacier-studded Prince William Sound. The cost for this adventure is $4,295. If you want a little less pedaling and a little more variety, try the 7-day Alaskan Adventure package, priced at $4,395. In this trip you'll take daily hikes, canoe trips, or sea-kayaking adventures, and you'll cycle an average of 30 miles per day. This trip, too, is topped off with a Prince William Sound cruise.

If you're a winter fan, Anchorage can be particularly fun. Organized sled dog races take place virtually every January and February weekend at the Tozier Sled Dog Track on Tudor Road. And nobody, but nobody, fails to feel the excitement when the biggest winter sled dog racing events of the year roll around in February and March.

First is the **Anchorage Fur Rendezvous** (907-274-1177; furrondy.net) staged in mid-February. This "Mardi Gras of the North" runs through two weekends and includes the **World Championship Sled Dog Race,** which begins and ends right downtown on Fourth Avenue. Thousands of cheering Alaskans line the way. The "Rondy" also features some rather outrageous activities among its hundreds of scheduled events, including an outhouse race with privies being pushed and pulled on skis. Of special interest is the blanket toss, an Alaska Native tradition in which one person sits on a skin blanket and everybody else pulls the edges of the blanket, lofting that person into the air. You're welcome to take a turn at tossing or being tossed. There are also snowshoe softball games, a footrace alongside reindeer, snow-sculpting competitions, a grand parade, dances, Native crafts fairs, and outdoor fur auctions.

Alaska's premier sled dog race takes place the first weekend of every March in Anchorage and draws thousands upon thousands of Alaskans and visitors alike to the state's largest city. The **Iditarod Trail Sled Dog Race** runs from Anchorage some 1,000 miles (1,609 kilometers) to Nome in Northwest Alaska, and features some of the world's finest mushers. The ceremonial start takes place in downtown Anchorage, where hundreds of Alaskan huskies lunge and howl and jump their way from the start, through town, to an equally ceremonial finish. After that, the dogs and sleds are trucked north to the small town of **Willow** for the official restart the next day.

The best way to view all the excitement is to simply head downtown on the Saturday morning of the race. Race enthusiasts can follow the mushers' progress via the Iditarod website at iditarod.com.

If you're really into seeing the race, though, you need to take to the air. **Rust's Flying Service** (907-243-1595; flyrusts.com) offers an Iditarod package, ferrying you to one of the early checkpoints at Finger Lake and back again. Call for their most up-to-date pricing. Rust's, one of the oldest and most reputable flying services in Anchorage, offers flightseeing, bear viewing, and fly-in fishing packages during the summer, too. One popular option is their Discover Denali National Park floatplane tour, starting at $575 per person.

Keep Your Mouth Shut

Once upon a time, when I was just getting started as an outdoors reporter for a local newspaper, I was told to go on a sled dog ride, interview the musher, and then write about it. The musher who agreed to take me out fit very well into the classic, taciturn stereotype; I was green and nervous. Pretty much the only communication we had before the ride was as she bundled me into the basket of her sled: "Keep your mouth shut."

What do you say to that? Nothing, really, if you want to follow instructions. Even less if you're already feeling intimidated, keenly aware that you're about to be at this person's mercy. So I kept my mouth shut as she pulled out the snow brake, which had held the sled motionless against the dogs' enthusiasm to run, and *hupped* the team into action.

It wasn't long before something whizzed by the side of the sled: A piece of sled dog poop, jettisoned from a recent owner who was so excited and delighted to be running, they wouldn't even think of stopping to do their business. I eyed the six or seven husky butts in front of me, all tails raised in excitement, and kept following what I now recognized had been very good advice: Keep my mouth shut.

The sled ride was short—maybe 10 or 15 minutes at most?—and I wasn't exactly caught up in a poopnado. But every so often a turd would fly by or, maybe for the less aerodynamic, plop down onto the trail somewhere behind its producer but in front of the sled, where there was an ever-present hazard of a couple dozen paws kicking it back at me.

By the time we got back to the musher's dog yard, I still hadn't said a word. "Now you understand?" she asked me, leaning over the sled with a twinkle in her eye. Mutely, I nodded: Yup. Mouth closed. Very important.

She laughed. And once she'd put the dogs away, we went inside for what turned out to be a very pleasant interview.

Prince William Sound

Curious thing about **Prince William Sound:** It took the nation's all-time awful oil spill—the *Exxon Valdez* disaster of 1989—for most people to learn about one of the continent's most gorgeously pristine regions. The vessel, you'll recall, went aground on Bligh Reef, ruptured its hull, and spilled more than 11.3 million gallons of North Slope crude oil onto more than 1,500 miles of coastline. The deadly pollution, killing uncounted thousands of birds and sea mammals in its path, extended as far as the Alaska Peninsula, 600 miles away.

Yet there's some good news. Although the sound will continue to suffer from subsurface oil contamination for decades to come, from a visual perspective it has largely recovered. Myriad glaciers, islands, and mountains await visitors aboard huge cruise ships, tiny kayaks, day boats, and state ferries. Whales of several species spout, roll, and sound in the waterways. Hundreds of thousands of birds again inhabit the trees and cliffside rookeries throughout the region. Bears wander along otherwise deserted beaches. Mountain goats frolic high (but visibly) on the peaks overhead.

As in Southeast Alaska, most of Prince William Sound's communities are not connected by road, but many who live there consider that a virtue. Actually, you can drive to the sound by first taking the Seward Highway from Anchorage to Portage, then driving, for a fee, through the tunnel to Whittier. Or you can drive on portions of the Glenn and Richardson Highways to Valdez. Cordova, the third of Prince William Sound's three principal communities, can't be reached by regular highway, but the state ferry regularly calls there as well as at Whittier and Valdez. Call 800-642-0066 or visit ferryalaska.com for more information.

Here's a rundown on these towns: *Whittier's* history runs back to World War II when it was used as a port for incoming military supplies, which were then loaded onto trains for further transport. Hemmed in by mountains, the gorgeous waters of Prince William Sound, and a patchwork of land-ownership challenges, the town remains small and friendly. It's particularly pleasant to visit when big cruise ships are *not* at the town's two berths, because the passengers from just one ship can easily outnumber Whittier's residents by a factor of ten to one.

The community contains an excellent dock and wharf area, a few waterfront buildings, and—dominating the scene—two very tall and prominent buildings (skyscrapers by Alaska standards) called Begich Towers and the Buckner Building. The U.S. Army built the structures during World War II to house servicemen and their families stationed at the site. Today the fourteen-story Begich Towers has been converted into condos, and most of the population of Whittier lives there. The Buckner Building is now vacant. Another building, Whittier Manor, houses most of the rest of Whittier's residents.

There are only a couple of hotels in town, and some condo rentals. The largest hotel, *The Inn at Whittier* (907-472-1007; innatwhittier.com), is still rebuilding after a serious flood, but should be open by the time you read this. It usually operates during the summer only. The other, smaller hotel, *The Anchor Inn* (907-472-2354; anchorinnwhittier.com), is open year-round and has the city museum on its first floor. Museum admission is $5. Rooms at the inn start from $155. They also own condo suites next door, which start from $220.

The Alaska Marine Highway System operates a ferry between Whittier and Valdez during the summer. Rates vary depending upon the length of your vehicle. Passenger rates can be obtained by calling 800-642-0066 or visiting ferryalaska.com. Because the ferry now uses dynamic pricing, the further in advance you book the cheaper your tickets will be. Commercial tour operators also operate between the two communities.

Phillips Cruises is one of the long-established day-cruise operators out of Whittier (907-276-8023; phillipscruises.com). Its 26 Glacier Cruise ($189) lasts 6 hours and tours active tidewater glaciers in the area. The 4-hour Glacier Quest Cruise ($149) explores Blackstone Bay and has an educational element for those eager for a learning experience.

If you don't plan to drive your car aboard the ferry for Valdez, don't bring it to Whittier. There's really nowhere for you to take it from there; Whittier is the literal end

southcentral alaska facts

Between 1911 and 1938, 1 billion tons of copper were mined from the Kennecott Copper Mine.

The northernmost rainforest in Alaska is in Girdwood, about 26 miles south of Anchorage on the Seward Highway.

The largest king salmon taken with sportfishing tackle weighed 97 pounds 4 ounces and was caught by Les Anderson in the Kenai River in 1985.

The highest mountain in the Chugach Mountains is Mount Marcus Baker at 13,176 feet. It is located at the tips of Matanuska and Knik Glaciers.

of the road. On the other hand, if you'd enjoy a really different circle trip from Anchorage, drive your car through the tunnel to Whittier, bring it aboard the ferry to Valdez, then disembark for a drive up the Richardson and Glenn Highways back to Anchorage, or stay on the Richardson all the way to Fairbanks. If time permits, take the ferry all the way to Cordova before disembarking at Valdez. This highway/ferry trip, of course, works in either direction.

In recent years, Whittier has absolutely blossomed with recreation options. One of the big highlights is *Glacier Jet Ski* (907-830-4001; glacierjetskiadventures.com), the first-of-its-kind Jet Ski adventure to the wild, untamed beauty of Blackstone Bay, where you can expect to see lots of glaciers. The price (from $380 per person) includes all the safety gear you'll need.

You can get the inside line on what it's like to really live in Whittier during a *Whittier Walks* (907-887-3896; whittierwalks.com) tour. Over 90 minutes, you'll learn about the World War II secrets still hiding in plain sight, and the epic wilderness all around you. Prices start at $40 per person.

When you visit such a pretty seaside town, it's practically required that you get out on the water. If you aren't raring to hop on a ferry, cruise ship, or Jet Ski, you might enjoy a sea kayak tour with *Sound Paddler* (907-472-2452; pwskayakcenter.com). Their options range from a 3-hour tour of bird rookeries and waterfalls (from $79 to $180 per person, depending on group size; smaller groups share the cost) to exploring stupendous Blackstone Bay (from $300 to $625 per person, depending on group size).

Now about **Cordova**. For travelers who enjoy "untouristy" destinations, it is a great little place for poking around, mixing with the locals, and exploring on one's own. Now mostly a fishing and fish processing town, Cordova had its start as the saltwater port for shipping copper ore brought down on the Copper River & Northwestern Railway from the Kennecott mines.

You can no longer drive to **Childs Glacier** or **Miles Glacier** due to an impassable bridge. However you can book boat tours to see the glaciers with **The Riverside Inn** and **Orca Adventure Lodge**. Childs Glacier, in particular, is extremely active in its calving. If you wander down to the level of the stream in front of the glacier and it calves off a big hunk of ice, run for higher ground. The surge wave can be sizable and dangerous. On the drive out from town, keep your eyes alert for bears. Other sights along the way: beaver dams, picturesque marshlands, lakes and mountain vistas, silver-salmon spawning streams, and trumpeter swans.

southcentralalaskatrivia

Prince William Sound has twenty active tidewater glaciers—the largest concentration in North America.

For die-hard adventurers who want a little help from the locals, **Orca Adventure Lodge** (907-424-7249; orcaadventurelodge.com) is a good place to stay. They offer pretty much every adventure tour you can ask for in Cordova, along with the option of staying in remote fishing cabins. Cruises aren't too hard to come by when you're in a coastal community; the key is finding the one that's perfect for you. And if you happen to be a birder, a whale watcher, or just an all-around adventurer, one of the cruises offered by Coast Guard–certified **Discovery Voyages** (907-202-1017; discoveryvoyages.com) will be just right. Captains Dean Rand and Megan Ciana of the twelve-passenger, 65-foot yacht *Discovery* offer one of the finest (albeit expensive) wilderness cruises in Alaska. This was the first wilderness cruise to be offered in Prince William Sound, and it remains a popular ecotourism-oriented adventure today. The *Discovery* originally was built for the Presbyterian Missions service to the Native communities in Southeast Alaska and today is fully renovated to house passengers comfortably and enjoyably. Trips aboard the *Discovery* range from a 3-day "classic" cruise for $2,900 per person to an 11-day bear-viewing tour for $8,950 per person. Rand also offers custom charters. He carries kayaks and skiffs for landing parties, and the yacht has private rooms, hot showers, and sumptuous food (including fresh seafood harvested on the trip).

The city of **Valdez** (Alaskans say "Val-DEEZ") calls itself the Switzerland of Alaska. Actually, that's not too far off the mark, as the range of Chugach Mountains that arch behind and around the city are certainly in a class with the Alps. But Valdez has at least one attribute the Swiss can only dream of: an ocean view of fish-filled waters and forested islands. The town boasts at least one additional distinction. The 800-mile **Trans-Alaska Pipeline** from Prudhoe Bay, in the Arctic, terminates here in a major, 1,000-acre terminal operated by **Alyeska Pipeline Service Company.** Alyeska loads more than a million gallons of crude oil daily onto huge oceangoing tankers docked at the site.

A good starting point for any visit to Valdez is the **visitor information center** (907-835-2984; valdezalaska.org) at 309 Fairbanks Drive downtown. You can view films about the 1964 Good Friday earthquake, which all but destroyed much of the old town near the water, and you can pick up a map showing the present location of historic homes from Old Valdez. Many were relocated when it was determined the old sites were no longer safe for occupancy. Nearby, at Chenega Street and Egan Drive, is the **Valdez Museum** (907-835-2764; valdezmuseum.org), where exhibits range from slot machines to gold rush gear and a restored 1907 fire engine. Admission costs $12.

There are several day tour and adventure options out of Valdez, and one of the longtime favorites is operated by Captain Stan Stephens, whose experience in the industry is unparalleled. His company, **Stan Stephens Cruises** (866-867-1297; stephenscruises.com), has been plying the waters of Prince William Sound for nearly 30 years. The company offers a 6-hour cruise to Columbia Glacier and surrounding areas, as well as a 7½-hour tour to the more distant Meares Glacier. Be on the lookout for sea lions, puffins, whales, and even the occasional bear. Prices start from $162 for the shorter cruise, and $185 for the longer outing.

If you're into people-powered water sightseeing, **Anadyr Adventures** of Valdez (907-835-2814; anadyradventures.com) provides deluxe charter boat–supported kayaking trips to remote and awesome parts of Prince William Sound. They offer a number of day trips ranging from paddling the shoreline along the port ($89) to a 10-hour paddle to and from Glacier Island ($329), where you may see horned and tufted puffins and sea lion pullouts. They offer multi-day guided expeditions, too, ranging from 2 days to nearby Shoup Glacier ($579 all-inclusive) to paddle from the Meares Glacier to the Columbia Glacier ($2,625 all-inclusive, including water taxi both ways).

If you've traveled this far into Alaska and still haven't taken a river rafting trip, this may be the place to do it. Valdez-based **Pangaea Adventures** (907-835-8442; alaskasummer.com) provides daily trips down the nearby Lowe River through high-walled Keystone Canyon, from $105. They also guided multi-sport adventures, a full range of sea-kayaking day trips and expeditions, and guided backpacking trips.

The Kenai Peninsula

Deep in the bowels of the Alaska State Library in Juneau resides a rare and trea-sured second edition of Jonathan Swift's *Gulliver's Travels,* an account written in 1726 about fictional Lemuel Gulliver's adventures in Lilliput, a nation of little people, and in Brobdingnag, the land of giants. What is especially intriguing about the book for Alaskans is Swift's map of Brobdingnag—a huge landmass extending westward from northern North America.

Remember that Vitus Bering and Alexei Shelikof, the men who happened upon Alaska while sailing for the Russian czars, did so in 1741. The second edition of Swift's book is dated MDCCXXVII—1727, fourteen years before the Russian voyages of that brought them to Alaska. Yet Swift's map bears a resemblance (some say a close resemblance; others say not really) to Alaska, complete with a little stretch of land that could be the Kenai Peninsula, extend-ing from Southcentral Brobdingnag.

The comparison becomes more intriguing still when you realize that in modern Brobdingnag/Alaska roam many of North America's "most giant-size" creatures, including record-size brown (grizzly) bears, even bigger polar bears, and large concentrations of enormous whales and walrus in adjacent seas. In addition, on the peninsula noted both in Swift's book and in modern guides, you can see and photograph huge moose.

The Kenai, probably more than any other locale, is where Alaskans them-selves play and recreate. Lake, river, and saltwater fishing is superlative. Hiking trails are widespread and wide ranging. Moderate-size and tiny communities offer traditional homespun Alaskan hospitality. Access is easy by highway, rail, and air from Anchorage.

Because the Kenai Peninsula is much used by Alaskans and visitors alike, particularly those coming from Anchorage, it's wise to avoid weekend and holiday visits, when traffic on the only road access from Anchorage, the Seward Highway, can be horrendous. Most of the time, however, the 127-mile asphalt road is more than pleasurable as it skirts saltwater inlets, circles around big and little lakes, and penetrates thick, vast forest expanses. It richly deserves its prestigious designations as an All American Road and National Forest Scenic Byway.

The Seward Highway: Anchorage to Tern Lake Junction

Following are some of the sightseeing opportunities along the several highways that serve the Kenai Peninsula, starting with the 127-mile *Seward Highway,* south of Anchorage. The mileposts you see along the side of the road, incidentally, measure the distance from Seward. So the parking area at Potter Marsh at mile 117.4, for instance, is 117.4 miles from Seward and 9.6 miles from Anchorage.

All along the highway be on the lookout for wildlife, especially moose. The Kenai is home to a national wildlife refuge, and the abundant moose population is the reason for it. At mile 117.4 and at mile 116 you'll see turnoffs for **Potter Marsh,** a state wildlife refuge where you can view extensive waterfowl, shorebirds, arctic terns, and bald eagles plus king, pink, and silver salmon in the creeks that flow into the marsh. A boardwalk crosses the marsh. Between mileposts 106 and 110 on the Seward Highway, look frequently to the craggy tops of the rocky cliffs that rise from the road. If you look carefully, more often than not you'll spot mama Dall sheep and their youngsters staring curiously down at you. Do not, of course, stop your car on the highway; there are several turnoffs where you can safely stop and then walk back for easy viewing. In fact, if you are on the road for sightseeing purposes, please respect your fellow travelers and obey the frequent signs asking slower vehicles to pull over. It is the law to pull over if more than five vehicles are behind you.

If you're interested in wildlife, stop at **Beluga Point,** at mile 110.3. Here, if you're just a little bit lucky, you may see the small white beluga whales that congregate in these waters. The best viewing is probably around high tide. At low tide the point is a good place to witness a bore tide (more on this phenomenon in a moment).

Bird Creek State Campground, just past mile 101, is not only a pleasant place to camp or picnic, it also provides one of the better vistas for watching one of Alaska's more spectacular natural phenomena—the **bore tide** that comes rushing through Turnagain Arm at low tide daily. Get a tide book (free at many service stations, sporting goods stores, and banks), and check the times for low tide at Anchorage. Then, to get the correct time for the Bird Creek overlook, add about 2 hours and 15 minutes to whatever time is listed. What you'll see is a frothing, foaming wall of seawater—sometimes as high as 6 feet—that comes surging into the constricted inlet. Don't, by the way, even think of wading out onto the mudflats that are exposed in these and other Cook Inlet areas. The mud is like quicksand, and innocently ignorant waders have drowned after becoming mired in the muck, held there until the incoming tide sweeps over them.

At mile 90, the Seward Highway connects with the 3-mile Alyeska access road to **Girdwood, Alyeska Resort,** and **Crow Creek Mine.** Girdwood is less a city and more a still-woodsy gathering place of some 2,000 Alaskans, most of whom love to ski (usually at adjacent Alyeska Resort) and many of whom work at shops, stores, or eateries either at the resort (907-754-2111; alyeskaresort. com) or nearby. Many Anchorage residents have condominiums here. The community isn't exactly planned or laid out, but it's small enough to be easy to wander around in. The residents are more than friendly and accommodating. At the resort (a world-class ski area in the winter months), you can take a tram ride (from $43) 2,000 feet up the mountain for hiking, for taking in sweeping views of Turnagain Arm, or for a gourmet dinner at **Seven Glaciers Restaurant** (907-754-2237), which is named for the seven glaciers you can see from the restaurant.

southcentralalaskatrivia

The popular skiing town of Girdwood was named for miner James E. Girdwood, who came to the area in 1896.

They currently offer prix fixe menus for roughly $125 per person, and if you have restaurant reservations the tram ride to get there is free.

At the **Crow Creek Mine** (907-229-3105; crowcreekgoldmine.com), you can pan for gold along creek beds still rich with the precious metal. The managers will even teach you how and point out likely areas for prospecting. Sure, it's sort of touristy, but there really is plenty of gold along these creek banks. Many Alaskans come here on weekends for recreational panning. Of course, you get to keep all the "color" you find. When you're through, you can refuel your body with sourdough pancakes or sandwiches in the **Bake Shop** (907-783-2831; thebakeshop.com) near Alyeska Resort—their sweet rolls and soups are legendary—or partake of the eclectic **Jack Sprat Cafe** (907-783-5225; jack-sprat.net) with meals both "fat" and "lean." The **Double Musky** (907-783-2822; doublemuskyinn.com), with its huge (14- to 20-ounce) French pepper steak, is another favorite among locals and visiting Alaskans. Arrive early or be ready to wait. The Musky is popular, and they don't take reservations.

If you're overnighting in Girdwood, consider **Carriage House Accommodations** (907-250-1279; carriagehouseaccommodations.com), a beautiful timber-frame house on California Creek. You'll enjoy the river-rock fireplace, hardwood floors with radiant heat, massive post-and-beam construction, and arched windows. Four rooms, two cottages, a hayloft, and a suite are available, all with private baths. Summer rates start at $250 per night.

Hostel enthusiasts can check out the **Alyeska Home Hostel** (907-783-2222; alyeskahostel.com) about 0.8 mile from the Alyeska Resort. This is a cozy house with eight-dorm bunks, two private rooms, and a seasonal cabin. Kitchen and shower facilities are shared. The charge is $30 for a bunk bed, $60 single occupancy for the smaller private room, or $140 for two people in a larger private studio. Additional guests in the private rooms cost $25 each.

To get there, drive the Alyeska Road past Glacier Creek, make a right turn on Timberline Drive, then the fourth right on Alta for about 0.25 mile. The hostel is on the left; you'll see the sign.

Back on the Seward Highway: At mile 79 you can take a driving tour of *Alaska Wildlife Conservation Center* (907-783-0058; alaskawildlife.org), the state's only drive-through wildlife park, to view moose, elk, buffalo, musk oxen, caribou, and other North Country creatures from your own vehicle. The nonprofit wildlife center cares for orphaned and injured animals and is a key participant in conservation efforts like reintroducing wood bison into rural Alaska. Admission is $25 for adults and $20 for children.

If you're heading for the port of *Whittier,* on fabled Prince William Sound, the *Anton Anderson Memorial Tunnel* (907-472-2584; dot.alaska.gov/creg/whittiertunnel) is the way to go. The tunnel is located on Portage Glacier Road and connects Whittier and Prince William Sound to the Seward Highway and the rest of Southcentral Alaska. At 2.5 miles, it is the longest highway tunnel in North America and also accommodates Alaska Railroad trains. The round-trip toll for driving the tunnel is $13 for general traffic.

Another option for reaching Whittier is to take the *Alaska Railroad* (800-544-0552; alaskarailroad.com) Glacier Discovery Train from Anchorage, which departs daily during the summer and costs $129 round-trip or $58 one way.

One of the most iconic trips out of Whittier is hopping aboard a sleek, comfortable catamaran for a *26-Glacier Cruise.* Operated by *Phillips Cruises and Tours* (907-276-8023; phillipscruises.com), this ship takes you on a 135-mile adventure into College and Harriman Fjords, where you'll likely see whales, sea otters, eagles, and harbor seals in addition to calving glaciers. Fun and fact-filled narration by the friendly crew, a hearty snack, complimentary coffee, and a guaranteed smooth ride make this a fabulous experience. Check out their seasonal rail/cruise special at $139 round-trip.

Also located on the 5.5-mile Portage Glacier Road is a visitor center dedicated to what used to be Alaska's most visited travel attraction, *Portage Glacier,* and perhaps Alaska's least-known wildlife species, the glacier iceworm.

Portage Glacier has long since receded past the point of visibility from the US Forest Service's *Begich-Boggs Visitor Center* (907-783-2326), but the center still makes a great observation point for beautiful *Portage Lake*—basically, a giant pool of meltwater from the glacier that just happens to be miles long and about 600 feet deep at its most profound. Once upon a time not that long ago, the lake was all but clogged with icebergs that had crumbled off the glacier face. Nowadays, it's rare to see a couple of icebergs bobbing near the visitor center. Incredibly, there are tiny but visible organisms, popularly called

Active Ice

There is something innately rewarding about gazing at, walking on, or even climbing on ice in the middle of summer—an activity made possible by the blue-white glaciers that, although receding, still linger across a good portion of the state. In fact, there are at least four well-known glaciers you can easily access by road in Southcentral Alaska.

Head south from Anchorage on the Seward Highway; 50 miles later you'll find the turnoff to Portage Glacier. Although you can no longer see the glacier from the visitor center, you can take a narrated boat tour to view it up close. Or you can hike to the nearby Byron Glacier to see how far it has receded up the valley wall; not that long ago, it was very easy to walk up to the glacier's edge. (*Warning:* Glacier ice is in constant motion and giant pieces have been known to break off, injuring or even killing unsuspecting people. Be very careful of this, as well as crevasses that you could slip into.)

Keep driving on the Seward Highway; 2 hours later you'll find yourself in the town of Seward, which is the jump-off point for some of the state's best tidewater glacier viewing, in Kenai Fjords National Park. You can also access an inland glacier, Exit Glacier, by road. Just drive the access road and take the roughly 2-mile round-trip walk to a designated viewing point that sits a safe distance from the toe of the glacier. You can hire guides to take you hiking or even ice climbing on the glacier, but absolutely should not try it on your own if you don't already have the technical skills for glacier travel. There's just too much risk of falling into a crevasse or moulin or being crushed by falling pieces of ice.

By far the most walked-upon glacier in Southcentral Alaska is the Matanuska, located just off the Glenn Highway some 46 miles northeast of Palmer. You used to be able to pay a nominal fee and hike out onto the glacier yourself, but nowadays you can only access it via a guided tour that provides all the safety equipment you need, along with a guide who has already thoroughly scouted the safe routes along the glacier surface. For an extra adrenaline rush, you can upgrade to ice climbing instead or trekking, or even come during the winter during which, rumor has it, you might be allowed to climb through ice caves and tunnels one wouldn't usually tackle in the summer.

For information on any of the other glaciers abundant in Southcentral Alaska, just ask at the Anchorage Log Cabin Visitor Information Center in downtown Anchorage. They'll get you pointed in the right direction.

iceworms, that live in glacial ice—although you have to get up very close to the ice to see them. They look sort of like black threads.

Even though the ice has receded out of sight from the visitor center, the center still has interesting exhibits inside that focus on the ecosystems of the valley around you. The center is open daily in summer 9:00 a.m. to 5:00 p.m.

The Gray Line of Alaska's sightseeing vessel **Ptarmigan** makes frequent 1-hour excursions from lakeshore to within 0.25-mile of Portage Glacier's glistening face. This is Alaska's most economical glacier cruise, at just $49 per person if you drive yourself there, or $119 if you need round-trip transport from Anchorage (888-452-1737; graylineofalaska.com). Forest service naturalists accompany each trip.

At mile 56.2 of the Seward Highway you have two somewhat confusing choices. If you're coming from Anchorage, turn right to access the Hope Highway or stay left to stay on the road to Seward. The Hope alternative is well worth exploring. The road leads to the community of **Hope** and one of Alaska's most celebrated backpacking experiences.

First, about the road and the community: At the turnout just beyond mile 2, you have at least a chance of seeing moose in the Sixmile Creek valley below. Just past mile 11 there's a big, paved turnoff with a view of Turnagain Arm. At mile 16.5, turn on Hope Road for "downtown" Hope, a picturesque little community of year-round homes for a handful of residents and getaway cabins used by urban Alaskans. The road leads past the post office, then to the waterfront, a popular site for anglers. The town had its start as a mining center in 1896. Today it offers a secluded base for hiking, fishing, and just getting away from it all.

Just past mile 16 and before you get to Hope, turn south on Resurrection Creek Road for the trailhead of the **Resurrection Pass Trail,** one of Alaska's finest backcountry hiking routes. It ends 38 miles later at about mile 53 on the Sterling Highway. In between, trekkers experience alpine ridges and lakes, scenic valleys, and vast panoramas plus the opportunity to observe moose, Dall sheep, mountain goats, and bears. Spaced about a half-day's hiking distance apart are seven US Forest Service public use cabins (877-444-6777; recreation.gov).

Back on the Seward Highway, between miles 47.5 and 44.5, you'll find numerous turnoffs that offer excellent photo ops for pictures of Upper and Lower Summit Lakes and the spectacular mountains that rise behind them. If you're driving from Anchorage to Seward in one day, the log cabin **Summit Lake Lodge** (907-244-2031; summitlakelodge.com), at mile 45.8, offers a good refreshment stop with moderately priced, old-fashioned eggs-meat-and-potatoes breakfasts plus full lunch and dinner menus. And if you like pie, this is the best place ever to get the pie of your choice. You name it, they make it.

Just before mile 38 you come to **Tern Lake Junction,** where the Seward Highway connects with the Sterling Highway; locals know this as "the Y" for its shape. If you're Seward-bound, continue straight ahead on the Seward Highway. If you're headed for Soldotna, Homer, and other such communities on the western Kenai Peninsula, turn right on what becomes the Sterling Highway. Locals always default to highway names instead numbers here, because the numbers are confusing and inconsistent—but the names almost always identify one of the major communities the road accesses, so they make good sense.

A Fall Ritual

There is never a bad season for hiking in Alaska. But there's something enchanting about walking in the crisp fall air, surrounded by yellowing leaves and ripe berries, that calls me out into the mountains and forests every autumn. We don't get brilliant reds and oranges in our trees as happens in other places, but those rich colors—and more—get splashed across the mountain tundra like a palette of spilled paints, usually starting around mid-September. Meanwhile, in the brushier, forested areas, you can enjoy the last of the summer berries *if* you know what's safe to eat.

This is also one of my favorite times of year for camping. Whether you're hiking into the backcountry with a tent, pitching that tent in a roadside campground, or even camping in the back of your car (which is honestly one of my favorite things to do), there's nothing quite like cozying into the warm cloud of a down camping quilt in blissful contrast to the crisp air that turns your breath into fog.

You get major bonus points if you remember to unzip your tent, or crack open a car window or sunroof, if you have one, and look out at the night sky: Once September hits, the night skies are dark enough to see banners of stars unfurling overhead. Or sometimes, if you're really lucky, you'll look up and see the northern lights dancing in the sky.

If the northern lights are really bright, you might see the bright greens, reds, and pinks that come through so beautifully in photographs. But our eyes don't gather as much light as a camera lens set to long exposure, so sometimes we'll see the aurora as a milky white that can be hard to distinguish from wispy clouds . . . except that clouds don't wave and dance like they're caught up in a spectral wind, or fade in and out of being like alternate dimensions coming in and out of focus.

The Seward Highway: Tern Lake Junction to Seward

Moose Pass, at mile 29.4, would be easy to miss if you blinked. It's an interesting little town (population about 200) and has a motel, general store, and restaurant. At **Estes Brothers Grocery** (907-288-3151; no website) there's a big waterwheel that turns a working grindstone. If you collect pictures of unique signs, the one here reads MOOSE PASS IS A PEACEFUL TOWN. IF YOU HAVE AN 'AXE TO GRIND' DO IT HERE. If you're looking for an interesting spot to stretch your legs, there's a 1.3-mile paved biking and walking trail that skirts the edge of Trail Lake. **Trail Lake Lodge** (907-288-3101; traillakelodge.com) offers steak and seafood dining right on the shore of its eponymous lake, and sometimes live music too.

If you're looking for a place to stay in Moose Pass, **Midnight Sun Log Cabins** (907-288-3627; midnightsunlogcabins.com) offer a quintessentially Alaska chic experience from $165 a night. The cabins have running water, private bathrooms and balconies or porches, and generally sleep two to four people depending on the cabin.

If you're traveling in a group or just like a lot of space, **Moose Pass Adventures** (907-599-0643; moosepassadventures.com) offers two yurts for rent. Named after local pioneers, the Nellie (named for famed female trapper Nellie Neal-Lawing) sleeps five people, and the Ed (named for local pioneer Ed Estes) sleeps up to eight.

The highway ends at mile 0 and the city of **Seward.** The community is relatively old by Alaska standards, having had its start in 1903, when railroad surveyors selected this site at the head of **Resurrection Bay** as an ocean terminal and supply center. Actually, there was a small Russian settlement there prior to 1903. Since 1923 the town has served as the farthest-south point on the 470-mile route of the Alaska Railroad and prides itself today on being the gateway to **Kenai Fjords National Park.**

Incidentally, the 4-hour Alaska Railroad trip aboard the **Coastal Classic Train,** from Anchorage to Seward, is one of the North Country's most rewarding excursions for $211 round-trip. The journey departs Anchorage at 6:45 a.m. daily in the summer and leaves Seward at 6:00 p.m. for the return trip. Sights along the way include the dramatic coastline of Cook Inlet, major lakes and streams, forest country, deep gulches and gullies, and frequent wildlife sightings of moose, bears and more. For information about rail-only travel or rail/sail combination tours that include cruising Resurrection Bay and Kenai Fjords National Park, call 800-544-0552 or visit alaskarailroad.com.

To get a quick glimpse of old downtown Seward, the small boat harbor, and all the history in between, hop aboard one of the vans with **Seward City Tours** (sewardcitytours.com). It only takes about an hour, and departs the depot shortly after your train arrives. Tickets start from $45. The same company offers a free or low-cost shuttle service that circulates between the rail depot, cruise ship terminal, and various points along the waterfront and within town; this service generally runs mid-May to mid-September.

Two hiking destinations, among many others, are especially notable. From a trailhead at about mile 2 on the Lowell Point Road, you can walk, at low tide, along a 4.5-mile forest and beach trail to **Caines Head State Recreation Area,** where World War II bunkers and gun emplacements serve as reminders of Alaska's strategic importance during a time when a Japanese invasion of North America was of genuine concern.

Mount Marathon, which rises from the community's edge from just above sea level to 3,022 feet, offers another satisfying trek. But if you don't like crowds, avoid this trail (and actually, the entire town of Seward) on Independence Day. On July 4 each year the town continues a tradition begun in 1909 with a wager between two "sourdoughs." The bet: whether or not a person could run from midtown to a high point on the mountain and back in less than an hour.

The outcome: Yes, it can be done—so far in a record time of 43 minutes, 23 seconds. These days competitors come from other towns, states, and even nations to scramble to the summit, then run, leap, slide, and fall during the helter-skelter descent witnessed by cheering crowds of spectators along the route. The runners' trail they use is distinct from the hikers' trail, although both end up at the same high point that serves as a turnaround. Unless you're training to run the Mount Marathon race yourself, I sincerely recommend taking the hikers' trail. It's much less likely to require a rescue.

A small but informative **National Park Service visitor center** (907-422-0500; nps.gov/kefj), with information on nearby Kenai Fjords National Park, is located at 1212 Fourth Avenue on the Seward waterfront. It sits among structures that house sightseeing, charter, fishing, and souvenir shops. The center operates 9:00 a.m. until 7:00 p.m. daily from Memorial Day weekend through Labor Day, offering slideshows, interpretive programs, other exhibits, and short walks.

You really won't find any hideaway eating places in Seward. But for lunch and dinner, locals and visiting Alaskans often choose **Ray's Waterfront** (907-224-5606; rayswaterfront.com) at 1316 Fourth Avenue at the small boat harbor, especially for fish and seafood. Prices are in the $20 to $30 range for lunch, $25 to $35 for dinner. Seats by the window are a must.

For a different sort of waterfront view, the **Seward Windsong Lodge** (907-224-7116; sewardwindsong.com) and accompanying **Resurrection Roadhouse** overlook the Resurrection River on the way to Exit Glacier. The rooms are comfortable and secluded, and the food, well, let's just say the food rivals the views you'll see out the roadhouse's windows. Try the white mushroom pizza—you won't regret it.

The Cookery (907-422-7459; cookeryseward.com) sits squarely in downtown Seward at 209 Fifth Avenue, so it's only a short distance from waterfront views, but you probably won't want to take your attention off your plate. Fresh oysters, local meats, local produce, and foraged finds all feature prominently in the creative meals here.

And for coffee lovers, if you're wandering the streets of downtown Seward, be sure to stop at what looks like a church but actually is **Resurrect Art Coffee House,** on Third Avenue (907-224-7161; resurrectart.com). The baked goods and espresso are all tasty. This is a relaxing place to read a newspaper, visit with locals, or just admire the artwork that adorns the former church's walls.

Exit Glacier is one of the few glaciers in Alaska whose face you can actually approach on foot. It's located at the end of Exit Glacier Road, also known as Herman Leirer Road, which junctions at mile 3.7 on the Seward Highway. En route to the glacier you initially pass by small clusters of homes, then drive through thick forests and a steep-walled valley for about 8 miles to a visitor parking area. A series of paths and trails lead to the snout of the 3-mile-long river of ice. *Caution:* You'll see whole groups walking right up to the ice to pose for photos; that's a foolish thing to do. Huge pieces of ice can fall at any time. Stay safely back to still get great pictures without the risk of dying.

If you're a hiker, you'll find two great trails here: the **Exit Glacier Trail** you hiked to get to that viewpoint, and the much longer, more challenging **Harding Icefield Trail** that takes you up a mountainside to the eponymous icefield—essentially the "headwaters" for Exit Glacier and many others.

There are bears and moose in the area, and you can find iceworms in the ice (they avoid the sun, so look for them in the early evening).

Of course, to really appreciate Kenai Fjords National Park, you need to see the fjords from the water. Several excellent day-cruise operators offer half-day or longer narrated excursions through Resurrection Bay to see whales, sea otters, a sea lion rookery, puffins, eagles, glaciers, mountains, and other features of the magnificent Kenai Fjords landscape. Times and rates vary.

You'll be surprised at the number of cruise-ship operators in Seward, and their names are all so similar sounding that it's easy to get confused. You probably won't go wrong with any of these operators; they're all reputable. But the two largest operations, and often the most affordable, are as follows:

Major Marine Tours (907-224-8030; majormarine.com) offers a great 4-hour wildlife and glacier tour from $140 plus tax (about $155 total) narrated by a National Park Service ranger. You'll have a chance to see puffins, sea otters, eagles, and all sorts of massive glaciers. Long cruises are available, ranging from 6 to 8 ½ hours; those options include a free deli lunch. **Kenai Fjords Tours** (907-224-8068; alaskacollection,com) offers a very similar range of trips. The shortest is a 4-hour cruise available only in the spring, then a 5-hour cruise that includes a stop for lunch on Fox Island (from $130 plus tax).

Resurrection Bay, and its surrounding smaller bays, also offers some of the best sea kayaking in the state. There are no shortage of kayak rental and tour companies to help you plan a memorable trip.

Sunny Cove Kayaking (907-224-4426; sunnycove.com) offers afternoon tours to 8-day guided sea-kayaking and camping expeditions. Prices start from $219 for a day trip that blends paddling with a scenic cruise aboard one of the local tour boats or, if you want to go camping, from $1,350 for a fully guided 2-night trip. Longer trips of up to 6 nights are available.

For accommodations plus kayaking tours and rentals in a beautiful, secluded setting, contact **Kayaker's Cove** (907-224-2662; kayakerscove.com) where rustic lodging will take you way off the beaten path and daily kayaking will invigorate your spirit. The lodge is located on Resurrection Bay, 12 miles from Seward. Hostel-style bunks cost $30, and cabins rent for $120 a night. Kayaks are available for $25 per person, per day.

Now, back to terra firma. It isn't off the beaten path—in fact, it's one of the largest buildings in Seward—but the **Alaska SeaLife Center** (907-224-6300 or 800-224-2525; alaskasealife.org) is certainly not to be missed. The facility, the crown jewel of this waterfront community, houses some of Alaska's most interesting animal life. Admission to this research and education center starts at $29 for adults, and is cheaper if you purchase in advance online. Once at the center you'll be able to see puffins, sea lions, seals, and other marine wildlife up close. There are daily films; a viewing platform overlooking the bay; behind-the-scenes experiences, like helping feed puffins, for an extra fee; and all sorts of exhibits.

If you'd enjoy sleeping in a National Historic Site, book yourself into the **Van Gilder Hotel** (907-224-5518; vangilderseward.com), a small but comfortable hotel in the older business district in downtown Seward. It was built in 1916 as an office building but became a hotel in 1921. The rates begin at $159 for a room with shared bath and just $10 more for a room with a private bathroom. Just scale your expectations to the setting: This property is charming and historic, but that also translates to thin walls and relatively basic accommodations.

The Sterling Highway: Tern Lake to Homer

Seward is as far as you can go by road on the Seward Highway, which covers the eastern side of the Kenai Peninsula. At its Tern Lake junction with the Seward Highway at mile 37, however, the paved Sterling Highway heads west, then south along the western side of the Kenai. Strangely, the mileposts along the Sterling Highway measure distances from Seward, even though the road doesn't go there. The road ends at its southernmost point, at the tip of the Homer Spit at mile 179.5.

For those who enjoy luxuries while traveling, the rustic but regal **Kenai Princess Wilderness Lodge** (800-426-0500; princesslodges.com) is accessible from the road at mile 47.7. Note the chandelier in the lobby made from deer antlers. Activities include horseback riding, river rafting, flightseeing, hiking, fishing, and touring from the lodge throughout the rest of the peninsula. Or just relax in a hot tub. The lodge is open from mid-May to mid-September; rates begin at $219 during the shoulder season, $499 during peak season.

The small town of **Cooper Landing,** spread out along the road before and after mile 48, is an outdoorperson's heaven. You'll find visitor facilities, including guided fishing trips, cabins, and shops, as well as countless trails to explore, an aquamarine lake to admire, and a fish-packed river waiting to be fished. For those who want to explore deeper into the woods, stop by Alex Kime's **Alaska Horsemen Trail Adventures** (907-595-1806; alaskahorsemen .com) and sign up for a day or overnight trip into the Chugach Mountains. Alex, a quintessential cowboy with a perpetual smile, is eager to share his world with guests atop the backs of one of his twenty-eight or so horses. Two-hour valley rides are $250, with a maximum of two people in the group, so you'll get lots of personalized attention. Alex also offers longer day trips and sometimes offers horsepacking wilderness trips; call to check pricing and availability for those.

Alaska Wildland Adventures (800-334-8730; alaskawildland.com) offers quality river trips from a launch site at mile 50.1. If you're looking for a bit of adventure, ask about their 7-hour Kenai Canyon raft trip through a remote, nonmotorized section of the Kenai River. It includes some spirited Class III rapids and a lunch on the shores of pristine Skilak Lake. The cost is $199. If you prefer a more peaceful trip, the company offers a Kenai River scenic float through a portion of the **Kenai National Wildlife Refuge,** where there are frequent sightings of moose, eagles, Dall sheep, waterfowl, signs of beaver, and sockeye salmon. The cost is $72. Alaska Wildland also offers half- or full-day Kenai River Sportfishing trips, on which you can angle for salmon, rainbow trout, and Dolly Varden. These trips are packaged with comfortable accommodations at **Kenai Riverside Lodge.** Costs vary from $2,375 for 3 nights to $7,095 for 8 nights and include everything from transportation from Anchorage to meals and gear.

Just down the road, at mile 50, Gary and Carol Galbraith's family-operated **Alaska Rivers Company** (907-595-1226; alaskariverscompany.com) offers a half-day scenic float excursion in rafts from $65, stand-up paddleboard floats from $80, or a full-day scenic, sometimes splashy, canyon experience for $175. Both trips include professional guides, excellent wildlife viewing prospects, and homemade picnic lunches. The Galbraiths also have log cabins—rustic but very comfortable—for rent on the shore of the Kenai River. The River House sleeps four and rents for $350 per night.

At mile 58 you have a choice to make and a **U.S. Fish and Wildlife Service Information Station** to help you make it. You can continue on the paved Sterling Highway westerly to mile 75.2, or you can take the southerly 19-mile gravel Skilak Lake Loop Road to its junction with the Sterling at mile 75.2. I recommend the latter, as long as the unpaved road looks to be in pretty decent shape. That always comes down to how recently the grader has gone through, and what the weather has been like: In wet weather the road can quickly become a serious mudpit, but in dry weather it's usually pretty decent. More importantly, the opportunities for photography, fishing, hiking, and wildlife spotting are excellent along this road, and there are some worthwhile hiking trails and small campgrounds, too.

A warning note: Beautiful **Skilak Lake,** like many of the large lakes on the Kenai, can be extremely dangerous. Horrific winds can arise suddenly on the water. If you plan to take out a small boat, stay close to shore and wear a life jacket.

After that intersection with Skilak Loop Road at mile 75.2, the Sterling Highway continues westerly to mile 83.4, where you have another off-highway choice. If you're transporting a canoe, the choice is an easy yes. The Swanson River and Swan Lake Roads head north, then east, for nearly 30 miles, accessing two of the most highly acclaimed canoeing routes in the North Country. The **Swanson River Canoe Trail** is 80 miles long and connects more than forty lakes with 46 miles of the Swanson River. Portages between lakes are short, less than a mile over relatively easy terrain. The **Swan Lake Canoe Trail,** separate from the Swanson River route, covers 60 miles and connects thirty lakes with forks of the Moose River. Both trails lie within the Kenai National Wildlife Refuge.

The opportunities for viewing wildlife—especially moose, eagles, trumpeter swans, and tundra swans—are enormous. For maps and additional information, call or visit the **Kenai National Wildlife Refuge Visitor Center** (907-260-2820; kenai.fws.gov) at the top of Ski Hill Road. Information is also available at the forest service cabin at mile 58, the Kenai National Wildlife Refuge Information Center in Soldotna, and at local information centers in Kenai and Soldotna.

At mile 94.2, you face still another vexing little decision. This time your options are three. You can continue westerly on the Sterling Highway to Soldotna (the city center is only a mile down the road), then keep driving southerly on the Sterling toward the end of the road in Homer. Or you can turn northerly at what is called the Soldotna Y on the Kenai Spur Highway to the city of Kenai, then drive on to **Captain Cook State Recreation Area.** The third choice is to drive on to Soldotna, visit that city, then backtrack the short distance to the Kenai Spur Highway. After you've finished exploring the spur road and the city of Kenai, you can then bypass Soldotna and drive southerly on Kalifornsky Beach Road to rejoin the Sterling at mile 108.8. I recommend the third choice.

First, about **Soldotna:** If you want to fish the Kenai River for king salmon and other species, this community of about 3,700 offers several charter-boat fishing services. You can also fish on your own from the shores of the river; many do. Among the sights to see is the **Soldotna Historical Society Museum** (907-262-3832; soldotnamuseum.com), which includes a small "village" of historic log buildings, among them the 1958 territorial school, the last one built in Alaska before statehood. Damon Hall, at the village site, contains an excellent display of Alaska wildlife mounts. Still other mounted wildlife displays can be seen at the **Kenai National Wildlife Refuge Visitor Center** (907-262-7021; kenai.fws.gov), at the top of Ski Hill Road. This is a prime location to get information about canoeing, hiking, camping, or just sightseeing in the refuge, which was established by President Franklin D. Roosevelt in 1941 as the Kenai National Moose Range.

Now retrace your steps back to the Y at mile 94.2 on the Sterling Highway, where the Kenai Spur Highway heads northerly. The city of Kenai lies about 11 miles up this road.

It's probably best to start a **Kenai** visit at the **Kenai Visitors and Cultural Center** (907-283-1991; kenaichamber.org) near Main Street and the Kenai Spur Highway. There you'll find a cultural museum and wildlife displays as well as friendly staff to give directions around the far-flung community.

Kenai, you'll find, is one of those curious cities that doesn't really seem to have a downtown, yet this is a site where Native peoples and Russian fur traders settled in centuries past. The Russian heritage is dramatically expressed in the **Holy Assumption of the Virgin Mary Russian Orthodox Church** (907-283-4122; holyassumptionkenai.org) not far from the visitor center. The original church was founded in 1846 by a Russian monk, Egumen Nicolai. The present three-domed structure was built a half century later and is one of the oldest Russian Orthodox houses of worship in Alaska. Tours are available, and in the summer you can usually walk right in. The nearby **St. Nicholas Chapel** was constructed in 1906 and covers the grave of the founding monk. In the same vicinity is **Fort Kenay,** a log structure built during the 1967 Alaska Purchase Centennial to commemorate the original 1869 U.S. Army installation. It housed some one hundred men and officers. Check at the visitor center for a copy of a self-guided walking tour.

Walk to **Beluga Lookout,** at the end of Main Street, for possible sightings of the white beluga whales that visit these waters.

Fishing for lunker king salmon, monster-size halibut, and other species is, for many visitors, what Kenai is all about. As in Soldotna, a large number of guides and charter boats call Kenai home.

Perhaps the best way to see the Kenai Peninsula and its surroundings is by plane. **Kenai Aviation** (888-505-3624; kenaiaviation.com) offers book-by-the-seat flightseeing tours, so you don't have to worry about splitting the cost for the entire plane—although you can do that, too, if you have a big enough group. Prices start at $250 for an hour-long tour overlooking the Harding Icefield, or $325 for a 90-minute tour with vistas of an active volcano, Mount Redoubt, and Lake Clark National Park.

The Captain Cook State Recreation Area, at the very end of the Kenai Spur Highway, is one of Alaska's relatively unsung state parklands—probably because it's at the end of a single road. But especially if you're a camper, it's well worth the drive. **Discovery Campground,** near the end of the road, merits special mention. Here you'll find a locale of rolling hills, wooded spruce plateaus, and beautiful vistas of the Alaska Range across Cook Inlet. The volcanic peaks Mount Spurr, Mount Redoubt, and especially Mount Iliamna stand out across the water (as do thirteen oil platforms).

Three warnings: First, on the tidelands, observe the warnings and don't let an incoming tide catch you off guard. Stay entirely off mudflats, which are made of silt ground up by glaciers and then washed downstream to the ocean. The mudflats might seem solid while the tide is out, but they more or less turn to quicksand as the water table rises. People have become trapped and died. Second, delicious berries are thick in the area, and they are there for the picking, but avoid the bright red or white poisonous baneberry, which are present here and in much of Alaska. And third, if you get into a standoff with a bear, leave the site and the berries to the animal. Don't even think of trying to shoo the bruin away.

After you've "done" the Kenai Spur Highway, you can retrace your travel to mile 94 of the Sterling Highway, then continue south on the highway. The more scenic choice, though, is to head west, then southerly, on Kalifornsky Beach Road. This takes you down the coast to the small, waterfront town of Kasilof, at mile 108.8 on the Sterling Highway.

The **Hungry Moose B&B** (907-252-9253; hungrymoosebandb.com) sits perched atop a hilltop, surrounded by gardens, greenhouses, and forest. The sunsets from the upper deck are beautiful. Their four rooms with shared baths start from $120 double occupancy ($20 for each additional person) and a private cabin—with running water!—starts from $140. If you would rather stay riverside, **Kasilof River Lodge** (907-262-6348; kasilofriverlodge.com) offers three lodge rooms (from $95 to $145), five cabins (from $105 to $165), and a yurt (from $95). Expect to share bathhouse facilities. Both of these properties just mentioned are happy to set you up with fishing trips, too, or a package rate that includes fishing; call or email them for details.

If you're neither a hunter nor an angler, but you'd still like to do something very Alaskan, stop at mile 117.4 and head for *Clam Gulch State Recreation Area* (where there are 116 campsites) to join hundreds of locals on the shore for the grand old Alaska sport of razor clam digging. *Three caveats:* Don't drive down the extremely steep beach road to sea level unless you have a four-wheel-drive vehicle. Don't go digging without a valid Alaska sportfishing license, available at various sporting and retail establishments. And, again, don't get stuck offshore on an incoming tide. The best clamming occurs on minus tides and varies from month to month. Locals are more than happy to share their knowledge and technique. You'll find similar clamming opportunities at the Ninilchik Beach Campground, which is part of *Ninilchik State Recreation Area,* at mile 134.5.

At about mile 135 you'll come to a side road that leads to the old original *Ninilchik Village* and the beach. Take the time to explore this site, which includes a few old log buildings. A white Russian Orthodox church, still in use, overlooks the village from a photogenic hilltop setting. Modern *Ninilchik* stretches down the road from roughly mile 135.5. If you don't like crowds, avoid the area on Memorial Day and other holidays, when thousands converge for the fishing thereabouts.

At mile 157 on the Sterling Highway, the collector of superlatives will want to turn off the main highway and drive on the Old Sterling Highway past the Anchor River to another turnoff, this one on the Anchor River Beach Road. At the end of this road lies the *Anchor Point State Recreation Site.* There, on an overlook platform facing Cook Inlet, stands a big sign that reads NORTH AMERICA'S MOST WESTERLY HIGHWAY POINT. You can't drive your car anyplace west of this point on the connected highways of the United States and Canada. Incidentally, more than a million razor clams are taken each year on the beaches between Anchor Point and Kasilof up the highway.

You come to *Homer,* one of my favorite places in Alaska, at mile 172 of the highway and beyond. At about mile 175, you can turn onto the famous Homer Spit. The Sterling Highway ends here, just under 142 miles from its beginning at the "Y," and nearly 233 miles from its start in Anchorage.

One of the nicest things about Homer, once you get past its scenery, art, food, fishing, and the friendly community vibe, is the weather: It's usually mild and pleasant, at least by Alaska standards, throughout the year.

Homer is small enough to be cozy but large enough to have everything you need. The hiking, fishing, photography, and nature-watching opportunities are enormous. There's lots of Alaska history (and prehistory) here, and the people—though individualistic to the core—are as open and friendly as you'll find anywhere.

First, a little orientation: Most residences, city services (hospital, fire department, library, city hall), and government offices are located in what you might call Homer proper. Nearby, the *Pratt Museum* (3779 Bartlett St.; 907-235-8635; prattmuseum.org), which emphasizes natural and cultural diversity on the Kenai Peninsula, has a botanical garden, a museum store, a fascinating historical cabin that functions as its own mini-museum, and a marine gallery

Homer Away from Home

As a longtime resident of Alaska, and in particular the "big city" of Anchorage, I'm endlessly fascinated by the divergence in how out-of-state visitors and other Alaskans see me. To folks from Outside (note the capital letter—anywhere outside Alaska), I pass very well as a local in almost any circumstance. But of course to residents of other, smaller Alaska communities, they spot me as an outsider (note the lowercase letter—anywhere outside their own community) right away because if I actually lived there, they would already know me.

But I sometimes still forget how obviously a stranger like me can stick out in small towns. So when a friendly Homer local leaned over my shoulder and offered a chipper greeting of "Hi, where are you from?" it took me a minute to catch up to the chain of (very correct) assumptions she had already made.

I was standing in line at one of my favorite bakeries, just like all the locals—and all the tourists—knew to do. (Just for the record, Two Sisters is the name of this supremely excellent bakery.) I wasn't wearing the brand-new adventure gear, or carrying a camera with a massive lens, that would brand me as fresh off a cruise ship. I wasn't from there, but I also wasn't exuding "new to here" vibes, so I hadn't just moved in. That left "some other Alaska community" as the only logical possibility.

"I'm down from Anchorage," I said with a smile, confirming the answer made most likely by sheer population size.

"Oh, what brings you to Homer?"

Thus the door opened to a lovely, if short, conversation. We covered a lot of ground as the bakery line crept forward, ranging all the way from which baked goods were best here (everything) to why I don't drink coffee, Homer's beautiful sand beaches, what the weather had been like lately, and her favorite hiking trails.

Often, I am the friendly Alaskan, spotting visitors and asking where they've come from and why, how they're liking the trip so far, and so on; it's just what a lot of us do here. People are interesting, and tourism brings us a never-ending stream of new ones to get to know. But in this instance, I was the one being greeted and made to feel at home and filled in on local attractions I just wouldn't know about unless I lived there. And it felt good.

So if you find yourself in a small Alaska town, or even a big one, please take the time to say hi and chat with the people you meet. You might just find that you have a lot in common, starting with how much you both love Alaska.

that includes a livestreaming webcam from a seabird rookery. Admission is $15, free for children under age 6. The hours are 10:00 a.m. to 6:00 p.m. daily during the summer.

Most visitor attractions and services are located on the narrow, 5-mile gravel bar called the **Homer Spit.** The spit, which never sat very high above sea level in the first place, dropped 4 to 6 feet during the 1964 Alaska earthquake. It nonetheless remains the site of countless visitor shops, eateries, commercial wharfs, docks for waterborne sightseeing and fishing cruises, parking places, campsites, and a prime port for the Alaska Marine Highway System's oceangoing ferries.

The **Salty Dawg Saloon** (907-235-6718; saltydawgsaloon.com), one of Alaska's best-known frontier bars, is located on the spit. Just a few doors down is **Homer Ocean Charters** (907-235-6212; homerocean.com), which has a fleet of boats and experienced captains to take you fishing for halibut, salmon, and rockfish (depending on the season). Prices start from $340 per person for a full-day halibut fishing trip during peak season, with discounts for shoulder season fishing.

Here's one of my favorite trips to take while in Homer: the evening **dinner ferry** aboard a beautiful repurposed wooden fishing boat, the **Danny J,** which motors past **Gull Island** and on to the artistic community of **Halibut Cove,** across the bay from Homer. You'll disembark there and explore the boardwalks that connect the homes and galleries in this isolated community. On a sunny Alaska summer evening, it feels like you've entered a postcard.

To top off your tour, eat dinner at Halibut Cove's sole restaurant, the **Saltry** (907-226-2424; thesaltryrestaurant.com), which has some of the best food you'll eat in Alaska—period. The seafood is, hopefully needless to say, fresh-caught; and the salads taste like they were just picked from a nearby garden. The cost of the ferry is $50 for a dinner sailing or $70 for a daytime sailing, meal costs not included. You can book the ferry through the Saltry's website.

If you enjoy nautical travel under your own steam, **True North Kayak Adventures** (907-235-0708; truenorthkayak.com) takes small groups of experienced and inexperienced kayakers into the wild beauty of Kachemak Bay for up-close encounters of the sea otter kind, plus porpoises, sea lions, and shorebirds. Day trips start at $150 per person. You can also rent sea kayaks (from $45 for a single, $60 for a double) or stand-up paddleboards (from $50).

Rainbow Tours (907-235-7272; rainbowtours.net), on Cannery Row Boardwalk on the Homer Spit, will book you for a guided all-day **Seldovia Wildlife Tour** that promises glimpses of some of the area's plentiful marine wildlife: You might see humpback whales, orcas, sea otters, bald eagles, and much more. The 65-foot MV *Rainbow Connection* or the *Discovery* depart daily at 10:30 a.m. for a 7-hour cruise that includes a 2½-hour visit to the isolated city of **Seldovia**—enough time to have lunch and briefly explore, if you so desire. The cost is $89 for adults, $69 for children.

Seldovia, on its city website seldovia.com, once billed itself as "307 Friendly People and a Few Old Crabs." It originated as a Russian sea otter hunting station and today relies on fishing, fish processing, some timber operations, and summer tourism. Seldovia's picturesque boardwalk dates to the 1930s. Birders can collect lots of views of bald eagles here, as well as of sea- and shorebirds, and sightings of sea otters from excursion boats are common.

If you're aiming to stay in Seldovia—which happens to be a great mountain biking destination—it's hard to resist lodgings right on the water. Two good options are the **Seldovia Boardwalk Hotel** (907-234-7816; seldoviahotel.com), with eleven rooms looking out over Seldovia Bay or, on the other side of the building, back into the mountains. Room rates start at $149 for a mountain view room with a queen bed or $159 for a waterfront view with a queen bed. For a more private-feeling experience, **Thyme on the Boardwalk** (907-440-2213; thymeontheboardwalk.com) offers a waterfront cottage for rent (from $350) and a waterfront suite (from $225). They also rent kayaks.

Once you've put your feet back on the ground in Homer, you may notice that it abounds in charter boats, especially for halibut fishing. In fact, the town calls itself the halibut fishing capital of the world. You'll see incoming anglers hang their halibut on scales at the dock and record catches in the 50-, 100-, even 200- to 300-pound classes. Homer Ocean Charters, mentioned earlier, has a large enough fleet that you can often get a seat with them, even when other charters are full.

Homer has many boutique lodging options, plus a few chain hotels. Although you'll usually pay a premium for ocean views, **Ocean Shores Resort** (3500 Crittenden Drive; 907-235-7775; akoceanshores.com) offers nice views from up on a bluff overlooking the water, with private bathrooms and friendly service, starting from about $180.

Another great, chain-free option is the two studio apartment rentals over **Sea Lion Gallery** (4241 Homer Spit Road; 609-602-8509, sealionart.com). They're fully set up for independent living, and you just can't beat the location partway down the Homer Spit. The apartments currently rent through AirBnB for about $140/night plus fees.

Seaside Farm Hostel (907-235-7850; kilcheralaskacabins.com) is many things: It's a large working homestead in the best Alaska tradition, a B&B, a campsite for tenters, a place to rent cabins, and a hostel with overnight accommodations in the main ranch house and a large cabin. There's an open-sided kitchen on site for hostelers and campers, and room to pitch a tent in the fields.

Call for prices and accommodation options, or find them as "Seaside Farm Stay" on Facebook or "Seaside Farm" on HipCamp.com.

My very favorite place to camp in Homer is a couple of walk-in, tent-only *city campgrounds* along the spit. As you drive along the spit, look for the open sandy spots on your right, between and beside stands of commercial buildings. It's not always immediately obvious which spots are meant for camping, but if you pull to the side of the road there are usually a few spots to put your car and a sign directing you across the street to a self-pay station. These city-owned spots on the spit cost about $20 per night, and there's a city campground information hotline, too: 907-235-1583.

Parks Highway— Southern Section: Anchorage to Denali National Park

Now, back to Anchorage. Truth to tell, it's a little difficult sometimes to know exactly which highway you're traveling on in Alaska. The **Parks Highway** between Anchorage and Fairbanks is a good example, because for the first 35 miles of the trip you're really on the Glenn Highway, which eventually takes you to Tok. The Parks Highway starts at its junction with the Glenn at about mile 35 on the latter road, but the mileposts on both show the distance from Anchorage. To read about places to see and things to do on the first 35 miles out of Anchorage, see the discussion of the Tok Cutoff in the Glenn Highway section of this chapter.

The Parks Highway, it should be noted, is among Alaska's best. You encounter some rough spots and frost heaves along a few portions (so keep driving speeds within safe limits), but generally it is among the wider and most modern in the state. It cuts through some of Alaska's most urbanized country as well as some of the state's wildest and most scenic. You can see Denali, North America's highest mountain, from a number of places, and the highway provides access to two of the state's most popular state and national parks.

About mile 39.5 you come to the **Wasilla** city limits and shortly thereafter Wasilla's Main Street. There your choices are several: Head north a block to 323 Main Street and visit the community's **Museum and Visitor Center** (907-373-9071, cityofwasilla.gov). Go north as well to access the Wasilla Fishhook Road to **Independence Mine State Historical Park** (Mile 17.3 Hatcher Pass Road; no phone; dnr.alaska.gov), or turn south across the railroad tracks to drive along the Knik Road. If you're interested in learning more about sled dog racing, head left on this road and drive for a couple of miles to the **Iditarod**

Trail Committee Headquarters and Visitor Center (907-376-5155; iditarod .com) at 2100 South Knik-Goose Bay Road. Look for the large, colorful sign. There, you can view historical mushing exhibits and films, see sled dogs, meet a musher, and shop for mushing souvenirs. The center is open daily in summer and does not charge admission.

Nearly 14 miles down the road from the Parks Highway junction and about 0.5-mile after you come to the village of *Knik,* you'll find the *Knik Museum and Sled Dog Mushers' Hall of Fame* (907-376-7755; wkhsociety.org). In addition to mushers' portraits, mushing equipment, and Iditarod Trail historical exhibits, you can see artifacts from Knik village's gold rush (1898–1916) beginnings. The museum building itself dates to that period. Admission is $3. It's open from May into October from 1:00 to 6:00 p.m., Wednesday through Sunday.

If you'd like to get up close and personal with some sled dogs and go for a spin on a sled equipped with wheels for summer travel, check out *Dream a Dream Sled Dog Tours* (907-606-0517; dreamsleddogtours.com) at 9373 N. Rappe Drive in Willow. Veteran musher Vern Halter opens his kennels to the public from May through September. An Iditarod presentation, kennel tour, and sled dog ride runs $249 per person. If you're really in love with the sport, you can stay on as a bed-and-breakfast guest (from $179, with private bathroom, fully equipped kitchen, and a king bed).

Another fun way to see the Valley is by horseback. *Alaska Horse Adventures* (907-229-4445; alaskahorseadventures.com) in nearby Palmer offers guided and unguided riding by the hour as well as covered wagon and sleigh rides, pack trips, and kayak rentals for use on nearby Jim Lake and Jim Creek.

Looking to overnight in the Valley? *Snowgoose Pond B&B* (281-686-4363; snowgoosepondbnb.com) offers an idyllic getaway with large front and back decks offering beautiful views of the mountains, a hot breakfast during the summer (you prepare your own breakfast during the winter), and a cozy, home-like atmosphere.

At mile 47, turn left on Neuser Drive for 0.75-mile to the road's end at the *Museum of Alaska Transportation and Industry* (907-376-1211; museum ofalaska.org). This museum features, in the words of the Mat-Su Visitors Center, "ten acres of neat ol' stuff," including airplanes, locomotives, farm and construction rigs, plus "trucks and vehicles that built Alaska." Admission is $8 for adults. Hours are 10:00 a.m. to 5:00 p.m. daily.

Just past mile 52 on the Parks Highway, the Big Lake Road leads to (you guessed it) *Big Lake* and any number of lodges, B&Bs, eateries, service stations, shops, fishing supply stores, public and private RV facilities, and several smaller lakes joined to the big one. *Suggestion:* Big Lake is one of Anchorage folks' favorite weekend getaway locales, so plan your own Big Lake visit Monday through Thursday to miss the relative crowds.

Nearing mile 99 from Anchorage, you come to a 14.5-mile spur road to **Talkeetna,** one of several Alaska communities often compared to the once-popular mythical TV town of Cicely on *Northern Exposure.* Busloads of tourists stop to check out this quaint Alaskan town, but if you want a real Alaskan view of the community, attend one of Talkeetna's quirky festivals. The famous **Wilderness Woman Contest and Bachelor Auction** (talkeetnabachelors.com) in December is a sterling example. For a calendar of events and comprehensive list of tour companies, visit talkeetnachamber.org.

Near the end of the spur road, stop in at the **Talkeetna Historical Society Museum** (907-733-2487; talkeetnamuseum.org), located on the village airstrip, which is almost in the middle of town. Formerly a schoolhouse built in the mid-1930s, the museum contains displays and information from its gold-mining past as well as items commemorating the life of famed bush pilot Don Sheldon. Over the years, the museum has grown to include several outbuildings and outdoor interpretive exhibits. Visit the main building first for a walking tour brochure. And don't miss the beautifully detailed scale model of **Denali,** the tallest peak in North America and often beautifully visible from Talkeetna, in one of the other buildings.

Talkeetna is definitely a walk-around town, so pick up a walking tour map at the museum, then wander about, taking pictures of the community's WELCOME TO BEAUTIFUL DOWNTOWN TALKEETNA sign, the historic old **Talkeetna Roadhouse,** the old **Fairview Inn** that is a hotbed of live music and evening entertainment, and various other log and clapboard houses and structures spread along Talkeetna's streets and paths.

Steve Mahay's **Mahay's Riverboat Service** (907-733-2223; mahaysriverboat.com) offers two very different sightseeing options out of Talkeetna: the Wilderness Jetboat Adventure, priced at $89 for adults, and the Devil's Canyon Adventure for $195. The former is a leisurely 2-hour, 10-mile adventure in which you will see how trappers lived at the turn of the twentieth century and visit an authentic trapper's cabin with its rustic furnishings. Your guide will display raw furs from the local area and demonstrate trapping methods. Naturalists will acquaint you with the wildflowers and plants that grow in abundance along the river system. The latter trip is 5 hours long and takes you roaring through the whitewater rapids of Devil's Canyon in a jet boat.

When they're not busy airlifting climbers to base camps on Denali in the spring and early summer, Talkeetna's excellent bush flight services take visitors on airborne flightseeing forays around North America's tallest mountain, sometimes even landing on a glacier's icy surface. Among the companies offering such services is Talkeetna-based *K2 Aviation* (907-733-2291; flyk2 .com), which offers statewide air tours and a variety of Denali National Park air tour options. Prices for flightseeing out of Talkeetna start as low as $305. The appropriately named Top of the World Tour takes you to 20,000 feet for a dramatic view of Denali (the mountain), plus Denali National Park and views of the Alaska Range extending north and west to the horizons. The 2-hour tour starts from $495 per person.

Talkeetna, incidentally, is also accessible by daily summer Alaska Railroad train service from Anchorage or Fairbanks (800-544-0552; alaskarailroad.com).

Denali National Park and Preserve, of course, gets lots of attention, and properly so. But there's another Denali, *Denali State Park,* which deserves more mention than it gets. You enter this park at mile 132 on the Parks Highway, and you're within its boundaries until mile 169. In between, you can enjoy fine dining or lodging with indescribable views of Denali at *McKinley View Lodge* (907-733-1555; mckinleyviewlodge.com) starting from $110 double occupancy. Or you can pitch a camp in the stellar lake, stream, and forest country at *Byers Lake Campground* at mile 147. The overnight fee is $20. *Caution:* Especially if you go hiking in the woods there, make noise and know what to do if you encounter a bear. Grizzlies roam this area frequently.

At roughly mile 210 on the Parks Highway you arrive at *Cantwell* and the junction of the Parks and Denali Highways. Before hurrying on to Denali National Park, spend a little time around this small community, which many pass by. (For details see the section on the Denali Highway, in the chapter on Interior Alaska.)

The entrance to Denali National Park and Preserve lies just past mile 237. For information about exploring and enjoying this grand national parkland, see the following chapter on Interior Alaska.

Glenn Highway: Anchorage to Glennallen

The *Glenn Highway* is one of the most traveled and most scenic routes in Alaska. The sky-piercing Mentasta and Wrangell Mountains abut this route as it dissects long, wide valleys of spruce, alder, and birch forests, and in the Matanuska and Susitna Valleys it courses through Alaska's principal agricultural districts. The Glenn provides the principal access between Anchorage and Tok, the first major Alaska community you'll encounter when arriving via the Alaska Highway.

Alaskans often talk about the Anchorage–Tok link as if it were one road. (And, indeed, the state Department of Highways designates it, plus part of the

Seward Highway and all of the Sterling, as Alaska Route 1.) To be accurate, however, we should note that the 328-mile route actually consists of two separate highways and part of a third—the Glenn itself, which extends 189 miles from Anchorage to Glennallen; a 14-mile portion of the Richardson Highway, from Glennallen to Gakona; and the 125-mile Tok Cutoff, extending from Gakona to Tok, where it connects with the Alaska Highway.

We'll explore the Glenn and Richardson sections of the highway in this Southcentral Alaska section of the book; you'll find the Tok Cutoff portion in the following chapter on Interior Alaska.

Leaving Anchorage on the Glenn, you pass access roads to Elmendorf Air Force Base and Fort Richardson, and about 13 miles out, you come to a community called *Eagle River,* the closest thing you'll ever find to a suburb of Anchorage, although many Eagle River residents are bent on differentiating themselves from the (relatively) enormous city next door. (By the way, if you happen to like sushi, skip all the choices in Anchorage and make the drive out to Eagle River. A great little place called *Shine's Sushi* (907-622-8889) has excellent sashimi and plenty of inventive rolls from which to choose.

From downtown Eagle River, drive 12.5 miles easterly on the Eagle River Road to the nonprofit *Eagle River Nature Center* (907-694-2108; ernc.org). There's lots of good information to be picked up here, including hiking maps and updates on recreation sites in one of Alaska's and America's largest state parks. Take a short hike on nearby trails, and check out nature walks and other get-togethers offered by area naturalists. The center also rents out a public use cabin and three yurts for $100 a night each; it's the perfect overnight getaway if you're not prepared for a long trek. The cabin, built in 1998, is only a little more than a mile down the trail behind the nature center. The yurt is a few minutes away from the cabin. All three have woodstoves, firewood, and sleeping platforms. Just bring yourself and a taste for the wilderness.

A bit of a warning: Bears are sighted here often, so be on the lookout and brush up on what to do in case of bear encounters. Also, make your reservations early. The sites are popular and book up fast. Parking at the center is $5, unless you're staying at the cabin or yurt, in which case it is complimentary.

Eklutna Village and *Eklutna Historical Park,* 26 miles from Anchorage, is another of those priceless little places that many pass by in their rush to get from Anchorage to some more publicized travel attraction. Through historical records, oral history, and archaeology, the Athabascan village can trace its occupancy of this area back an astonishing 350 years. To get to the park, exit left off the Glenn Highway at Eklutna. The road leads to the nearby park. When park tours are available, they start with an orientation in the Heritage House, which has art displays and lifestyle exhibits. The tour then leads, on a guided gentle walk, to a tiny little Russian Orthodox church built in the 1830s. Visitors then move on to a more modern church and finally to the village cemetery, where the dead lie buried beneath small, colorfully painted spirit houses.

A great getaway is just a few miles away at **Eklutna Lake,** where you can rent a kayak and paddle beneath the vistas of Twin Peaks. Mountain-bike rentals also are available, all from on-site vendor **Lifetime Adventures** (907-746-4644; lifetimeadventures.net). They have also started offering a shuttle from downtown Anchorage for anyone who wants to explore the lake but didn't rent a car.

Just before mile 30 on the Glenn, you have the opportunity to turn right onto the Old Glenn Highway. Both the Glenn and the Old Glenn end up in Palmer, but the older route offers options such as a view of **Bodenburg Butte,** access to a nice view of Knik Glacier, and the opportunity to see original Matanuska Valley colony farms. At the **Williams Reindeer Farm** (907-745-4000; reindeerfarm.com) on Bodenburg Loop Road (which begins at mile 11.5 on the Old Glenn) you can see, pet, and feed reindeer. The farm also now boasts other species, including a moose, elk, bison, yaks, and alpacas. Admission starts at $15.

At the end of the Old Glenn Highway, and at mile 42 on the Glenn, lies **Palmer,** borough seat for the Matanuska-Susitna Borough and a major hub for trade and agriculture in the Mat-Su Valley. It's also the site of the **Alaska State Fair** (alaskastatefair.org) during the 11 days preceding Labor Day each year. Other celebrations in the state share the "state fair" designation, but none other is so large and well attended. It's here, incidentally, that you can see and photograph the valley's huge and famous vegetables, including cabbages that often reach more than 100 pounds. There are lots of other food and animal exhibits as well as carnival-type rides and a whole smorgasbord of entertainment options.

Just beyond Palmer, the partly paved, partly gravel **Fishhook Road** at mile 49.5 on the Glenn Highway offers a delightful side trip to wide-open spaces and vistas, soon changing names to **Hatcher Pass Road** as it winds toward the eponymous pass. The main attraction along the road is fascinating **Independence Mine State Historical Park** (dnr.alaska.gov), about 17 miles from the Glenn Highway junction and maybe a mile from the pass. It's currently under management by an excellent tour company based in Anchorage, **Salmon Berry Travel & Tours** (866-681-0209; salmonberrytours.com). Unsurprisingly, they offer tours. But you can also park and explore the park's many interpretive exhibits on your own for just a few dollars.

There's no charge for gold panning in the park, and staff at the visitor center (the old mine manager's house) will direct you to the best prospects. Located on a private inholding within the 761-acre park is the A-framed *Hatcher Pass Lodge* (907-745-1200; hatcherpasslodge.com), perched at a 3,000-foot elevation and offering lodge rooms (from $160 per night), meals, and rustic A-frame cabins (from $185 per night). Some great biking can be had around Hatcher Pass for those who like fat-tire cycling. For rentals and trail advice, visit *Backcountry Bike & Ski* (907-746-5018; backcountrybikeandski .com), a full-service bike and ski shop in nearby Palmer.

There's also fantastic hiking, with the family-friendly *April Bowl Trail,* which sets out from the very summit of the pass, as one of the most popular trails. Another great option is the (relatively) short, easy hike to *Gold Cord Lake,* which starts out just across the access road from Independence Mine.

southcentralalaskatrivia

Eagle River, which flows 9 miles north of Anchorage, heads at Eagle Glacier and was named in 1916. Before that, miners and trappers called it Glacier River and Sitk Creek. Before that, Alaska Natives called it Yukla-ina. Today a thriving community lies along the banks of Eagle River, about 15 miles north of Anchorage.

Eventually the 49-mile Fishhook Road joins with the George Parks Highway at Willow—or you can backtrack to the Glenn Highway. Just off the Glenn Highway at about mile 50, a former farm from the old colony days now houses the *Musk Ox Farm* (907-745-4151; muskoxfarm.org) in Palmer, the only one of its kind in the country. About seventy of the animals (sort of a scaled-down water buffalo with long hair) live there. Their highly prized qiviut, the musk oxens' very fine undercoat, is knitted into hats, scarves, and other items. An ounce of qiviut is eight times warmer than an equal amount of sheep's wool, and you can buy spun yarn of qiviut—either pure, or blended with other fibers to bring down the cost—in the gift shop. The farm is open year-round; their hours shift slightly with the seasons, but they're usually open at least noon to 5:00 p.m., with longer hours during the summer. Admission is $14.

If you'd like to walk on a glacier—minus the expense of a high-priced helicopter tour—the *Matanuska Glacier* offers a rare opportunity to do so. Turn off the Glenn Highway at mile 102 and take unpaved South Glacier Park Road for a couple of miles to reach the lodge for *Glacier Tours on the Matanuska* (907-745-2534; glacier-tours.com), where you can take a guided tour on the glacier for $150 per person, with all the gear you need provided. You can also book more activities on the glacier—including hiking, ice climbing, snowmachine tours by winter, and even helicopter tours—through *MICA*

Guides (907-351-7587; micaguides.com). They even offer helicopter-assisted glamping on the glacier.

Other ways and places to view the glacier include the *Matanuska Glacier State Recreation Site* and camping area ($20 per site or $25 per camping vehicle) at mile 101, the state highway pullout just past mile 101.5, and *Majestic Valley Wilderness Lodge* (907-746-2930; majesticvalleylodge.com) at mile 114. According to one of our faithful readers, Majestic Valley is immaculately well kept and with a comfortable family room for reading and rooms starting at $245 double occupancy. Make reservations ahead of time and the owner will make a wonderful home-cooked dinner for $40 to $60.

At mile 113.5 lies *Sheep Mountain Lodge* (907-745-5121; sheepmountain .com), established nearly a half century ago. If you can tear yourself away from the lodge's hot tub and sauna, there's great sheep viewing by telescope as well as excellent hiking and skiing in the area. From the lodge you can head out on over 12 miles of cleared trails leading into the mountains. Visit in late summer or early fall and you may come away with a great stash of wild blueberries and cranberries (remember that not all berries are safe to eat; baneberries are not and can be bright red or white). Rates start at $239 for a double-occupancy cabin and $119 for a double-occupancy cabin with a shared bathhouse a short distance away.

Another worthwhile side trip, just short of 20 miles each way, takes you to *Lake Louise* via the Lake Louise Road, which begins just before mile 160 on the Glenn Highway. Several fine fishing and outdoor lodges as well as a state recreation area and campgrounds are located on this lake in one of the North Country's premier water/mountain/glacier settings.

Evergreen Lodge (907-822-3250 summer, 907-390-0027 winter; alaska evergreenlodge.com) is located on beautiful Lake Louise and provides lodging and B&B accommodations from Memorial Day weekend to October 1. The long-established lodge also operates flightseeing tours and guided fly-out fishing. After a hearty breakfast, guests can enjoy boating, swimming, and hiking in and around the lake. If you're lucky you'll catch a glimpse of a moose, caribou, or bald eagle. Dinner at the lodge must be arranged in advance. *Lake Louise Lodge* (907-822-3311; lakelouiselodge.com) also offers year-round accommodations, including rustic cabins and rooms with decks overlooking the lake. To fully enjoy the lake, paddle out in the canoe included with your stay. Rates start at $150 for a room in the lodge, or $120 for a dry cabin (no running water).

If you're tenting or driving an RV, *Tolsona Wilderness Campground* (907-822-3900; tolsonacampground.com) lies 0.75-mile north of the noise and traffic of the highway at mile 173 and is set in the forest beside Tolsona Creek. One of its attractions is a primitive 1-mile hiking trail to an active mud spring, where gases bubbling up from lower Cretaceous and upper Jurassic formations carried fine particles of silt to the surface to form a 2,075-foot hill from which the spring emerges. The spring itself flows year-round and is a source of water for wildlife, especially in the cold and frozen months of the year. Also, be sure to check out the proprietor's varied collection of turn-of-the-twentieth-century artifacts. It's a museum tour—for free! Camping fees are $30–$35 for tenters, $39–$45 for RV hook-up campsites.

southcentralalaskatrivia

Though the Alaska summer is short, the long daylight hours produce incredibly large vegetables. Each August, gardeners bring their biggest to the Alaska State Fair in Palmer, where the produce is weighed in. The largest cabbage wins its grower $2,000. To date, the record holder weighs 138 pounds.

The Glenn and Richardson Highways meet and blend at Glennallen. Beyond this community, for 14 miles you're really traveling on the Richardson Highway and therefore the mileposts indicate miles from its start at Valdez. Then, at Gakona Junction, the Richardson continues north to Delta Junction and Fairbanks, while the **Tok Cutoff,** on the Anchorage–Tok route we're discussing here, courses northeasterly. You're right, it can be a little confusing, so be alert.

And . . . not to confuse you further, beyond Glennallen you're really traveling in Interior Alaska. So for information about the more northerly portions of this route, refer to the chapter on Interior Alaska.

The Richardson Highway—Southern Section: Valdez to Gakona Junction

When you drive on the 368-mile Richardson Highway, you're traveling along a historic gold rush route first pioneered in 1898 as the Valdez–Eagle Trail. The trail at that time, however, began with a treacherous start literally over the ice of Valdez Glacier, a fact that devastated or turned back many a would-be prospector before he ever started his trek to the gold fields. The following year Captain W. R. Abercrombie created an alternate route through Keystone Canyon and across Thompson Pass, bypassing the glacier. The route—first a sled dog and horse trail, now paved and fully modern—has been a major Alaskan land link between Prince William Sound and the Interior ever since. Today the Richardson connects Valdez with Delta Junction and Fairbanks. Now in its second century, a few of the road's pioneer (but now renovated) roadhouses remain along the way, reminders of the era when warm, welcome accommodations were spaced a day's horse- or dog-team travel apart.

As you head north, check out the **Crooked Creek Salmon Spawning Viewing Area** at mile 0.9 of the Richardson Highway. In July and August the creek is teeming with salmon, and you can get a close look with the underwater video cam inside the U.S. Forest Service Station.

The canyon drive into or out of Valdez is one of Alaska's most spectacular, with high, steep walls and no small number of breathtaking waterfalls. The surrounding mountains are likewise high, rugged, and spectacular. Of special note are **Bridal Falls** at mile 13.8 of the Richardson Highway and **Horsetail Falls** at mile 12.8. These make for good photo ops, plus there's a nice interpretive plaque on gold rush history at the Bridal Falls pullout. If you have some time to stretch your legs, take the 2-mile **Valdez Goat Trail,** a restored section of the military pack train trail that allowed miners to bypass the more hazardous route over glacial ice.

It sounds pleasurable and it is: **Blueberry Lake State Recreation Site,** with loop entrances at both mile 23 and mile 24 along the Richardson, is a visual delight and a favorite campground for Alaskans. An alpine area situated above timberline, the site offers a sweeping lookout over Keystone Canyon as well as close-up views of dwarf plants and other flora usually associated with northern tundra. It's also the natural habitat for Alaska's state bird, the willow ptarmigan. Flocks of dozens are not uncommon. The state camping fee is $25 per night.

At mile 26 you come to 2,678-foot **Thompson Pass,** where winter snowfall totaling nearly 1,000 inches has been recorded. The long, tall poles alongside the road guide snowplows and snowblowers in the snowy season. About 2.5 miles beyond the pass is **Worthington Glacier State Recreation Site,** where you'll find displays and exhibits explaining the huge river of ice. You can walk a paved trail to views of the glacier.

At about mile 83 you come to the paved 35-mile Edgerton Highway to **Chitina** (pronounced CHIT-na; the second "i" is silent), which connects at the highway's end with the 60-mile gravel McCarthy Road. This road, in turn, leads over a former railroad bed to the near-ghost towns of **McCarthy** and **Kennicott** within **Wrangell-St. Elias National Park.** Take the time to drive at least to Chitina, stopping en route perhaps at **Kenny Lake Mercantile and RV Park** (at mile 7.5) to top off your gas tank or, if you're pulling a rig, to drop off your RV and proceed unencumbered. In fact, you can even leave your car and RV here if you wish. This is a pickup point for scheduled van service to McCarthy and Kennicott. Call (907) 822–3313 for details. Electric hookups are available. If you enjoy collecting scenic landscape photos, stop at mile 23.5 at bubbling, forested Liberty Creek and thunderous Liberty Falls in **Liberty Falls**

State Recreation Site. The highway itself bisects rolling hills and offers views of wide, forested valleys, grand lakes, and the imposing peaks of the Wrangells. If you're really lucky, you may even see bison herds across the Copper River.

Wrangell-St. Elias National Park (907-823-2242; nps.gov/wrst) has a ranger office in Chitina, and the staff there can tell you about park and local attractions as well as conditions on the McCarthy Road, which begins where the Edgerton ends. Picturesque Chitina is almost a ghost town—just ask the locals, who have painted humorous, ghostly pictures on a few of the town's abandoned turn-of-the-twentieth-century structures. Hand-hewn log cabins, western-style stores, and rusting old cars, trucks, and wagons give testimony to the town's gold rush past.

If you're game, by all means continue beyond Chitina on the McCarthy Road, but be advised that it can be a slow, bumpy, and narrow. It can also be pretty muddy in the rain. Still, the rewards are many when you make it to the road's end at the Kennicott River and, after all, this is off-the-beaten-path travel at its best. McCarthy, the town for which the road is named, lies across the river and you can access it easily by a footbridge across the water.

About two dozen hardy souls call McCarthy their permanent home, including the owners of *Ma Johnson's Historical Hotel* (907-554-4402; majohnsonshotel.com), circa 1916. Visitor rooms are in the early-twentieth-century tradition, long and slender and furnished in Victorian decor. The hotel does, however, offer modern shared baths. The $319 rate for two includes custom bathrobes and slippers for use at the hotel (907-554-4402; visit mccarthylodge.com). The same friendly folks run *Lancaster's Backpacker Hotel,* with rates starting at about $239 for a single or double-occupancy room.

The *McCarthy Museum,* housed in the old railway depot, displays items and photographs from the community's mining glory days. Five miles down the road (van pickup is available) lies the abandoned town of *Kennicott* and the old *Kennecott Copper Mine* (the difference in spellings is supposedly due to a long-ago clerical error). There you'll also find *Kennicott Glacier Lodge* (907-258-2350; kennicottlodge.com), a thoroughly modern, thoroughly elegant thirty-six-room lodge, most of it built in the style and decor of the surrounding old structures. Rates for the Kennicott Glacier Lodge start at $245, with an option to purchase a meals package if you plan to eat exclusively at the lodge. There's lots of exploring and poking around to be done in this National Historic Landmark community.

One bush flight service based in McCarthy and another based in Glennallen offer a wide variety of flightseeing, hiker drop-off, and transportation services, including flights to Kennicott and Kennicott Glacier Lodge. McCarthy-based **Wrangell Mountain Air** (907-554-4411) will ferry you from Chitina to McCarthy (thus relieving you of a long, bumpy ride along the McCarthy Road) for about $210 round-trip. Backcountry drop-offs range anywhere from $285 to $1,000+ per person, depending on group size and destination; and flightseeing trips start from $315 per person. Meanwhile, Glennallen-based **Copper Valley Air Service** (907-822-4200; coppervalleyairservice.com) can shuttle you from Glennallen to McCarthy starting from $360 round-trip, air-taxi you to remote backcountry destinations, take you flightseeing (from $350 per person), and offer fly-in fishing trips.

St. Elias Alpine Guides (907-231-6395; stellasguides.com) offers a wide selection of options, including a Root Glacier hike from $115 per person. This 4- to 6-hour trek allows you to explore the ice formations, waterfalls, and blue-water pools that make glaciers so exotic. Other day-trek adventure options include river rafting, learn-to-climb instruction, fly-in hikes, history tours, and backcountry skills seminars. Multi-day rafting and mountaineering adventures are available. Call for current prices.

Back on the Richardson Highway, just beyond mile 100 you come to the turnoff for **Copper Center**, a community that grew out of a nineteenth-century trading post. The highway officially bypasses Copper Center, but *you* shouldn't. Turn right onto the *Old* Richardson just past mile 100. The historic old **Copper Center Lodge** burned down in 2012, but the original outbuildings remain, and one of them has been turned into the **Old Town Copper Center Inn & Restaurant** (907-822-3245; oldtowncoppercenter.com). The inn offers four rooms for travelers (call for prices) and a restaurant. Another outbuilding, the **George Ashby Memorial Museum,** houses mining, trapping, Alaska Native, and pioneer relics and displays. Half the cabin is an authentic old log bunkhouse. And within the museum you can walk through the actual iron doors of the old Copper Center Jailhouse. There is no charge, but donations are accepted.

Driving north from Copper Center, the old segment of the Richardson Highway connects with the north end of the bypass at mile 106, and you're officially back on the Richardson.

The park headquarters and visitor center for the **Wrangell-St. Elias National Park and Preserve** (the nation's largest, at 13.2 million acres) is located at mile 106.8 on the Old Richardson Highway, just north of Copper Center. The park, which is the size of six Yellowstones, contains nine of the sixteen highest peaks in the nation—not to mention countless glaciers, forested valleys, and many species of wildlife. The headquarters is your source of information about park hiking, camping, road access

I before E, Unless You're a Miner

Is it Kennecott with an "e" or Kennicott with an "i"? The river and glacier, deep in the Wrangell Mountains, are spelled Kennicott, named for Robert Kennicott. The town also goes by the same name. But the much-photographed mine, with its deep-red buildings, is known today as Kennecott due to a misspelling made in 1906.

The Kennecott Mines Co. established a camp and offices on the bank of National Creek, meaning to take its name from the Kennicott Glacier 3 miles to the north. But inadvertently its owners dropped the "i" and added an "e." It stuck. During its heyday the Kennecott mined more than 590,000 tons of copper ore, making it the richest copper mine in the world. By 1938 copper prices had crashed and the company closed the mine.

To visit the mine, you must make a sometimes harrowing drive to the town of McCarthy. From Glennallen follow the Edgerton Highway 66 miles to the hamlet of Chitina, population 49. After crossing the steel-span bridge over the Copper River, you're on the McCarthy Road, which follows the old Copper River and Northwestern Railway built between 1907 and 1911 to carry copper to the town of Cordova on Prince William Sound.

The 60-mile McCarthy Road is unpaved and often bumpy. In dry weather it's dusty. In rainy weather it's muddy. For most people, the top speed on the road is 20 mph (although, to be fair, it's not as bad as it used to be).

For years the final stage of the journey to McCarthy and Kennicott was the hand-pulled cable car used by locals and visitors alike to cross the braided Kennicott River. In 1997, safety concerns finally forced the construction of a railed footbridge to replace the cable car. Leave your vehicle on the near side of the river, then walk across the bridge into McCarthy, where there is always at least one local shuttle option (sometimes more) to help you get around.

(extremely limited), and attractions (907-822-7250; nps/gov/wrst for more information).

At mile 115 the highway meets at **Glennallen** with the Glenn Highway from Anchorage. For the next 14 miles, the Richardson Highway and the Glenn Highway–Tok Cutoff route are the same. Near mile 129 and Gakona Junction, the Tok Cutoff heads northeast, while the Richardson continues north to Delta Junction and Fairbanks.

And now, although there's no official boundary between Southcentral Alaska and the Interior, this is probably a good place to separate the two regions. For information about the northern portion of the Richardson Highway, see the next chapter on Interior Alaska.

Places to Stay in Southcentral Alaska

ANCHORAGE

Base Camp Anchorage Hostel
1037 West 26th Avenue;
907-274-1252;
basecampanchorage.com.
A well-run outdoorsy hostel.

Camai Bed and Breakfast
3838 Westminster Way;
907-333-2219;
camaibnb.com.
One of the most budget-friendly options, but not downtown.

Historic Anchorage Hotel
330 E Street;
907-272-4553;
historicanchoragehotel.com.
A famously historic, and some say haunted, property.

Hotel Captain Cook
939 West Fifth Avenue;
907-276-6000;
hotelcaptaincook.com.
One of Anchorage's nicest hotels, with great gift shops.

Parkside Guest House
1302 West Tenth Avenue;
907-683-2290;
parksideguesthouse.com.
You can't beat this central downtown location.

Susitna Place
727 N Street;
907-274-3344;
susitnaplace.com.

Stunning views within a reasonable walk of downtown.

Tutka Bay Lodge
Fly-in accommodations;
907-274-2710;
withinthewild.com.
A remote lodge with some of the finest food you'll ever have.

CORDOVA

Orca Adventure Lodge
907-424-7249;
orcadventurelodge.com.
A nice lodge with some of the most prolific tour offerings in Cordova.

GIRDWOOD

Alyeska Resort,
1000 Arlberg Avenue;
907-754-2111;
alyeskaresort.com.
Luxury in the heart of the Girdwood skiing community.

HOMER

Land's End
4786 Homer Spit Road;
907-235-0400;
lands-end-resort.com.
At the end of the Homer Spit.

Ocean Shores Resort
3500 Crittenden Drive;
907-235-7775;
akoceanshores.com.
Friendly service and ocean views at a reasonable price.

Sea Lion Gallery
4241 Homer Spit Road;
609-602-8509;
sealionart.com.

Two studio apartments over an art gallery; currently rented via AirBnB.

Seaside Farm Hostel
907-235-7850;
kilcheralaskacabins.com.
Quirky B&B located on a large, working homestead.

KASILOF

Hungry Moose Bed & Breakfast
20900 Tustumena Lake Road;
907-252-9253;
hungrymoosebandb.com.
Great views from atop a hilltop.

Kasilof River Lodge
53270 St. Elias Avenue;
907-262-6348;
kasilofriverlodge.com.
Three lodge rooms and a yurt with shared bathrooms.

MOOSE PASS

Midnight Sun Log Cabins
907-288-3627;
midnightsunlogcabins.com.
Rental cabins with running water and private bathrooms.

Moose Pass Adventures
907-599-0643;
moosepassadventures.com.
Rental yurts that can accommodate groups.

SEWARD

Salted Roots
13690 Beach Drive;
907-599-0533;
saltedrootsalaska.com.

A-frame cabins at the water's edge.

Seward Windsong Lodge
Mile 0.5, Exit Glacier Road;
800-808-8068;
alaskacollection.com.
On the road to Exit Glacier, just outside Seward.

Van Gilder Hotel
907-224-5518;
vangilderseward.com.
Small, comfortable, and a National Historic Site.

SOLDOTNA

Alaska Silvertip Lodge and Cabins
35930 Janota Circle;
907-262-4450;
silvertiplodgeandcabins
.com.
Cabin suites, with running water, fish processing, and a great selection of all-inclusive or à la carte tour packages.

Aspen Hotels Soldotna
326 Binkley Circle;
907-260-7736;
aspenhotelsak.com/Soldot
na.
The most comfortably hotel-like of Soldotna's options, this local chain offers rooms, suites, and freezer storage for your fish.

Soldotna B&B Trophy Lodge
48520 Funny River Road;
877-262-4779;
alaskafishinglodges.us.
Fishing-oriented lodge rooms with blackout blinds, a private dock on the Kenai River, and lots of tour options.

Places to Eat in Southcentral Alaska

ANCHORAGE

Arctic Roadrunner
5300 Old Seward Highway;
907-561-1245.
Local favorite for great burgers.

Glacier Brewhouse
737 West Fifth Avenue;
907-274-2739;
glacierbrewhouse.com.
Great Alaska seafood and freshly prepared side dishes that are artful and tasty.

Gwennie's Old Alaska Restaurant
4333 Spenard Road;
907-243-2090;
gwenniesoldalaska.shop.
Huge portions and a borderline outrageous level of Alaskana, but still loved by many locals.

Jens' Restaurant
701 West 36th Avenue;
907-561-5367;
jensrestaurant.com.
Some of the city's best creative fine dining.

Lucky Wishbone
1033 East Fifth Avenue;
907-272-3454;
luckywishbonealaska.com.
They do fried chicken fast and right.

Moose's Tooth Pub & Pizzeria
3300 Old Seward Highway;
907-258-2537;
moosestooth.net.
Gourmet pizza and microbrew.

Ristorante Orso
Fifth Avenue and G Street;
(907) 222–3232;
orsoalaska.com.
Heartly Italian dining in downtown Anchorage.

Snow City Cafe
1034 West Fourth Avenue;
907-272-2489;
snowcitycafe.com.
Creative breakfasts and lunches in slightly Bohemian atmosphere. Wonderful weekend brunches.

EAGLE RIVER

Kim's Cuisine Asian Fusion Bistro
12400 Old Glenn Highway;
907-622–8889.
Extensive menu of sushi, sashimi, and cooked Japanese fare.

HOMER

La Baleine Café
4460 Homer Spit Road;
907-299-6672;
labaleinecafe.com.
Breakfast and lunch from one of Alaska's best chefs.

The Boat Yard Cafe
5075 Kachemak Drive;
907-299-9297;
boatyardcafehomer.com.
Quaint eatery with a focus on local ingredients.

The Saltry,
on the dock at Halibut Cove,
across from Homer on Kachemak Bay;
907-226-2424;
thesaltryrestaurant.com.
Fresh-caught Alaska seafood in a beautiful, remote setting.

Two Sisters Bakery
233 East Bunnell Avenue;
907-235-2280;
twosistersbakery.net.
A local favorite for very good
reason.

SEWARD

The Cookery
209 Fifth Avenue;
907-422-7459;
cookeryseward.com.
Local ingredients, foraged
finds, and all-around
delicious.

**Resurrect Art
Coffee House**
320 Third Avenue;
907-224-7161;
resurrectart.com.

A church turned coffee shop
and gift shop. It's good!

**Resurrection
Roadhouse**
31572 Herman Leirer Road;
800-808-8068;
alaskacollection.com.
Broad menu but the pizza is
the best.

Interior Alaska

From one point in Alaska's interior region—the summit of Denali—climbers can literally look down on every other mountaintop, hill, ridge, valley, and plain in North America. (Although McKinley was for a long time the name the federal government officially recognized for the continent's highest peak, Alaskans, noting that President William McKinley, of Ohio, never once laid eyes on even a small mountain in Alaska, have always preferred to use the beautiful Athabascan name for the peak, *Denali,* which means "the high one." The view from Denali may explain why Interior Alaskans speak in such expansive terms about their region of sky-piercing mountains, rolling hills, long and mighty rivers, subarctic tundra lands, and vast taiga forests.

This is gold-mining country, and has been since Felix Pedro's 1902 strike near present-day Fairbanks. It's oil country as well, at least in the sense that a large share of the 800-mile Trans-Alaska Pipeline passes through the Interior on its way from Prudhoe Bay to the coast at Valdez. And the Interior is grand traveling country. It's a land of long roads and riverways and remote fly-in lodges and cabins. It is a place with a rich Athabascan culture, and a place of grizzlies, moose, caribou, wolves, and scores of smaller species. It's a warm and balmy

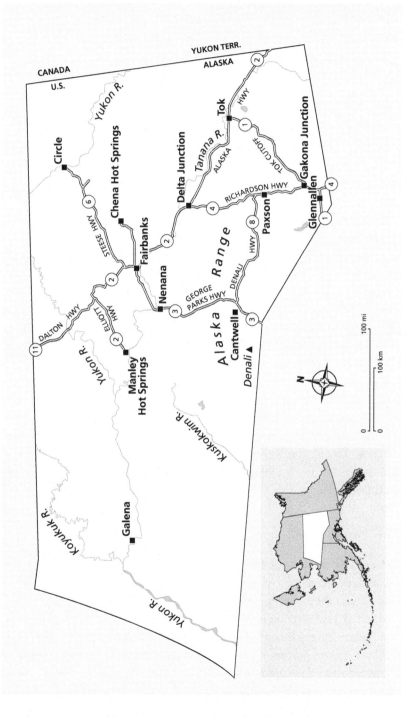

TOP 10 PLACES IN INTERIOR ALASKA

Camp Denali	Husky Homestead
Chena Hot Springs Resort	Rika's Roadhouse
Denali Highway	Tangle Lakes Lodge
Denali National Park and Preserve	A Taste of Alaska Lodge
Fox 'n Fireweed Bed and Breakfast	University of Alaska Museum of the North

region in the summer, though temperatures can plummet to sixty *below* in the winter.

Fairbanks, about 300 miles from the Canadian border and the second-largest community in Alaska, serves as transportation and travel hub for the region, and for that reason we describe the many facets of Fairbanks at the beginning of this chapter. We then deal with pleasurable things to see and do along Interior Alaska's roads and highways, most of which (but not all) lead to or from Fairbanks. We will examine the Interior portions of the state's four multi-region highways in the same order in which they appeared in earlier chapters. Specifically, we'll describe the Alaska Highway from the border (where we left off in the Yukon chapter) to the highway's end at Delta Junction.

We'll examine the northern portions of the Parks Highway connecting Anchorage and Fairbanks and the Glenn Highway–Tok Cutoff route, which runs from Anchorage to Tok. And of course we will cover the northern portion of the Richardson Highway, which begins at Valdez and ends in Fairbanks. We'll look, too, at the Steese Highway from Fairbanks to Circle City on the Yukon River. Not to be omitted in these pages are the smaller and often-overlooked Denali Highway and the Elliott Highway.

Fairbanks

Fairbanks is a bustling, dynamic city on the banks of the Chena River. Fairbanksans call it the Golden Heart of Alaska, and it was indeed gold that brought about the founding of the town in the early 1900s.

When in 1901 Captain E. T. Barnette set out from St. Michael, at the mouth of the Yukon River, aboard the stern-wheeler *Lavelle Young,* he intended to establish a trading post in the gold prospecting area at Tanana Crossing, about halfway between Valdez and Eagle. He didn't get that far, however. The ship couldn't navigate the shallow Chena River beyond present-day Fairbanks, so he established his post there. A year later Felix Pedro, an Italian prospector, found gold in the area, and a "rush" to Fairbanks soon followed.

The *Morris Thompson Cultural and Visitors Center* (907-456-5774; explorefairbanks.com), right downtown at 101 Dunkel Street, provides lots of current information on things to see and do, places to go, restaurants, and overnight options, with some interpretive displays that rank it right up there with other "naturalist" galleries in the state. For a free visitor's guide to the Golden Heart City, call 800-327-5774. For the traveler seeking offbeat options, an even more important resource is the *Alaska Public Lands Information Center,* also located in the Morris Thompson building. This is the place to get information about the Interior's outdoor touring, camping, and recreational opportunities.

The *Riverboat* Discovery *Cruise* (907-479-6673; riverboatdiscovery.com) now sees large numbers of cruise ship passengers every day, so it isn't as off-the-beaten-path as it used to be. But it still feels rather like you're exploring off the beaten path and just happen to be taking many dozen new friends along with you on the eponymous riverboat, which is maintained by a family that's lived along the river for five generations. The *Discovery* is an actual stern-wheel paddleboat that sets out from the docks at 1975 Discovery Drive (southwest of downtown) for a cruise down the Chena and Tanana Rivers.

En route, as the hustle and hurry of Fairbanks fades farther and farther behind, passengers learn about the Native Athabascan peoples of this area, as well as the history of gold rushes and oil booms and homesteading hereabouts. They watch as huge fish wheels, powered by stream currents, scoop fish into large holding baskets from the rivers they're cruising. If they're lucky they even see moose in the woods along the shore. Finally the vessel stops at a river island for a visit at *Old Chena Village,* a re-created glimpse into how Alaska Native people in Interior Alaska smoke fish, tan wildlife hides, sew leather, bead garments, and live in a harsh but bountiful environment. Sled dog mushing demonstrations, often including visits with pups, are part of the fun. Tickets start from $90.

If you're interested in birds, *Creamer's Field Migratory Waterfowl Refuge* (907-459-7307; friendsofcreamersfield.org), a mile from downtown, provides great viewing of huge flocks of ducks, geese, and sandhill cranes in the spring and fall. Toward the end of August, when up to 3,000 cranes may grace the fields at any given time, you can enjoy the festivities at the annual

interioralaskatrivia

Between 1926 and 1957 the Fairbanks Exploration Company mined approximately $70 million worth of gold from the Fairbanks area.

Tanana Valley Sandhill Crane Festival, featuring a guest speaker, guided nature walks, workshops, and dinner. At other times you can walk along a 2-mile self-guided nature trail and visit the restored farmhouse that now serves as visitor center. The start of the trail is located at 1300 College Road, which is one of Fairbanks's principal east-west thoroughfares.

Close by Creamer's Field, at 2600 College Road, you can shop at the *Tanana Valley Farmer's Market* (906-456-3276; tvfmarket.com) for fresh veggies, meats, bakery items, flowers, and craft goods on Wednesday from 11:00 a.m. to 4:00 p.m., Saturday from 9:00 a.m. to 4:00 p.m. It's the only market of its kind in Interior Alaska, open during the summer months only.

At the *University of Alaska Museum of the North* (907-474-7505; uaf .edu/museum), on the UA Fairbanks campus, northwest of downtown, you can view natural and historical exhibits, such as an incredible 36,000-year-old Steppe bison that was almost perfectly preserved in Alaska's permafrost until its excavation in the twentieth century. Also on display are contemporary wildlife mounts (including a really humungous brown bear and the skeleton of a 42-foot bowhead whale), the state's largest exhibit of gold, Native art, and an exhibit on the aurora borealis (northern lights). The $42 million museum building is by far the most dramatic architecture in Fairbanks. In the new art gallery, you'll see the full spectrum of Alaskan art, from primitive carvings to contemporary pieces. Don't miss the photo opportunity in the "designer outhouse," crafted from found items that offer a whimsical take on local culture. Plan at least 2 to 4 hours for your visit, especially if you're going to take in one of their excellent short movies in the theater. Museum admission is $20, with discounts for seniors and youth 6 to 17 years old. The museum is open daily.

For your photo collection of strange beasties of the Arctic, tour the university's considerably less visited *Large Animal Research Station* (907-474-5724; uaf.edu/lars), off Yankovich Road north of the main campus. Tours are offered several times a day from Tuesday through Sunday during the summer, at $15 per adult and $10 for each youth. There, among other animals, you'll find the shaggy, horned wood bison, once hunted to extinction within Alaska. With the help of imported animals from Canada, the species is making a comeback. UAF also offers Wednesday afternoon tours of the *Geophysical Institute* (907–474-7558), where scholars ferret out knowledge of the earth's deepest regions and the heaven's northern lights. And for the botanically inclined, the Agricultural and Forestry Experiment Station's *Georgeson*

TOP ANNUAL EVENTS IN INTERIOR ALASKA

Tanana Valley Sandhill Crane Festival

Held in late August at Creamer's Field Migratory Waterfowl Refuge, this festival celebrates the thousands of sandhill cranes and other waterfowl that congregate at the refuge at part of their southerly migration (friendsofcreamersfield.org).

Ice Art Competition

Held each March in Fairbanks, this world-class competition features intricate ice sculptures by the world's best ice carvers (833-442-3278; icealaska.com).

World Eskimo-Indian Olympics

Held every July in Fairbanks, this 4-day festival celebrates and promotes the cultural expertise and Native traditions of Alaska, Greenland, Siberian, and Canadian Inuit and Native peoples, through a series of challenging games

that are also serious athletic events (907-452-6646; weio.org).

Deltana Fair and Music Festival

Held every July in Delta Junction, this festival brings together music acts and a country-style fair ambiance, including a parade, horse show and games like the cutest baby contest and a memorial pet show (907-895-3247; deltanafair.com).

Tanana Valley State Fair

Summer brings all sorts of state fairs to Alaska, but this one in Fairbanks is the largest in the Interior. The fair begins in early August and features Alaska's famous giant vegetables along with a large midway, live entertainment, and animal exhibits (907-452-3750; tvsfa.org).

Botanical Garden offers lots of material to support a self-guided tour. Call 907-474-5211. Admission is $8.

In 1967, wanting to commemorate the one hundredth anniversary of Alaska's purchase from Russia in a lasting way, the people of Fairbanks and the State of Alaska created a 44-acre pioneer theme park called Alaska 67. Later renamed Alaskaland, now it's called *Pioneer Park* (907-459-1087; fnsb.gov/462/pioneer-park) and continues in business on Airport Way. There's no admission charge to enter, but there are fees to visit some portions of the park. Among various things to see and do, especially during the summer months, you'll find a genuine stern-wheeler riverboat (the SS *Nenana,* a National Historic Landmark), the Gold Rush Town of relocated and restored homes and stores from Fairbanks's early days, the frontier Palace Theatre and Saloon, a miniature mining valley, a pioneer air museum of early aircraft, plus one of the two best salmon bakes/barbecues in Alaska. (The other is in Juneau.) Circling it all is the *Crooked Creek & Whiskey Island Railroad:* not terribly authentic, perhaps, but it is fun and a good way to get the lay of the land before you start wandering around the acreage.

Here's a chance to collect another Alaska superlative. If you're a golfer and want to play some really far-out golf, be aware that two courses in Fairbanks lay claim to being the farthest north golf course in the world. Friends in the city tell me that the *Midnight Sun Golf Course* (907-415-1264; midnightsungolfak.com) is

interior alaska trivia

Sled dogs, like wolves, foxes, and coyotes, curl up to protect less heavily furred parts of their bodies from extreme cold. Often these sleeping canines will allow falling or drifting snow to cover them, providing more insulation from the cold air.

actually a tad more northerly (though on the opposite side of the city) than the *Fairbanks Golf Course* (907-479-6555; fairbanksgolfcourse.com)—but who's measuring? The thing to do is play them both. You'll find Midnight Sun northeast of town off Old Steese Highway on Golf Club Drive. The Fairbanks Golf Course is located northwest, near the intersection of Farmers Loop Road and Ballaine Road.

Historic *Gold Dredge Number 8* (907-479-6673; golddredge8.com), at mile 9 on the Old Steese Highway, is a restored relic from an important mining era in Alaska's gold country. Between 1928 and 1959 this huge, floating hulk, five decks high and 250 feet long, scooped $3 billion worth of gold from creeks near Fairbanks. You can take a guided tour of the now-inoperative dredge for $55, which includes the tour, a video presentation of the dredge in action, and gold panning. For a more hands-on gold panning experience, I really enjoy *Gold Daughters* (1671 Steese Highway, 907-347-4749; golddaughters.com), which is just a couple miles south of Dredge Number 8.

If you get to Alaska and wish you had brought your bike or canoe or what have you, be sure to stop by *CanoeAlaska* (907-457-2453; canoealaska .com) near the Peger Road entrance to Pioneer Park. The company has 30 years of experience in renting out just the thing you'll need for your outdoor experience.

One of the most versatile local tour companies operating out of Fairbanks is *Northern Alaska Tour Company* (907-474-8600; northernalaska .com) They offer day trips and overnight excursions across the northern portion of the state, including aurora-viewing, exploring the Yukon River, flightseeing, a cultural visit to the remote community of Fort Yukon (from $589), and an opportunity to dip your hands (or whole body) into the Arctic Ocean in Utqiagvik, the northernmost community in the United States (from $779).

Alaska is one of those places where, even if you don't imbibe, you really ought to visit a few of the more colorful frontier saloons. In Fairbanks at least two watering holes match that description: the **Palace Theatre** at Pioneer Park (907-452-7274; akvisit.com/palace-theatre) and the **Malemute Saloon** (malemutesaloon.com) at the Ester Gold Camp just off mile 351.7 on the Parks Highway. Both the Palace and the Malemute offer great shows in the summer, and a cover charge or ticket fee sometimes applies (call for details). The Malemute one of those atmospheric places frequented by locals as well as visitors where patrons throw peanut shells on the sawdust floor and gawk at the artifacts and the art junk on the walls.

interioralaskafacts

The geographic center of Alaska lies 60 miles northwest of Denali (the mountain), at 63 degrees-50 north, 152 degrees west.

The Yukon River is Alaska's longest river. It runs 1,400 miles from Canada to the Bering Sea.

The first oil pumped through the 800-mile Trans-Alaska Pipeline took 38 days, 12 hours, and 54 minutes to arrive in Valdez.

Anaktuvuk Pass is the last remaining settlement of Nunamiut people, the inland Inupiat whose ancestors date to 500 B.C.

The Brooks Range includes nine groups of mountains, but not Denali, which is in the Alaska Range.

Warbelow's Air Ventures, Inc. (907–474–0518; warbelows.com) partners with the already-mentioned Northern Alaska Tour Company to offer tours around the northern part of the state. They also offer a stand-alone "Bush Mail Flight" tour in which you literally ride along with the pilot as he delivers mail to remote villages. You won't get tours in the villages, but you do get to enjoy a true slice of life in rural Alaska (from $199 per person).

For a charming experience and close-up view of reindeer, the very close domesticated cousin of our wild caribou, visit **Running Reindeer Ranch** (907-455-4998; runningreindeer.com). This 2-hour tour isn't any more complicated than a wander through the forest in the company of the reindeer and then having tea with the proprietor, but it's always a memorable experience.

Koyukuk National Wildlife Refuge (fws.gov/refuge/koyukuk), which totals almost four million acres, is home to excellent birding ventures, though access can be a challenge. The area encompasses a vast floodplain containing fourteen rivers, hundreds of streams, and thousands of lakes. More than 400,000 ducks and geese migrate south from the refuge each year. Check with local air-taxi services for access to the area, or call the refuge headquarters in Galena at 907-656-1231.

If you're looking for a classic, woodsy Alaska wilderness-type lodge located 20 minutes from downtown, *A Taste of Alaska Lodge* at 551 Eberhart Road off Chena Hot Springs Road (907-488-7855; atasteofalaska.com) is the answer to your quest. The main lodge is a 7,000-square-foot natural log structure featuring six guest rooms and two suites, all with private baths. Other accommodations on the 280-acre spread include a two-bedroom log house with private hot tub, a one-bedroom frame house, and a five-person hot tub building. Guests enjoy views of Denali, the Alaska Range, and the Trans-Alaska Pipeline. Year-round rates range from $215 per night for single or double occupancy; there is a charge of $35 per night for additional guests. The rates include a full breakfast, cable TV and WiFi, plus access to an aurora-viewing yurt during the winter. You can also purchase an excellent dinner.

interior alaska trivia

The town of Glennallen derives its name from the combined last names of Captain Edwin Forbes Glenn and Lieutenant Henry T. Allen, who explored the Copper River region in the late 1800s.

For a different sort of adventure, consider staying in the quaint, interesting *Alaska Heritage House* (907-388-9595; alaskaheritagehouse.com) at 410 Cowles Street in downtown Fairbanks. Once the largest and most elegant house in the Alaska Territory, this home was—in its day—remarkable for having coal-fired central heat and an indoor bathroom with cold *and* hot running water. Now it's been repurposed into a boutique hotel located at 410 Cowles Street; each room has its own unique character and history. Prices vary, with the least expensive being $295 for the triple-occupancy Blanche Cascaden Room.

For standard Alaska fare that is prepared nicely, try the *Pumphouse Restaurant* (907-479-8452; pumphouse.com), at 796 Chena Pump Road. The seafood is particularly good. *Pike's Landing* (907-456-4500; pikeslodge.com), on the Chena riverbanks, at 4438 Airport Way, is another favorite. We usually choose the casual outdoor setting on the large deck. Or try the *Two Rivers Lodge* (907-488-6815; tworiverslodge.com) at mile 16 on the Chena Hot Springs Road, where your choices range from seafood to steaks and Cajun cuisine.

The Alaska Highway: U.S. Border to Delta Junction

Now, back to the Alaska Highway, where, in the Yukon chapter, we left off at the U.S.-Canada border. Your first stop in Interior Alaska, mandatory if you're coming in from Canada on the Alaska Highway, is the U.S. Customs and

Immigration Station at mile 1,221.8, right at the international boundary. The station sits sort of out in the middle of nowhere, with no large community nearby.

At mile 1,229, similarly situated, the U.S. Fish and Wildlife Service maintains a log cabin visitor center with an observation deck and outdoor exhibits about Alaska's wildlife. There's more of the same indoors, along with animal mounts and lots of good information about Alaska's fish, birds, and other wild critters.

At mile 1,302 you come to the Tetlin Junction, a meeting of the Alaska Highway and the Taylor Highway, which extends north to Eagle. The Taylor, in turn, provides access to the Canadian Yukon Territory's Top of the World Highway to Dawson City, Yukon. For information about these roads, see the sections after Dawson City in the chapter "Canada's Yukon."

You'll come to the next major highway junction at mile 1,314, right in the middle of **Tok** (rhymes with joke), where the Alaska Highway, heading sort of west, meets the Tok Cutoff from southwesterly Anchorage. Just before the junction you'll see the ***Alaska Public Lands Information Center*** (907-644-3661; nps.gov), where you can get tons of information about state and federal lands, waters, and outdoor recreation. Audiovisual aids, wildlife mounts, and helpful staff will provide you with the latest about places and things to do both on and off the beaten path. Also worth a visit is ***Alaska's Mainstreet Visitor Center*** (907-883-5775; tokalaskainfo.com), operated by Tok's chamber of commerce. The center, also at the above-mentioned junction, is located in the largest one-story log structure in the state and features mounted wildlife and birdlife dioramas. The visitor center opens in May and offers free trip-planning services to walk-ins.

For a quiet retreat after days on the road, check out ***Fox 'n Fireweed Cabins*** (907-505-0214; foxnfireweed.com), which is in a black spruce forest with bike trails nearby. They offer a handful of cabins and rooms in the main house. You can borrow a bike, fish, or go for a hike. Rates start at $80 for a room and $160 for a cabin.

Here in Tok, the locals take sled dog racing, Alaska's official state sport, very seriously. You can see mushing equipment and puppies at the ***Burnt Paw Gift Shop and Cabins*** (907-251-5885; www.burntpaw.com) at mile 1,314.3 on the Alaska Highway, or stay overnight and get to spend quality time with the animals. You can ride a dogsled pulled by an ATV at ***Mukluk Land Theme Park*** (907-883-2571; muklukland.com) Admission is $5.

interior alaska trivia

The lowest body temperature recorded in a living mammal is minus 2.9 degrees Celsius in hibernating arctic ground squirrels. A high sugar condition may keep the animals' blood from freezing.

Speaking of sled dog racing, winter visitors can see mushers and their dogs almost any weekend working out or racing on the **Tok Dog Mushers Association Trail,** which starts at their log headquarters building at mile 1,312.8 on the Alaska Highway. Spectators can view the 20-mile course from many points along the highway.

If you'd like to start your day and your visit in a thoroughly Alaskan way, try the all-you-can-eat sourdough pancake breakfast with Alaska reindeer sausage at the **Sourdough Campground** (907-883-5543; sourdoughcampground .com), 1.5 miles south of the junction on the Tok Cutoff. They have a cafe that serves lunch and dinner from 11:00 a.m. to 7:00 p.m., and of course you can stay there, too. A tent-only spot starts from $28, electric-only RV spots start from $46, with full hookups for $65. Recently, the campground also added a couple of hotel-style rooms with private bathrooms, starting from $129 for one queen bed or $149 for a room with two queen beds.

For a tasty end to your day, try **Fast Eddy's Restaurant** (907-883-4411; fasteddysrestaurant.com), at about mile 1,313, which serves rib-eye steaks, king crab legs, beer-battered halibut, prawns, and more.

If you're traveling by RV or roughing it in a tent, **Tok RV Village** (907-883-5877; tokrv.net) at mile 1313.4 of the Alaska Highway is a good choice. They offer 160 sites with showers, vehicle wash, TV and Internet terminals, pull-throughs, and double pullouts. There's also a gift shop on site.

Flightseeing can be had through **40-Mile Air** (907-883-5191; 40-mileair.com), which will take you over the Alaska Range to see glistening glaciers. Their one-hour flightseeing trips offer you an opportunity to see moose, bears, and Dall sheep, starting from $340 per person for a two-person group, or $225 per person in groups of three or four. You can also hop aboard the mail plane to Chisana for $210 per person. That gets you beautiful landscapes, too, but also an opportunity to participate in an important, and unusual, part of normal life in remote, rural Alaska.

When you get to **Delta Junction,** at mile 1,422, you've come to

interioralaskafacts

The three highest mountain peaks in North America are in Alaska: the South Peak of Denali (20,310 feet), the North Peak of Denali (19,470 feet), and Mount St. Elias (18,008 feet).

At six million acres, Denali National Park and Preserve is about the size of Massachusetts.

Collared pikas, tiny members of the rabbit family, can be found in both the southern Brooks Range and the Alaska Range.

Fairbanks is the state's second-largest city, with a population of nearly 86,000 in the greater Fairbanks area.

The earliest recorded breakup date and time for the Nenana Ice Classic was April 20, 1940, at 3:27 p.m. The latest breakup occurred May 20, 1964, at 11:41 a.m.

the end of the Alaska Highway. From that point on north, the road to Fairbanks is the Richardson Highway, and the mileposts beside the road indicate distance from Valdez. Delta Junction's Richardson Highway milepost is 266. For information about the Richardson from Delta Junction north, see the section in this chapter on the Richardson Highway.

The Parks Highway—Northern Section: Denali to Fairbanks

The Parks Highway, you'll recall, runs for nearly 360 miles from near Anchorage on the shores of Cook Inlet, to Fairbanks. In our Southcentral chapter, we followed the course of this excellent highway to Denali National Park and Preserve, where this section picks up this road once more.

For many, Denali National Park and Preserve is the high point of an Alaska vacation. (No pun was intended, but as a matter of fact, the top of Denali, at 20,310 feet, is the highest point in North America.) And in the surrounding parklands, visitors may well see more game—moose, grizzly bears, caribou, Dall sheep, perhaps even wolves plus any number of smaller creatures and birds—than anywhere else they travel in the state.

It should be noted, however, that much of the park and its environs are by no means off the beaten path. In particular, the strip along the Parks Highway near the mile 237 park entrance overwhelms with hotels, lodges, motels, cabins, RV parks, and varied visitor services. Most of the overnight accommodations there are roomy, nice, and comfortable, like *Denali Crow's Nest Log Cabins,* at mile 238.5 (907-683-2723; denalicrowsnestcabins.com). Some of them, such as the *Denali Princess Wilderness Lodge* (800-426-0500; princesslodges.com) and *Grande Denali Lodge* (907-683-5100; grandedenalilodgealaska.com), are quite superior. But the sheer numbers of such places provide ample evidence that many thousands of visitors beat down this path every summer. So where, if you're a dedicated offbeat traveler, can you stay? And what can you do away from the crowds?

Actually you have options, not the least of which is to pitch a tent or park your RV at one of seven National Park Service campgrounds within the park itself, then hike in the backcountry hills, valleys, mountain slopes, and open spaces in splendid isolation. Isolation, that is, from the human sort: Such an adventure creates high odds of close encounters with wildlife. Be aware, however, that overnight backcountry hikes require a permit, and the number of backcountry users permitted in a given area is limited.

Another caution: Campsites within the park are often hard to come by, so it's wise to reserve months ahead if you can by calling the reservations line,

800-622-7275 or 907-272-7275. If all advance-reservation camping slots have been assigned for the days you plan to visit, you may be able to reserve space up to two days in advance on a first-come, first-served basis at the Denali National Park Service Visitor Center on the main park road, 0.5 mile inside the park boundary. Thirty percent of the sites are set aside for these walk-in reservations.

If you enjoy day hikes, check the bulletin boards and with the ranger on duty at the information center for the times, location, and degree of hiking skills required of various ranger-escorted treks not only in the park entrance area but at bus-accessible points along the single road that bisects the park and at the **Eielson Visitor Center** and **Wonder Lake,** near the road's end.

Also important: As of this writing, the Denali National Park road—the single thread of gravel roadway that takes you out to many of the park's campgrounds—is still closed at mile 43, or roughly its midpoint. That is due to an ongoing landslide that, for years, could be repaired fast enough to keep up with the damage and thus keep the road open. However, in late August of 2021, the slide was moving too quickly for repair crews to keep up with it. The road was closed until a solution could be identified.

That solution—a bridge spanning the slide area at a wide enough distance to remain safe and stable—has been found, but it's taking longer than expected to implement. At the moment, the project is expected to wrap up in late 2026. Hopefully, the full length of the road will be open in 2027.

Denali's Wife

Traveling through Alaska, you'll notice reference to a mountain called Foraker, a 17,400-foot peak at the head of Foraker Glacier in Denali National Park and Preserve. It was named in 1899 for Joseph Benson Foraker, a U.S. Senator from Ohio. It wasn't uncommon at the time to name mountains, valleys, and towns after political officials, even if they had never stepped foot on Alaska soil.

But Foraker wasn't always singled out. When Russian explorers first observed North America's highest peak, Denali, they saw Foraker in its shadow and thought it to be part of the same mountain. They called the two, collectively, Bolshaya Gora, or "Big Mountain." Likewise, before the Russians, the Tanana people of the Susitna River Valley also considered Foraker and Denali one mountain, calling the massif *Denali,* meaning "the great one" or "the high one."

However, the Tanana people in the Lake Minchumena area had a broadside view of the massif and could differentiate the two peaks. They referred to Foraker as *Sultana,* the "woman," or *Menlale,* meaning "Denali's wife."

If you're not a camper, consider spending a few days at award-winning **Camp Denali** (907-683-2290; campdenali.com) at the western end of the park road. This is one of Alaska's best-loved backcountry ecotourism lodges and has been since its founding more than a half century ago. Even with the park road closed, you can still get here—you'll just have to up the adventure factor by taking a small plane from the Denali National Park Entrance. Staff will help you arrange that part of the trip and, once you reach the lodge, your $1,375 per person, per night accommodations fee covers everything else, including meals and activities.

Guests at Camp Denali enjoy breathtaking views of Denali and other peaks of the Alaska Range from hillside log cabins. Meals are served family-style in the main lodge building. Short walks and wildlife-viewing hikes, guided by experienced wilderness interpreters, provide fascinating insight into the nature of things. Canoeing, biking, rafting, flightseeing, gold panning, and evening natural history talks provide further options.

Opportunities Taken and Missed

I don't think I'll ever forget what must be, to date, my very favorite experience in Denali National Park, even if it wasn't exactly in Denali. I'd taken the train north to the park in the early shoulder season—my absolute favorite way to travel—and booked a horseback riding tour that takes place just on the fringes of the park. I ended up being the only person on the tour, but in those days minimum head counts weren't as common as they are now, so I and one guide swung up onto the horses and headed off into the wilderness.

It's important to note here that while my mother grew up barrel racing and riding in parades in a small New Mexico farming town, I was mostly raised in the city. I knew which end of a horse was which and the very basics of riding, but that was about it. Still, I must have shown some signs of competence as the wrangler guide took us up and down increasingly rough terrain, giving me a heads up on when and how to shift my weight to help my horse maintain its balance.

Nothing I've done since has compared to that experience: It was just us, the horses, and endless miles of wilderness spilling around us in every direction, rich with the sounds of wind, birds, hooves on the ground . . . and nothing else. Of course since I wasn't used to sitting in a saddle, once we'd rambled our way back to the barn it was all I could do to unfreeze my legs from the stirrups and swing myself off the horse. I was proud of myself for *not* collapsing to the ground in a puddle of newly discovered muscles.

So perhaps you can imagine my surprise when the business owner walked right up, before I'd even relinquished the horse's reins, and offered me a job. I already had another job that I very much liked (the newspaper column that launched my writing career), so I politely declined—and I certainly can't complain about where that newspaper job took me. But to this day I wish I'd found a way to take the riding job too, or at least asked what inspired her to make the offer. It's a real mystery to me and to my very amused cousins, some of whom still farm for a living.

Also at the far western end of the road lies **Kantishna Roadhouse** (907-374-3041; kantishnaroadhouse.com) and the former gold-mining town of Kantishna, now a wilderness resort owned by Alaska Natives. The accommodations are in a log lodge and cabins. Attractions include the Smokey Joe Saloon, escorted nature walks, hiking, mountain biking, gold panning, and fishing. Rates start at $1,450 per person, per night, and *do* include round-trip transportation from the park entrance by small plane.

Another all-inclusive option is **Denali Backcountry Lodge** (877-376-1992; alaskacollection.com), also in Kantishna. Until the park road reopens they offer helicopter transfers from the park entrance, included in your all-inclusive rate of $1,650 per person, based on double occupancy. This rate also includes all your meals, lodging, gear, and activities.

Within Denali National Park itself, you'll spot most wildlife during bus or motorcoach tours that run daily on the single park road. There are three free bus routes circulating near the park entrance, taking you as far as Savage River at mile 15 of the park road. But if you want to travel the rest of the way into the park, you're going to need to buy a bus ticket. Bus prices tend to shift a bit every year, and locals or frequent visitors tend to prefer the less-expensive, non-narrated transit bus option, which starts from about $34 per adult; children 15 and under ride for free. If this is a once-in-a-lifetime trip for you, you might prefer the **Natural History Tour** (from $117) or the **Tundra Wilderness Tour** (from $144), both of which are driven and narrated by trained naturalists. Those ticket prices include the $15 park entry fee, but the non-narrated transit bus tickets do not. You can reserve tickets for any of these buses online at reservedenali.com, or by phone at 800-622-7275.

Denali National Park is one of my favorite places, and I've been there at least half a dozen times. I often wish I lived there, especially if it could be somewhere like Denali musher Jeff King's home. Four-time Iditarod Sled Dog Race champion Jeff King and eighty-plus dogs live on a ridge just south of the park, and a tour of this world-class musher's dog yard is a must-see on your itinerary. Called **Husky Homestead** (907-683-2904; huskyhomestead.com), it offers a ninety-minute narrated kennel tour with an in-depth look at dog mushing with one of Alaska's best mushers. King knows how to get to you. As you step out of the van that will take you to his home, you'll be greeted by fluffy, soft-eared, gentle-eyed sled dog puppies—known as Alaskan huskies to those in the sport—that you can cuddle to your heart's content. You'll see summer training in action and learn about what it takes to mush dogs 1,000 miles from Anchorage to Nome. Jeff has lots of interesting stories to tell from his 20-plus years of mushing—don't be shy, just ask him. Tours are held three times a day in the summer and cost $64 for adults.

If you're looking for some rugged adventure but hiking's not your thing, try some four-wheeling with **Denali Jeep Excursions** (907-683-5337; denalijeep.com). Your guide will take you from the park entrance to the Denali Highway (*not* the Denali Park Road) by Jeep. The Denali Highway once served as the only access route into the park and unlocks very similar, broad swaths of wilderness like what you'd see in Denali National Park. You can also just rent a vehicle and drive it on the highway yourself—but most major car rental companies don't allow this, due to the roughness of the road. Prices start from $179 per person and for every group of two people who go in a Jeep, one person will have to drive.

Also worth a visit at mile 238 on the Parks Highway, north of the park entrance, is **Denali Raft Adventures** (907-683-2234; denaliraft.com), which offers an iconic 2-hour Canyon Run raft trip through such exotic-sounding rapids as Cable Car, Coffee Grinder, and Ice Worm. There is also a milder (but still splashy) Wilderness Run tour. Both tours start from $130.

This kind of raft trip will work up your appetite, and if it does, skip the hungry crowds at the park entry eateries and drive south on the Parks Highway to mile 224 to **Denali Perch Resort** (888-322-2523; denaliperchresort.com), a local favorite that offers great seafood and steaks in a wooded surrounding. They also run a pizza pub with hand-tossed pizza. Cabins are available for rent, starting from $150.

The best and most peaceful lodging, just north of the park entrance, can be had at the **Earth Song Lodge** (907-683-2863; earthsonglodge.com), run by Jon and Karin Nierenberg. You can stay in one of twelve tastefully built log cabins with private baths. There is a naturalist on staff and evening programs in the coffeehouse.

Denali Hostel & Cabins (907-683-7503; denalihostel.com), near Carlo Creek about a dozen miles south of the park, offers bunking for those with backpacks or on a budget. Bunks in shared rooms start from $60, and private cabins start from about $190.

Another nice option nearby is **Carlo Creek Cabins** (907-683-2576; denaliparklodging.com). They offer budget-friendly dry cabins with a shared bathhouse (from $189), or you can rent a private cabin with its own bathroom (from $300), or a lodge room with a private bath (from $195).

There are, in addition to hikes led by park rangers, several quality commercial firms that offer treks and climbs in Denali National Park that vary from tender to tough. If you want to go all the way to North America's highest peak—a rigorous, dangerous climb that only strong and experienced mountaineers should attempt—or you want a less-demanding but equally adventurous backcountry wilderness trek, locally owned **Alaska Mountaineering School**

Who Really Climbed Denali First?

The debate rages on. Who climbed North America's highest peak, Denali, first: adventurer Frederick Cook in 1906 (not to be confused with Captain James Cook, who explored much of Alaska's coastline and named its prominent features in the late 1700s)? Or Hudson Stuck in 1913? Cook attempted to climb the mountain twice in 1906. He acknowledged defeat on the first attempt but claimed that he made it to the mountain's summit on the second attempt. Many people doubted him, but not having climbed the mountain themselves, they had no way to prove it.

In 1910 a group of Alaskan old-timers, during a discussion in a bar, decided they, too, doubted the truth of Cook's story. They decided to climb the mountain themselves and maybe make a rightful claim to fame. So off went Tom Lloyd, Charles McGonagall, Pete Anderson, and Billy Taylor, who, with little climbing experience but lots of Alaska hardscrabble toughness, reached the north peak summit—not realizing that it was actually lower than the south peak—and planted a spruce pole there to prove they had made it. So their ascent wasn't acknowledged either, but it sure gained them lots of respect.

Three years later, along comes the Reverend Hudson Stuck, Episcopal archdeacon of the Yukon, who decided he, too, would get a little closer to God and make his way up 20,310-foot Denali. He and three other men began the ascent—Harry Karstens, Robert Tatum, and Walter Harper—and reached the summit in June 1913. Their photographs were deemed authentic, and Hudson, for the most part, has claimed this spot in history. As far as being the first man in that group to reach the summit, though, it was Harper who first stood atop the summit. And perhaps rightly so. The name Denali is an Athabascan word for "the high one" or "the great one"—and Harper was Athabascan.

Today, as many as 1,000 people a year attempt to climb Denali each spring between April and June, but only a small percentage succeed.

(907-733-1016; climbalaska.org) can get you on track. They also offer multi-day backpacking trips for adventure travelers. For day hikes, check out the free ranger-led programs first. If they don't have what you want, **Walk Denali Backcountry Guides** (830-266-9255; walkdenali.com) probably do. They offer everything from easy walking tours to heli-supported backcountry hikes.

Another fun option for getting up close and personal with Denali is to sign up for one of the small group classes, research internships, or field seminars offered each summer by the **Denali Education Center** (907-683-2597; denali .org). Check out their courses online.

Back on the Parks Highway, roughly 300 miles north of Anchorage, you come to **Nenana,** on the Tanana River. (Nenana is pronounced nee-NAN-a; Tanana is TA-naw-naw.) Don't breeze through without stopping at least to see the **Alaska Railroad Museum** in the 1923 railroad depot building alongside the tracks on Front Street. The old-fashioned pressed-tin ceiling is a particular curiosity, and if you happen to be a pin collector, you can pick up lapel pins commemorating not only the Alaska Railroad but various other U.S. and Canadian rail systems as well.

Also worth a look-see is the 1905 log **St. Mark's Episcopal Church,** whose altar is adorned with elaborate Athabascan beadwork. It's located at Front and A Streets, east of the depot. At Nenana's sod-roof log **visitor center** on A Street, just off the Parks Highway, volunteers will tell you about Alaska's most popular annual statewide guessing game—the Nenana Ice Classic, in which the winner can earn more than $300,000 by predicting when the ice will break up on the Tanana River. For information call 907-832-5446 or visitnenanaakiceclassic.com.

interioralaskatrivia

The first land- and sea-grant university in Alaska was in Fairbanks, and it was called the Alaska Agricultural College and School of Mines. It opened in 1917 and in 1935 was renamed the University of Alaska. Today there is the University of Alaska Fairbanks, University of Alaska Anchorage, and University of Alaska Southeast, as well as feeder campuses spread across the state.

If you work up an appetite as you head up the road, you'll want to stop at the **Monderosa Bar and Grill** (907-832- 5243; no website) at mile 309 of the Parks Highway. Folks have been known to drive 50 or 60 miles to order up one of the famous "mondo" burgers. They've got a beautiful natural log building along with patio dining in the summer, and they serve beer, wine, cocktails, steak, and shrimp in addition to their famous burgers.

If you turn off the highway at mile 351 and stay to your right, you'll be at the old gold mining town of Ester. Miners worked the Old F.E. (Fairbanks Exploration) Company dredges here until into the 1950s, and while most of the gold may be gone, this tiny community still shines with local color and unusual characters.

The self-proclaimed "Republic of Ester" is a hodgepodge of dirt roads, cabins, and quirky studios worked by talented artists.

interioralaskatrivia

The language of the Athabascan people who inhabit the Interior is closely related to that of the Navajo and Apache.

Nenana means "a good place to camp between two rivers."

Glenn Highway–Tok Cutoff—Northern Section: Glennallen to Tok

A word of review about the Glenn Highway–Tok Cutoff from Anchorage to Tok. The route, you'll recall, is actually three segments: 189 miles of the Glenn from Anchorage to Glennallen, 14 miles on the Richardson, and a final 125 miles on the Tok Cutoff. This section begins where the section in the South-central Alaska chapter left off, at Glennallen, where the Copper Valley Chamber of Commerce operates a log cabin visitor center. The center itself is worth a stop and a picture, since plants actually grow from the cabin's sod roof. This is authentic Alaskana. Many a sourdough used this same material for insulation on log cabins.

Fourteen miles farther, at the Richardson Highway's mile 128.6, the Tok Cutoff begins. *Gakona Junction* is mile 0. Tok, our destination, is located at milepost 125. At mile 2, stop at least for an evening meal (no lunches) at the *Carriage House* dining room of the *Gakona Lodge & Trading Post* (907-822-3482; gakonalodge.com). The lodge, built in 1905, originally served travelers on the old Richardson Trail and is now on the National Register of Historic Places.

At mile 32.7 of the Tok Cutoff, *Red Eagle Lodge* (907-822-5299; redeaglelodge.com) offers six homestead-style cabins that blend rustic Alaskana with comfort: You'll spend the night cozied up with down bedding and handcrafted quilts in a queen bed near a crackling wood stove. Rates start at $85 for a cabin with access to a shared bathhouse.

Just past mile 65 you come to the 45-mile Nabesna Road and one of your few opportunities to actually drive into Wrangell-St. Elias National Park, one of the wildest, most mountainous and least developed in the U.S. park system. Just beyond the junction, at *Slana,* you'll see the *Slana Ranger Station* (907-822-7401; nps.gov/wrst). Inquire about road conditions, especially the last dozen miles or so, which can be quite rough. Just before mile 4 you enter the park itself. For the dedicated backwoods aficionado, *Huck Hobbit's Homestead Campground and Retreat* (907-259-3196; no website) has a few 12-by-12-foot log cabins to rent and is just finishing construction on a new cabin retreat with hydroelectric power and peaceful ponds around it.

To get to the homestead, turn left on the side road at mile 4, drive 3 miles to the signed parking place for your vehicle, then walk an additional 0.5 mile of trail to Steve & Joy Hobbs's wonderful, rustic getaway. Steve will meet you at the trailhead if you feel nervous about the hike or if you have lots of gear to haul. He will also rent you camping space and a tent if you need one, has canoes available, and will point you in the direction of the best fishing and berry picking.

There are several other lodges and overnight accommodations toward the end of the road; the ranger station can fill you in on current options. Heads up: If it's been raining a lot, creeks can flood the road.

The Glenn–Richardson–Tok Cutoff route from Anchorage to Tok ends at mile 125. (For information about Tok, see the section in this chapter on the Alaska Highway.)

The Richardson Highway—Northern Section: Gakona Junction to Fairbanks

In this section we take a look at the northern portion of the historic Valdez-to-Fairbanks Richardson Highway, commencing at the Gakona Junction where the Richardson meets the Tok Cutoff at mile 128.5.

The terrain along the Richardson continues to reveal tall, majestic mountains, countless big and little lakes, and thick forests. You stand a good chance of seeing moose alongside the road (pay special attention to small ponds, where a huge animal may rise up and break the surface after having scoured the pond's bottom for succulent plantlife) as well as caribou and perhaps grizzly bears. The Trans-Alaska Pipeline shows itself at various times.

If you missed out on king salmon fishing either in Southeast or Southcentral Alaska, *Salmon Grove Fishing Guide Service and Campground* (907-822-5822 or 907-255-4601; klutinariver.com) can help you make up for it on the Gulkana, Klutina, Tonsina, and Copper Rivers. Options include full-day, half-day, and multi-day expeditions, with day trips being offered via foot, raft, or jet raft. The overnight expeditions tend to be float trips. They also have a campground on the shores of the Klutina River. Tent sites start from $30, and dry RV sites are $35, or $45 with basic electric (you'll need a 15-amp adapter).

The Richardson Highway connects with the *Denali Highway* at *Paxson* at mile 185.5. If you don't plan to drive all 135 miles to Cantwell and Denali National Park, at least consider round-tripping some of the first 21 paved miles of the road. The panoramic views—of glaciers, lakes, and majestic, snow-covered peaks—from the tops of hills, rises, and turnoff viewing areas are just breathtaking.

If it's time to stop for the night, *The Lodge at Black Rapids* (907-388-8391; lodgeatblackrapids.com), located at mile 227.4 of the Richardson Highway, is splurge-worthy. The massive, beautiful building offers stunning views and personal attention from the owner who will, if time allows, bring out her guitar and sing for you. Although this lodge offers quite a bit of luxury, it's still well off the beaten path, and very "Alaskan" in the way the owners have simply put things together and figured them out as they go. The result is personal, personalized, and truly one of a kind.

At mile 266 the Richardson Highway and the Alaska Highway meet at *Delta Junction.* Actually, this is where the Alaska Highway ends. The Richardson continues north to Fairbanks and mileposts beside the road continue to measure distance from Valdez.

The *Delta Junction Information Center* (907-895-5063; deltachamber.org), at the junction of the two highways, is a good place to stop for visitor information and road condition updates. Especially if you had your picture taken at the Alaska Highway milepost 0 monument in Dawson Creek, British Columbia, you'll want to do the same at the highway's end monument at the information center. You can also pick up an "End of the Alaska Highway" certificate to commemorate your journey.

For campers or RV travelers, there are private and state-owned campgrounds just north and south of town. *Delta State Recreation Site,* at mile 267, is a good, convenient choice that offers twenty-four sites on the banks of the Delta River with views of the Alaska Range. The campground has the basics—water, toilets, and a covered shelter with tables. And at $15 per night, it's more than affordable.

More conventional lodging in Delta Junction can be a little hit or miss, as facilities are sometimes rented out for work crews and government employees. For the more luxurious end of things, try the *Alaska Frontier Inn* (from $200) or, for basic but clean accommodations, try the *Delta Lodge* (from $79 with a shared bath). Both are run by *Delta Lodging* (907-895-1266; deltalodging.com).

Among Alaskans, at least, Delta Junction is probably best known for its herd of 500 or so bison (American buffalo). They're the outgrowth of small numbers of the animals established there in the 1920s and roam freely over the 70,000-acre *Delta Bison Range.* Occasionally the bison spill over into adjacent barley farm fields, and farmers are not amused. If you want to see the herd, you stand a pretty good chance at the visitor viewpoint just past mile 241 on the Richardson. If you'd like to see the *Trans-Alaska Pipeline,* a terrific photo op awaits where the pipeline crosses over the Tanana River at mile 275.

Not to be missed is *Rika's Roadhouse* at *Big Delta State Historical Park* (907-895-4201; dnr.alaska.gov), just upstream from the pipeline river crossing. The roadhouse is right out of Alaska's history. Built in 1910 and purchased by Rika Wallen in 1923, it served for decades as a major overnight stop on the Richardson wagon road and highway for travelers between Valdez and Fairbanks. Recently the roadhouse has been undergoing another round of restoration, but even if you can't go in the buildings it's fascinating to wander the park grounds and take in the interpretive signs.

Harding Lake, 1.5 miles off the Richardson Highway from mile 321.5, is a great place to swim, have a beach picnic, or camp overnight. Avoid it Friday night through Sunday, however. Lots of Fairbanksans drive down for the weekend, and it gets pretty crowded. The camping fee is $20 per night.

As you approach Fairbanks, don't let your desire to get there lead you to bypass the *Chena Lakes Recreation Area,* accessible from a 2-mile side road at mile 346.7. Whether you're RV camping or simply looking for a superb picnic spot, this place is definitely worth a look-see. (It's not to be confused, incidentally, with the Chena River State Recreation Site in Fairbanks, nor with the Chena River State Recreation Area on the Chena Hot Springs Road.) The Chena Lakes Rec Area is a sprawling, lake-oriented, 2,178-acre site with scores of campsites, lots of picnic areas, swimming beaches, even a children's playground. There's at least one island with camping and picnic facilities. Again, local Alaskans tend to use it most heavily on weekends and holidays.

Also worth a stop before you arrive in Fairbanks is *Santa Claus House* (907-488-2200; santaclaushouse.com) in (where else?) *North Pole, Alaska*. The large shop, located at mile 349, is packed with Christmas-type gifts, including Santa Claus letters for kids that Santa will mail and postmark from North Pole in December.

The Richardson ends at mile 364. If you started your Alaska Highway–Richardson trip in Dawson Creek, British Columbia, you've traveled 1,520 miles.

interioralaskatrivia

North Pole was named by a development company that hoped to attract a toy manufacturer that could advertise that its toys were made at the North Pole, Santa's home.

The Steese Highway: Fairbanks to Circle City

Although it's paved for only 44 of its 162 miles from Fairbanks, the Steese Highway is one of the most satisfying among the backroads in Alaska. Along the way you see the sites of old mining camps and new ones, hot springs spas, gorgeous rolling hills and mountains, small authentic Alaska communities, some of the most intensely colorful wildflower viewing to be found anywhere, and the Chatanika and Chena River Recreation Areas. We've found midweek travel easier, with less gravel dust in the air than on weekends, when many Alaskans head for hot springs spas and good fishing along the route.

You've barely been traveling northwest along Steese Highway from its beginning at the junction of the Richardson and Parks Highways when, at mile 4.9, you come to the *Chena Hot Springs Road.* The road is paved and generally well maintained but drive carefully; it can be bumpy. For a good portion of its nearly 57 miles, the road travels through the *Chena River Recreation Area,* with lots of scenic spots for camping, picnics, fishing, and wildlife viewing.

About 20 miles or so down the road, you'll approach the Two Rivers area, which can accurately be described as sled dog country. Some of the state's most dedicated mushers come from this area. Keep going roughly 9 miles

more to reach the *Chena Outdoor Collective* (907-799-4420; chenaoutdoorco
.com), where a cooperative of local mushers bring their dogs for day tours in
summer, fall, and winter. Tours start from $100 during the summer and $90
during the winter.

At road's end you'll find lodging, a restaurant, bar, and other facilities at
Chena Hot Springs Resort (907-451-8104; chenahotsprings.com), with its
spring-fed pool, hot tub, and 2,800-square-foot redwood deck with ten-person
spa. Accommodations include hotel rooms starting at $220. Besides soaking,
horseback riding, canoeing, hiking, mountain biking, and hayrides, the resort
also features the *Aurora Ice Museum,* the largest year-round, manmade ice
structure in the world. The inside of the museum is decorated with sculptures
by an award-winning husband-and-wife team of ice artists.

Back on the Steese Highway, one of the best places to see the Trans-Alaska
Pipeline up close is about 10 miles north of downtown Fairbanks, just off the
highway. The pipe, in fact, is elevated, so you can stand right under it and have
your picture taken while countless gallons of crude oil flow over your head.

Also at the site is an *Alyeska Pipeline Service Company Information
Center* with interpretive displays.

At the junction of the Steese and Elliott Highways lies *Fox,* a tiny town
with a couple of great local hangouts. If you're looking for great prime rib and
seafood, nothing beats the *Turtle Club* (907-457-3883; turtleclubfairbanks.
com) at mile 10 of the Steese Highway. Be sure to call ahead for reservations,
unless you're content to eat in the bar. And speaking of bars, you can't visit
Fox without stopping next door at the *Howling Dog Saloon* (907-456-4695;
howlingdogsaloonak.com), another popular local hangout. The patrons are
almost as colorful as the memorabilia, and there's usually live music and dancing on weekends.

Across the street in what used to be the old Fox Roadhouse is the *Silver
Gulch Brewing Company* (907-452-2739; silvergulch.com), which produces
microbrews with a thriving following.

The *Chatanika Gold Camp* (chatanikagoldcamp.com), at mile 27.5, is
right out of Alaska's glory mining days. This camp was originally operated by
the Fairbanks Exploration Company from 1922 to 1964, and is today on the
National Register of Historic Places. On site you'll see lots of artifacts from the
'40s, '30s, and earlier. As I write this, the camp is just getting set to reopen after
having been closed for some time, so you'll have to check their website for
contact information and lodging rates.

If you happen to be traveling on the Steese Highway about the time of
the summer solstice (June 20 or 21), plan to celebrate the change of seasons
the way many Fairbanksans do—by driving to *Eagle Summit* (mile 108) for

a midnight picnic and a view of the sun dipping close to the horizon but not quite setting, then rising again to start a new day and a new summer season. The summit lies south of the Arctic Circle, but this phenomena is possible because of the summit's 3,624-foot elevation.

The Steese Highway dead-ends at mile 162, at the picturesque community of *Circle*, a community of mostly Native Alaskan residents. The town got its name when early prospectors thought it straddled the Arctic Circle. It doesn't— the circle lies 50 miles north—but the town does sit on the banks of the Yukon River, which made it a busy transportation and trading hub during the early and middle years of the twentieth century.

Camping can be had at the end of the road on the banks of the Yukon River. There are tables, toilets, and a parking area.

interioralaskatrivia

Vast portions of the Interior were not glaciated during the last ice age. Therefore they remain in a state similar to that which they were during the Pleistocene era.

Elliott Highway: Fairbanks to Manley Hot Springs

Most of the travelers you'll meet on the Elliott Highway, especially beyond the road's mile 73.1 junction with the Dalton Highway to Deadhorse, will be Alaskans. And chances are they'll be heading to or coming from one of Fairbanks's favorite getaway destinations, *Manley Hot Springs.* It's one of two popular hot springs spas in the region, the other being Chena Hot Springs at the end of an access road off the Steese Highway.

The Elliott Highway takes off from the Steese about 11 miles north of Fairbanks, and for the first 30 miles it's paved. Beyond that it's gravel, but not a bad road at all, although it gets slick in places when it rains. There are some roller-coaster rises and falls, but if you keep your speed at a reasonable rate, it's no problem.

At mile 1.2 on the Elliott, you come to El Dorado Gold Mine, a worthwhile stop that's both a commercial operation and a visitor attraction. (For a description, see the Fairbanks section.)

At about mile 72, you come to a junction with a 2-mile access road to *Livengood.* It was a major gold camp at times in the first half of the twentieth century, but now only one hundred or so people live in the area. Just past mile 73, the Elliott meets with the Dalton Highway supply road to the North Slope, Deadhorse, and Prudhoe Bay.

At mile 94.5 you come to a generous double pullout on the south side of the road. From here you have a good view of Minto Flats, the Tanana River, and the foothills of the Alaska Range. After mile 97 keep your eyes peeled northerly for great views of Sawtooth, Wolverine, and Elephant Mountains. At mile 110 the highway joins an 11-mile access road to the Native village of **Minto** (there's a lodge that provides meals and a general store, if you're looking for a place to eat or buy snacks), and 40 miles farther down the Elliott, you come to Manley Hot Springs.

Very Alaskan, this place. ***Manley Roadhouse*** (907-672-3161; manleylodge .com) is one of a vanishing breed of accommodations that once were common along the sled dog and horse trails of the north. This one was built in 1906, when the community served as a trading center for mining districts in the area. The roadhouse accommodated riverboat crews, miners, and commercial travelers. Today owner Robert E. Lee offers visitors the chance to revisit those days in his roadhouse with single and double sleeping accommodations, a rustic, antiques-filled sitting room, and the Roadhouse Bar, with Alaska's largest back bar. Rooms start at $110 for a standard room with a shared bathroom, $130 for a cabin with no plumbing.

interioralaskatrivia

Caribou populate the whole of Interior Alaska. They are the only type of deer in which both sexes grow antlers. One of their characteristics is wide hooves, which enable the animal to cross snow, ice, and slippery slopes.

Denali Highway: Paxson to Cantwell

They used to call the ***Denali Highway*** one of the worst roads in Alaska. It's still bumpy in places, a washboard in others, and you do have to watch for potholes. But if you keep your speed down and your eyes open, you can drive its 136 miles from Paxson on the Richardson Highway to Cantwell on the Parks Highway without fear or foreboding. At its Cantwell end it's only a few minutes to the entrance of Denali National Park. Because of the road's relatively high elevation, right at timberline or a bit above, you can enjoy lots of high tundra views. Sights of Alaska Range peaks are frequent and fabulous.

Perhaps because the Denali's old and unsavory reputation won't quite die, the road receives surprisingly less traffic than you would expect, considering its location. And because of its sparse traffic, the highway today is much appreciated by stream and lake anglers who don't care for bumper-to-bumper "combat fishing" crowds. There are several state and private RV campgrounds along the way as well as private lodges.

Off-road vehicle enthusiasts enjoy its designated routes, and mountain bikers and hikers also regard highly its marked and unmarked trails. *A caution, though:* If you're heading far off the road, be sure to carry a compass and know how to use it. It's distressingly easy to get turned around in the woods, or even in open tundra if clouds close in. From your first entry onto the road at Paxson (mile 0), keep your eye out for grizzly bears, moose, and other wild critters. They're often spotted.

The Denali is paved at its start, but the asphalt ends at mile 21. ***Tangle Lakes Lodge*** (907-822-4202; lodgeattanglelakes.com) is located at mile 22. A fire destroyed the original lodge and bar in 1998, so the present structure was newly built to greet guests in beautiful surroundings that include one of the best arctic grayling fisheries in the state. If you're a birder, this is the place to find all sorts of species, including ptarmigan (which is Alaska's state bird, not the eagle as many people assume), arctic warblers, gyrfalcons, wandering tattlers, and many others. Cabin rates start from $150 per night, with less-expensive bunkhouse options available. If you just want a canoe or kayak, they offer day rentals. If you would rather stay near the midpoint of the highway, ***Alpine Creek Lodge*** (907-398-9673; alpinecreeklodge.com), at mile 68 of the highway, offers simple, comfortable cabins and queen rooms from $120, suites from $250.

At mile 135.5 you've arrived in ***Cantwell,*** which began life as a rail-line flag stop and continues to be served by the Alaska Railroad on its run between Anchorage and Fairbanks. Newer businesses are located near the intersection of the Denali and Parks Highways, but if you want to preserve that feeling of beautiful remoteness you get while on the Denali Highway, you could pull in for the night at the peaceful ***Backwoods Lodge*** (907-987-0960; backwoodslodge.com) at mile 133.7 of the Denali Highway, just before you reach Cantwell and the relative bustle of the Parks Highway that runs north and south between Fairbanks, Denali National Park, and Anchorage. Their rooms range from $120 to $200, depending on the season.

Places to Stay in Interior Alaska

CANTWELL

Backwoods Lodge
Mile 133.7, Denali Highway;
907-987-0960;
backwoodslodge.com.

A peaceful, remote-feeling lodge just off the Parks Highway.

CHATANIKA

Chatanika Gold Camp
Mile 27.75, Steese Highway;
chatanikagoldcamp.com.

A historic mining camp, just reopening after an extended closure; see website for details.

CHENA HOT SPRINGS

Chena Hot Springs Resort
Chena Hot Springs Road;

907-451-8104;
chenahotsprings.com.
Several lodge options and a
rock-lined hot springs pool.

DELTA JUNCTION

Alaska Frontier Inn
907-895-1266;
deltalodging.com.
Clean, comfortable
accommodations with
private bathrooms.

Delta Lodge
907-895-1266;
deltalodging.com.
Basic rooms with shared
baths.

Delta State
Recreation Site
Mile 267, Richardson
Highway.
Twenty-four state-owned
campsites on the banks of
the Delta River. Amenities
are water, toilets, and a
covered shelter.

The Lodge at
Black Rapids
Mile 227.4 Richardson
Highway;
907-388-8391;
lodgeatblackrapids.com.
A gorgeous, hand-built
lodge with personalized
offerings.

DENALI HIGHWAY

Alpine Creek Lodge
Mile 68, Denali Highway;
907-398-9673;
alpinecreeklodge.com.
Simple, comfortable cabins
and rooms, even a few
suites.

Tangle Lakes Lodge
Mile 22, Denali Highway;
907-822-4202;
lodgeattanglelakes.com.
Cabins and affordable
bunkhouses.

DENALI NATIONAL
PARK

Camp Denali
Western end of Park Road;
907-683-2290;
campdenali.com.
Log cabins and family-style
dining.

Carlo Creek Cabins
Mile 224, Parks Highway;
907-683-2576;
denaliparklodging.com.
Budget-friendly cabins and
lodge rooms, some with
private bathrooms.

Denali Backcountry
Lodge
Western end of Park Road;
877-376-1992;
alaskacollection.com.
All-inclusive packages.

Denali Crow's
Nest Log Cabins
Mile 238.8, Parks Highway;
907-683-2773;
denalicrowsnestcabins.com.
Roomy, comfortable cabins.

Denali Hostel
& Cabins
142 Cleft Road, about a
dozen miles south of
Denali National Park;
907-683-7503;
denalihostel.com.

Denali Princess
Wilderness Lodge
Mile 238.5, Parks Highway;
800-426-0500;
princesslodges.com.
Superior lodgings alongside
cruise ship crowds.

Doyon, Limited
800-622-7275;
reservedenali.com.
A booking service for shuttle
buses and tours in Denali
National Park.

Earth Song Lodge
Mile 4, Stampede Road;

907-683-2863;
earthsonglodge.com.
Cabins and dog sled
expeditions, just north of the
park in Healy.

Grande Denali
Lodge
238 Parks Highway;
907-683-5100;
grandedenalilodgealaska
.com.
Superior—if
bustling—accommodations.

Kantishna
Roadhouse
Western end of Park Road;
907-374-3041;
kantishnaroadhouse.com.
Alaska Native–owned
wilderness resort, with lots
of great activities.

National
Park Service
campgrounds
Seven locations in the
park;
800-622-7275 or
907-272-7275.
For the DIY camping
experience; some are
walk-in only.

FAIRBANKS

Alaska Heritage
House
410 Cowles Street;
907-388-9595;
alaskaheritagehouse.com.
A carefully restored
historic home with lots of
personality.

A Taste of
Alaska Lodge
551 Eberhart Road;
907-488-7855;
atasteofalaska.com.
A wonderful large lodge with
homey rooms and vintage
memorabilia.

GAKONA

Red Eagle Lodge
Mile 32.7, Tok Cutoff;
907-822-5299;
redeaglelodge.com.
Cozy, comfortable
homestead-style cabins.

MANLEY HOT SPRINGS

Manley Roadhouse
Mile 152, Elliot Highway;
907-672–3161;
manleylodge.com.
A genuine roadhouse, just
like back in the day.

SLANA

**Huck Hobbit's
Homestead
Campground
and Retreat**
Mile 4, Nabesna Road;
907-259-3196;
no website.
Log cabins for rent.

TOK

**Fox 'n Fireweed
Cabins**
0.5 Sundog Trail;
907-505-0214;
foxnfireweed.com.
A favorite, longtime lodging
option under a new name.

Places to Eat in Interior Alaska

CHATANIKA

**Chatanika
Gold Camp**
Mile 27.75, Steese
Highway;
chatanikagoldcamp.com.
They're just reopening after
a long closure; check their
website for details.

DENALI HIGHWAY

Alpine Creek Lodge
Mile 68, Denali Highway;
907-398-9673;
alpinecreeklodge.com.
Remote dry cabins (no
running water), lodge
rooms, a full-service
restaurant, and custom
hiking and Jeep tours.

Tangle Lakes Lodge
Mile 22, Denali Highway;
907-822-4202;
lodgeattanglelakes.com.
Remote lodge with cozy dry
cabins, a bunkhouse, a full-
service restaurant, and great
river floating.

DENALI NATIONAL PARK

Denali Perch Resort
Mile 224, Parks Highway;
888-322-2523;
denaliperchresort.com.
Tasty fish, pasta, and
steaks, away from the
thickest park crowds.

ESTER

Malemute Saloon
Mile 351.7; Parks Highway;
907-479-2500.
malemutesaloon.com.

FAIRBANKS

Pike's Landing
4438 Airport Way;
907-456-4500;
pikeslodge.com
Delicious Sunday buffet.
Overlooks the Chena River.

Pumphouse Restaurant

796 Chena Pump Road;
907-479-8452;
pumphouse.com.
Good seafood.

Two Rivers Lodge
Mile 16, Chena Hot Springs
Road;
907-488-6815;
tworiverslodge.com.
A former homestead, rebuilt
with a solarium and a full-
service restaurant with a
sunny deck.

FOX

Turtle Club
Mile 10, Steese Highway;
907-457-3883;
turtleclubfairbanks.com.
Fine dining.

GAKONA

Carriage House
Mile 2, Tok Cutoff;
907-822-3482;
gakonalodge.com.
Part of the Gakona Lodge
& Trading Post, a 1905
lodge now on the National
Register of Historic Places.

TOK

Fast Eddy's Restaurant
Mile 1313, Alaska Highway;
907-883-4411;
fasteddysrestaurant.com,
Everything from ribeyes to
crab legs and halibut.

Alaska's Far North

Alaska's Far North, more than any other region, is a land of extremes. As its name implies, this region lies farther north than any other in the state or nation. It's the only part of the United States lapped by the Arctic Ocean's summer waters and barricaded by its winter pack ice. At its northernmost reaches, the region enjoys the country's longest period of daylight— 84 continuous days of constant daylight from May 10 to August 2. In contrast, during the dark days of winter, the sun literally does not rise for 67 days. At least one of the region's wildlife species, the polar bear, can be found nowhere else in the nation. And, of course, Alaska's Far North is home to one of North America's largest oil fields, Prudhoe Bay.

Although some may imagine the Far North as drab and lifeless, the tundra country is ablaze with wildflowers, berries, and other colorful plantlife in summer. Millions of birds migrate to the northern tundra from North and even South America each spring. Especially during flightseeing tours, but during road trips as well, you stand a good chance of seeing grizzly bears, caribou, and moose.

Among Native peoples of the region, there are two groups who might call themselves Eskimos (although visitors generally

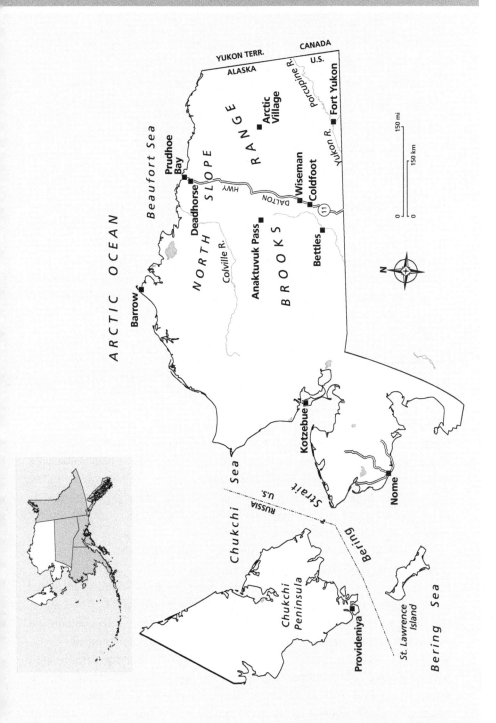

TOP 10 PLACES IN THE FAR NORTH

Arctic National Wildlife Refuge	Great Kobuk Sand Dunes
The beaches of Nome	Iditarod Trail (of the Sled Dog Race)
Bettles Lodge	Northernmost tip of Point Barrow
Coldfood Camp and the Dalton Highway	Pilgrim Hot Springs
Gates of the Arctic National Park	Serpentine Hot Springs

should not, as this word has also been used as a slur): the Inupiat on the shores of the Alaska mainland and the Yup'ik, who reside in Gambell and Savoonga on St. Lawrence Island, a large island in the Bering Sea only 40 miles from Russian Siberia. A small number of inland Nunamiut peolpe live at Anaktuvuk Pass, about 260 miles north-northwest of Fairbanks, while Athabascan communities may be found as far north as Arctic Village in the Brooks Range, 290 miles north of Fairbanks and roughly 100 miles north of Fort Yukon.

Major Communities of the Far North

Utqiaġvik, formerly known as *Barrow,* is just about as far off the beaten path as you can get and still have your feet planted on U.S. soil. Located 330 miles north of the Arctic Circle, the mostly Inupiat town is, in fact, the northernmost community in the Western Hemisphere. That's only one of the superlatives you can collect during a visit here. Utqiaġvik is also the seat of government for the North Slope Borough, which, at 88,000 square miles, ranks as the largest municipality in the world. (A borough, in Alaska, is rather like a county in the Lower 48, but much of the state is not part of any municipality or borough.)

In spite of its remoteness, you can get to Utqiaġvik easily. Alaska Airlines provides daily jet service from Anchorage and Fairbanks, and once you've arrived, you'll find several ground tour organizations with 1- and 2-day excursions designed to maximize your time at the "top of the world." The biggest and most consistent tour company is *Tundra Tours,* which also operates the fully modern *Top of the World Hotel* (907-852-3900; tundratoursinc.com). The Tundra Tours day tour is an excellent opportunity to become familiar with both Utqiaġvik and its culture; you will visit a nearby cultural center, explore the tundra to find ancient remains of traditional sod huts, and tour many of Utqiaġvik's iconic sights, including the famous whalebone arch, the shore of the Arctic Ocean, and the artificial-turf football field that plays a pivotal role for local students. If you stay in the hotel, high-season rates start at $355.

Northern Alaska Tour Company (907-474-8600; northernalaska.com) offers village tours, emphasizing the Inupiat culture with a program of traditional dance and song plus demonstrations of skin sewing, Native games, and the blanket toss. The tours also explore Arctic shores. Overnight tours of Utqiaġvik start at $779 if you're coming from Anchorage, or $829 if you're coming from Fairbanks, with a $150 single supplement.

Once in Utqiaġvik you may want to get around on your own for some even more off-the-beaten-path destinations, and you'll need wheels to do that. Try **UIC Car Rental** (907-852-2700; uicalaska.com). Prices are on the high side—but, hey, how else are you going to get wheels this far north?

You could put that daily car rental fee toward a good guide instead, who will do all the driving for you. Try Inupiat-owned **71 North Tours** (907-382-1000; 71northtours.com), who will take you to the northernmost point in Alaska, literally, as you go where the tour buses can't—to the original **Point Barrow**. You might even see polar bears there.

My very favorite hotel choice in Utqiaġvik is the **King Eider Inn** (907-852-4700; kingeider.net), located just across the street from the town's small airport, with rooms starting at $235 per night, kitchenettes available for an extra $35. King Eider also rents cars and SUVs to overnight guests.

Sam & Lee's (907-852-5556; no website) is a longtime staple of Utqiaġvik dining, offering Chinese and American food and a great view of the town's famous whalebone arch near the ocean shore. For the finest dining in town, head for **Niġġvikput** in the Top of the World Hotel.

A Place to Celebrate

Shaped like a giant ulu knife, the Inupiat Heritage Center in Utqiaġvik is a place for young and old Inupiat people to share their culture and pass on traditions. It cost almost $12 million to build. The building has four rooms: a 20,000-plus-volume consortium library, a room where Inupiat artists can work on their art, an exhibit room to show off some of the results of their labor, and a multipurpose room for demonstrations and lectures. The creations that can be seen at the center include umiaks (skinboats) and dogsleds, ivory carving, and skin sewing.

In building such a monument to their way of life, the Inupiat people are showing they are a culture steeped in tradition. In fact, during the building's dedication, a ceremony in which strips of baleen were placed at the corners of the building symbolized the passage of the cultural traditions of the elders to the young people in the community.

Alaska's largest Inupiat community, **Kotzebue,** lies 26 miles north of the Arctic Circle, 550 air miles from Anchorage, and 200 miles from the shores of the Russian Far East. The Inupiat have lived in this area for 10,000 to 15,000 years, and the village of Qikiktagruk, now called Kotzebue, served as a trading center. In 1818 German Admiral Otto Von Kotzebue, sailing for the Russian Navy, arrived in the sound. Today Kotzebue is the service center for the **Northwest Arctic Borough,** which includes areas around Kotzebue Sound, portions of the Brooks Range, and parts of the Seward Peninsula.

With a population of 7,600, 75 percent of whom are Inupiat, the borough is approximately the size of the state of Indiana. Its boundaries also encompass the Noatak and Kobuk Rivers, favorites of anglers looking for a true wilderness fishing experience. In addition, Kotzebue serves as the access point for the **Red Dog Mine,** which lies 90 miles to the north. Red Dog contains the world's largest concentrations of zinc. The metal is mined year-round and held at Kotzebue until the four-month ice-free shipping season begins in late spring.

You can get oriented to Kotzebue, Inupiat culture, and nearby attractions in the **Northwest Arctic Heritage Center** (907-442-3890; nps.gov/kova). This understatedly sleek, pretty building serves as a combination cultural center, visitor center, and museum.

Kotzebue is the jumping-off point for some genuine wilderness adventures. Alaska Airlines offers several flights a week from Anchorage, and if you plan to stay overnight, you can do so at the **Nullaġvik Hotel** (306 Shore Avenue; 907-442-3331; nullagvikhotel.com), where the rack rate for a double room starts at $279. By chartering out of Kotzebue, you can fly over **Selawik Wildlife Refuge,** the **Great Kobuk Sand Dunes,** and **Kobuk Valley National Park.** For more information contact **Arctic Backcountry Flying Service** (907-442-3200; arcticbackcountry.com).

farnorthalaskatrivia

The oldest frame building north of the Arctic Circle is the Cape Smythe Whaling and Trading Station, built in 1893 in Browerville, a whaling community near Utqiaġvik.

Serious anglers can opt for a week of remote fishing at the foot of the Brooks Range, where the average Dolly Varden can be over 7 pounds, with 20-pound lunkers showing up every so often. Kotzebue-based **Golden Eagle Outfitters** (alaskawildernessexpeditions.com) can fly you to the best fishing spots; they also offer flightseeing tours.

For another travel adventure, check out *LaVonne's Fish Camp* (907-442-6013 from late June through August; 907-296-0976 in the off-season; fishcamp .org), a one-of-a-kind opportunity to stay in a traditional Inupiat fish camp and spend time with locals, learning about their culture and how they traditionally harvest and then store fish as part of a subsis-

farnorth alaska trivia

If you're outside of the village of Kivalina, north of Kotzebue, and want to go camping, don't pitch your tent at Siniktagnelik on the right bank of the Wulik River. The word *Siniktagnelik* means "no camping place because one cannot sleep because many years ago some people mysteriously died here."

tence lifestyle. Activities include hiking, beachcombing, helping harvest tundra plants, bird-watching, and much more. At the end of each day, you'll dine family-style with your hosts, guests, and any locals who might have stopped in for a visit, with fresh local salmon and a large salad every night, plus some more familiar American foods for picky eaters.

Lower 48 residents seem to know at least three things about *Nome*. First, it was the site of a lively gold stampede from 1898 through the early years of the twentieth century. Second, each year in March the 1,000-mile *Iditarod Trail Sled Dog Race* finishes there under a massive timber-burled winner's arch, having started some 9 days to 2 weeks earlier in Anchorage. And, third, Nome lies in the far, far north, well above the Arctic Circle.

Well, two out of three's not bad.

Although virtually everyone thinks of Nome as an Arctic community, it's actually a bit south of the Arctic Circle. The town does, however, experience Arctic weather, especially in the wintertime. Seas freeze solid off its shores well into late spring, and in most winters the *"Nome National Forest"*

An Arctic Desert

Above the Arctic Circle, northwest of Kotzebue, lie the shifting sands of the Great Kobuk Sand Dunes. This, the largest active dune field in the Arctic, is composed mainly of glacial silt. Some of the dunes reach heights of 100 feet, and summer temperatures there can reach ninety degrees Fahrenheit.

The dunes are part of the Kobuk Valley National Park, a 1.7-million-acre area set aside in 1980 to protect them. During the ice age the Kobuk Valley remained ice-free, providing a corridor adjoining the Bering Sea land bridge, which once linked Alaska and Siberia. Little has changed in this valley since then. The cold, dry climate remains, and plant life resembles the flora of the late Pleistocene era.

springs up on that frozen ice. Once done as a prank to confuse visitors who came to Nome to watch the end of the Iditarod, the yearly habit of hauling everyone's old Christmas trees out onto the ice and "planting" them in lifelike positions, often with cut-outs of animals spaced among them, has become a beloved tradition.

Nome, with a population of 3,600, more than half of them Alaska Native, is a fair-size city by Alaska standards, but except for an occasional "far out" cruise ship, you can get there only by air. The air service, however, is excellent. Alaska Airlines jets fly to the city several times daily. And here's one of Alaska's best-kept secrets: Once you've arrived here on the shores of the Bering Sea, there are hundreds of miles of good roads to explore. Places to visit and things to see include former gold mining sites, Native villages, impressive scenic vistas, even a hot springs. Nome is also one of the few places in North America where you can take a side trip to Russia.

A little history: One unconfirmed account records that Nome got its start in 1897, when John Hummel, an aging prospector suffering from scurvy, arrived in the area to search for gold, which many had predicted would be found there. But unlike others, Hummel did his panning on the beach, more hopeful of curing his ailments in the sun and salt air than of anything else. Incredibly, while sifting the beach sands he found gold. More incredible still, as he tested up and down the shoreline, he continued to see precious metal in every pan. In no time the rush was on! Another more substantiated version of Nome's beginning states that "three lucky Swedes"—Jafet Lindberg, Erik Lindblom, and John Brynteson—started the rush by finding gold in Anvil Creek in 1898 and that the beach finds came a year or so later.

Top Annual Event in the Far North

Iditarod Trail Sled Dog Race: The main event in a monthlong celebration in Nome. The race starts in Anchorage on the first Satruday in March, but mushers begin arriving any time after the ninth day in Nome. A Mushers and Miners Ball and a statewide basketball tournament are held during March, too. Contact the **Nome Convention and Visitors Bureau** (907-443-6555; visitnomealaska.com) for more information.

However the rush began, it hasn't stopped yet, even if these days the rush consists of tourists eager to see where all the excitement took place. When you arrive in town, your first stop should be the ***Nome Convention and Visitor Bureau's Visitor Information Center*** (907-443-6555; visitnomealaska. com), located downtown on Front Street, across from Nome City Hall. Lots of free brochures, walking maps, restaurant menus, antiques, and historic photos are available or on display Monday through Friday. Less than a mile away on Seventh Avenue, you'll find the beautiful new home of the *Carrie McLain Museum* (907-443-6630; nomealaska.org/memorial-museum), with its wide variety of Alaskan artifacts and historical memorabilia.

Any time of the year, your most vivid memories of Nome may well be the gold dredges. One old and abandoned dredge is within walking distance of town. The huge, lumbering behemoths once created their own ponds as they crept and floated across the tundra, scooping up ore and extracting gold. And, of course, what could be more fitting for a visit to Nome than to buy a gold pan at one of the local stores and pan for some "color" of your own on the beaches where thousands once labored for nuggets and fortunes?

About those highways: For a place you can't drive to, Nome has lots of miles to tour by auto. Three major roads offer access to wildlife viewing, rivers to fish, mining ruins to examine, plus awesome seascapes and landscapes to photograph. Nowadays, you have two choices for vehicle rentals: from the *Dredge No. 7 Inn* (907-304-1270; dredge7inn.com) or from *Stampede Vehicle Rentals* (907-443-3838; aurorainnome.com). Cab service can be had by calling *Nome Checker Cab* at 907-443-5211.

The *Nome–Council Road,* which extends 72 miles east from Nome's main thoroughfare, Front Street, follows the coast for about 30 miles, then moves inland past rivers and sloping hills to the village of *Council.* About halfway out you'll come to the former community of *Solomon,* with its picturesque graveyard of old abandoned railroad engines and cars. Locals call this the Last Train to Nowhere. The 73-mile *Nome–Teller Road* leads to the village of *Teller* (population 200). You reach this highway from the west end of Front Street by turning north on Bering Street, which leads into the northwest-heading Teller Road.

A shorter driving option (about 3 miles one way) takes you to the top of *Anvil Mountain,* near an inoperative communications site. The rewarding view takes in the city of Nome, the Bering Sea, Sledge Island, and a colorful expanse of Arctic tundra.

Perhaps most rewarding, you can drive to *Pilgrim Hot Springs* on the Kougarok Road, which is accessible about 2 miles north of town by turning north off Bering Street. The experience offers a lot of natural history, mining history, and vast fields of tiny colorful flowers growing wild on the tundra. The 36-mile drive will take about 45 minutes one way. Pack a snack to enjoy on the shores of Salmon Lake at the Bureau of Land Management campground. Farther down the road comes historic Pilgrim Hot Springs—once the site of a Catholic mission orphanage—and experimental gardens where tons of beets, carrots, turnips, cabbage, kale, rutabagas, rhubarb, onions, and potatoes were harvested from the hot springs–heated ground. Visitors are welcome to soak up the local atmosphere by spending quality time in a Pilgrim Hot Springs hot tub. (Bring your own towel.) There's time, as well, for bird-watching, trail hiking, and

farnorthalaskafacts

The sun does not set in Utqiaġvik between mid-May and mid-August, and it does not rise between mid-November and late January each winter.

Cape Prince of Wales, at the tip of the Seward Peninsula, is the westernmost point of mainland Alaska. Cape Mountain (2,289 feet), which rises above the village of Wales, is the terminus of the Continental Divide.

angling for trout or grayling in the Pilgrim River. During a drive north on the Kougarok Road, you'll pass through the Nome River Valley, where it's not uncommon to spot musk ox, moose, and reindeer.

If you'd prefer to have a local expert along to show you the sights, contact the convention and visitors bureau to see who's currently hosting tours. If they're available, **Roam Nome** is a favorite, and **Beyond Captured** (907-304-1420; beyondcaptured.com) offers photo tours, city tours, and ground-based tours of the surrounding area—which is great if you don't want to tackle the often-bumpy highways outside Nome on your own.

Deja Vu Sled Dogs (no phone; dejavusleddogs.com) offers summer tours of their working sled dog kennel on a farmstead near Nome, plus 90-minute "Learn to Mush" tours during the winter, along with sled dog rides, kicksled tours, and an offer to customize your very own adventure. This is a one-of-a-kind opportunity to get up close with sled dogs in a place that is famous for being the endpoint of the Iditarod sled dog race.

If you think Nome is fascinating by foot or vehicle, try seeing it from a few thousand feet above ground. **Bering Air** (907-443-5464; www.beringair .com) is one of your best options for flightseeing, and its pilots can take you to such locales as **Bering Land Bridge National Preserve,** one of the most remote national park areas in the country and a remnant of the land bridge that connected Asia with North America more than 13,000 years ago. While there, unwind in the naturally occurring **Serpentine Hot Springs.** The majority of this land bridge, once thousands of miles wide, now lies beneath the waters of the Chukchi and Bering Seas. Call 907-443-2522 or visit nps.gov/bela for more information on the springs. Or try a flight-see over ancient lava beds—yup, you can find just about anything if you look hard enough in Alaska.

Arranging to see Nome and its surrounding area by air is only a phone call away if you want the planning done for you. Again, *Bering Air* (907-443-5464; beringair.com) is your best local resource. If you're interested in the Iditarod, you might enjoy taking to the air with *Rust's Flying Service* (907-243-1595; flyrusts.com) or *K2 Aviation* (907-733-2291; flyk2 .com). Although these air services are based in Anchorage and Talkeetna, respectively, they both offer "Chase the Race" flightseeing trips that give you a true bird's-eye view of the race, also landing you at a checkpoint so you can watch the mushers and dogs in action. The Rust's tour starts from $995, and the K2 tour starts from $725.

Several hotels offer lodging and dining accommodations in Nome, including the *Nome Nugget Inn* (on Front Street; 907-434-6474; nomenuggetinn. com), where most of the airline tourists stay. Rooms there start at $195 during the summer, and $290 during Iditarod season. If you like more informal surroundings, consider the *Dredge No. 7 Inn* (907-304-1270; dredge7inn .com), which has rooms in a collection of clean, comfortable, homey-feeling buildings in several places around town. Their prices start from about $300 per night.

Another comfortable option is the spacious *Aurora Inn and Suites* on Front Street (907-443-3838 or 800-354-4606; www .aurorainnnome.com). Opt for a standard or premium room with

farnorthalaskafacts

Don't be surprised if you see Pacific walrus during a visit to Nome. They migrate between the Chukchi and Bering seas. A bull walrus can weigh up to two tons.

When you're standing at the Arctic Circle on the summer solstice, the sun never sets. And if you're standing there on the winter solstice, the sun will not rise above the horizon.

farnorthalaskatrivia

Continuous permafrost reaches depths of 2,000 feet in the Far North and can wreak havoc on buildings whose heat causes partial thawing. To remedy the problem, many buildings in the Far North are built on ground that is kept frozen during the summer with refrigeration coils. It is easier to cool the ground for a few months each year than deal with the repairs caused by shifting ice and sagging structures.

or without kitchenette or choose an executive suite. Rates start from about $250 per night. There's a guest sauna on site, as well as vehicle rentals through Stampede Rentals.

While these places offer ample creature comforts, if you're prepared to do without, call and ask the visitors center (907-443-6555) about **beach camping** on the east side of town. Historically it's been free, although sometimes patches of beach are considered private property—so it's always best to ask for up-to-date information.

The **Polar Cafe** (907-443-5191; no website) has good breakfast omelets. **Bering Tea & Coffee** (907-387-0352; no website) is a cafe where you can grab a drink or a bite to eat. And **Pingo Bakery and Seafood House** (907-387-0654; pingobakery-seafoodhouse.com) is very good for breakfast and lunch. It's also very small, so you might end up sharing a table.

Another dining option is **Milano's Pizzeria** on Front Street (907-443-2924; no website) which, as is common in remote places, offers an interesting combination of cultural fare. In this case, it's Japanese and Italian, making this one of the few places in the world where you can get a California roll, pepperoni pizza, and lobster all in one place.

Life on the Beach

I lie on my sleeping bag with my head propped up, reading a book and relaxing. It's bedtime, but I can still feel the warmth of the sun through the tent fly. Of course, this is to be expected when you're camping just below the Arctic Circle in the middle of the summer. The sun barely sets this time of year. I am in Nome, Alaska, on the Bering Sea coast, and I'm camped on the beach. All I hear are the waves lapping tamely along the shore or an occasional bird that still hasn't settled for the evening.

Then I hear something different, a soft swoosh every now and then, like a stocking-footed child padding into a room. I peek outside my tent and am amazed to be surrounded by what must be at least a hundred reindeer making their way to the water's edge. These animals are part of several reindeer herds owned by Native Alaskans living in the region. The locals have told me not to be surprised to see them. They'll often visit the beaches, not for fun in the sun, but to seek refuge from the hordes of mosquitoes that plague them inland.

I'm a bit daunted by the sight of these big creatures encircling my little blue tent, but there's not much else I can do but get back under cover and hope they don't decide to stampede. In the morning I awake and they are gone, with fading impressions of their hooves left in the sand the only evidence that it wasn't a dream.

—Melissa DeVaughn (author of previous editions)

Villages in the Arctic

Since 1948 the small Brooks Range outpost called **Bettles** has been the base of operations for **Bettles Lodge** (907-692-5111; bettleslodge.com) now registered as a National Historic Site. Longtime Alaskans Dan and Lynda Klaes owned the lodge from 1982 to 2014; in 2014 they sold the lodge to the current owners, Heather and Eric Fox, who continue the tradition of offering accommodations and customized tours in a part of Alaska that less than 1 percent of the state's visitors get to enjoy.

It's hard to ballpark the cost of tours or lodging at Bettles Lodge, because each trip is customized to some degree. If you call or email them with specifics of what you're hoping to do, they can set you up with a quote for an all-inclusive stay. Possible summer activities include floats along the Koyukuk River and other backcountry excursions, and visiting nearby national parks. Fabulous fly-out fishing is one of the specialties here, with sheefish, arctic grayling, lake trout, arctic char, chum salmon, and northern pike all for the taking. This lodge operates year-round, and during the winter they offer northern lights viewing, dog sledding, and flightseeing among other options.

There are more options in the Brooks Range. **Chilkat Guides** (907-313-4420; chilkatguides.com), of Haines, offers an 11-day hiking/boating adventure for $9,300 on the seldom-traveled **Kongakut River.** The trip originates with a bush flight from Fairbanks. Another outstanding option is backpacking the Arrigetch Peaks of **Gates of the Arctic National Park** with **Alaska Alpine Adventures** (907-351-4193; alaskaalpineadventures.com). This 10-day adventure is a great late-summer trip and a perfect time to view the fall colors and perhaps see the migrating Western Arctic caribou herd. Pricing starts from $6,495 per person.

Another Gates of the Arctic option well worth visiting is **Peace of Selby** (907-672-3206; alaskawilderness.net) on Selby/Narvak Lake in the Brooks Range. Fully furnished, comfortable lodge accommodations, with meals included, are $500 a night per person. Available for $300 per person per night are cabins on Nutuvukti and Minakokosa Lakes and on the Kobuk River. Guided float trips, canoeing, day or overnight hikes, and fishing expeditions are available. This is a photographer's or bird-watcher's heaven. Also popular at Peace of Selby are winter adventures, ranging from cross-country skiing to snowshoeing to watching the caribou migration. Access, of course, is by air from Fairbanks.

For those who enjoy bird-watching, not just to check off another species on their list but to see birds in their most natural environment, **Wilderness Birding Adventures** (907-299-3937; wildernessbirding.com) offers an exciting assortment of possibilities from Shuyak State Park on Kodiak Island to the far north Arctic. Among the latter are float trips of the Colville River as well as floats or base camp adventures on a small island of mountains protruding from the Arctic coastal plain in the *Arctic National Wildlife Refuge.* A 12-day float down the Marsh Fork/Canning River on the western edge of the refuge offers a chance to see many species of birds. The company also packages tours of Gambell on St. Lawrence Island, and of Nome, where rare species fly over from Siberia. Tours are priced as low as $2,750 for a 5-day excursion on Kodiak Island to $6,350 for a 9-day trip in Fairbanks.

Jim Campbell and Carol Kasza, husband and wife, have hiked and climbed mountains around the world, but to establish their own guiding business, *Arctic Treks* (907-455-6502; arctictreksadventures.com), they selected the Brooks Range. They offer wilderness hiking, backpacking, and rafting options from 7 to 11 days. They take only six to nine clients per trip.

Established in 1847 by the Hudson's Bay Company, *Fort Yukon* is today one of Alaska's oldest settlements and the largest Athabascan village in the state. The Gwich'in Athabascans have lived in this area for literally thousands of years. The town, which the people call Gwichyaa Zhee (meaning "house on the flats"), lies 8 miles north of the Arctic Circle and about 140 miles northeast of Fairbanks. You can get there by air via three scheduled carriers and four charter outfits or by boat. No roads lead to Fort Yukon.

farnorthalaskatrivia

Any part of Alaska that can't be reached by road is called the bush. A community that can only be reached by sled, snow machine, airplane, or boat is called a "bush village."

If you enjoy buying souvenirs at the source, check out the *Alaska Commercial Company* store for beaded moose-skin accessories. Most visitor services are available. One of the principal visitor attractions is a *replica of the original Fort Yukon.* Nearby is the old Hudson's Bay cemetery. Hudson's Bay built the fort not for protection from Alaska Native people, but as a safeguard against the Russians who "owned" Alaska until 1867. Be sure also to see the *Old Mission School,* which is on the National Register of Historic Places. Ask to visit *St. Stephen's Territorial Episcopal Church,* where you can view exquisite and colorful Athabascan beaded embroidery on the altar cloth. The Athabascans are renowned for their beadwork designs, which decorate boots, moccasins, jackets, and gloves.

The Dalton Highway

This road—the only overland route into the Arctic from Alaska's highway network—is not for the timid or the unprepared. But the *Dalton Highway* is one of the last great adventure roads in the United States. If you have the right vehicle and plan ahead, it can be one of the most satisfying drives of a lifetime.

Alaska began construction of the 414-mile road in April 1974 and had it operational that fall in order to expedite construction of the 800-mile pipeline from Prudhoe Bay to Valdez. The Dalton today is gravel, two lanes, hilly in places, bumpy in many more, lonely (you may not see another car for hours), and has few service facilities along the way. If you break down you may not get help until an Alaska state trooper comes by on patrol. That's the bad news. The good news is that it is safely negotiable if you use common sense, and it opens up some of the most awesome northern mountain and tundra country in the world.

If you want to experience the highway but you don't want the hassle of planning, preparing, or driving the Dalton on your own, there's an easy option: Book reservations with one of several tour companies, large and small, that schedule motorcoach or van trips all summer long. Several of these offer 3-day drive/fly itineraries during which you cruise the highway in one direction and fly between Fairbanks and Prudhoe Bay in the other. Among the companies that offer this and other options are *Northern Alaska Tour Company* (907-474-8600; northernalaska.com) and *Alaska Tours* (907-277-3000; alaskatours .com). Prices vary with the different companies, points of origin, and whether you're traveling in a high or "shoulder" season. Northern Alaska offers a taste of the Dalton Highway with a 1-day drive/fly round-trip package from Fairbanks to Coldfoot, 60 miles north of the Arctic Circle.

If you decide to drive the road yourself, make sure your car is in top mechanical condition. It's a good idea to call the Alaska Department of Transportation (907-451-5311) or visit 511.alaska.gov before you leave to find out the current road conditions. 511 isn't always fully up to date so, when in doubt, go ahead and call. To be safe, carry two mounted spare tires. Chances are you'll need at least one. Especially if you're camping out along the way (in fact, even if you're not), bring lots of bug dope and a head net to help keep swarming mosquitoes away from you. And by all means, pack plenty of power banks for your phone and/or digital camera. It's a long, long drive to the nearest electrical outlet. If you don't plan to camp, make sure you've called ahead and reserved motel space in Coldfoot and Deadhorse. Be aware that gasoline is available along the way only at the Yukon River (mile 56), at Coldfoot (mile 175), and at Deadhorse at road's end (mile 414).

Whether you're in the family vehicle or an air-conditioned motor coach, the adventure begins when you leave the Elliott Highway past mile 73 and head north on the Dalton. Four miles later you're descending a steep incline into Lost Creek Valley, with the pipeline visible (as it frequently will be) to your right. From time to time the pipe will crisscross under the road. Sometimes the line will be buried for many miles, and you won't see it at all.

About 48 miles out you begin your descent to the Yukon River, and at mile 55.6, there it is: the storied Yukon and an impressive 2,290-foot wood-decked bridge that rises (or falls, depending on which way you're driving) at a 6 percent grade.

Across the river on its northern bank, you can top off your fuel tank at **Yukon River Camps** (907-947-3557; yukonrivercamp.com) as well as eat a restaurant meal and overnight in a motel. An overnight stay in a spartan room with two twin beds and shared restrooms down the hall starts at $259 for one or two people.

At mile 115.3 you can take a photo you'll be proud to hang on your living room wall. Here you will officially cross the Arctic Circle at 66 degrees, 33 minutes north latitude, and there's a big sign there to prove it.

At mile 175 you'll come to **Coldfoot,** which started life as an old-time mining camp and exists today as the major overnight spot for truckers and visitors on the Dalton Highway. The name, according to local legend, came about when early gold stamped-ers got this far north, then got "cold feet" and retreated south.

farnorthalaskatrivia

Don't be surprised if you hear locals call the Dalton Highway the "haul" road. This 414-mile scenic but often rough road was built in 1974 as a transport road during the construction of the Trans-Alaska Pipeline, and it is still used to "haul" materials to keep the pipeline in operation.

For accommodations, try **Coldfoot Camp** (907-474-3500; coldfootcamp .com) which has very basic work camp–style lodging (from $259 for one or two people in a small room with twin beds and a private bathroom), as well as gas, food, and even flightseeing. You're asked to be mindful of your noise levels in the hallways, as you're sharing accommodations with truckers who might be cramming in a few hours of sleep before continuing north or south on the highway. In the work camp dining room, you might see the same people during meals and may easily find yourself sharing a table with new friends. In remote places like this, the art of conversation has not been lost—and in fact, it's valued.

The National Park Service, Bureau of Land Management, and U.S. Fish and Wildlife Service maintain the beautiful *Arctic Interagency Visitor Center* in Coldfoot, offering road and travel updates as well as programs each night about the patchwork of public lands across the Arctic.

Approaching mile 189 along the highway, you join a short access road to *Wiseman.* Like many others of its kind, this community once thrived as a trading center for prospectors and miners. These days about two dozen determined souls still live there year-round, joined by others in the summer. The *Wiseman Museum* is a good place to stop and check out old mining artifacts and photos. And if you don't want to tent out, call *Arctic Getaway Bed & Breakfast* (907-799-4455; arcticgetaway.com). It's not fancy, but hosts Berni and Uta Hicker will make you feel at home. Also in Wiseman is *Boreal Lodging* (907-888-9785; boreallodge.com). Four rooms at the lodge share two bathrooms and a kitchen, while the Boreal Cabin has a private bath.

At mile 235.3, just south of a highway turnoff, you'll see the northernmost spruce tree in Alaska. No others grow beyond this point. This is also the start of a long and very steep grade—10 percent. Be sure to give any downhill-traveling trucks you meet their full half of the road.

Another steep ascent begins just beyond mile 242 and ends at Atigun Pass, which at 4,800 feet is the highest in Alaska. Watch for Dall sheep, especially on Slope Mountain.

About 75 miles later you'll see a pingo 5 miles west of the road. These curious circular mounds, more common the closer you get to the Arctic Ocean's shores, rise dramatically from surrounding tabletop-smooth terrain. They're caused by frozen water beneath the surface.

At mile 414 you've arrived at *Deadhorse,* the gathering point where crude oil from Prudhoe Bay, Kuparuk River, and other lesser oil fields is brought in by a network of smaller pipelines and directed into the 48-inch Trans-Alaska Pipeline for transport to Valdez, 800 miles to the south.

Truth to tell, you'll probably judge Deadhorse a pretty bleak and dreary place. Some of the oil company buildings (with self-contained dorms, cafeterias, libraries, and recreation centers) are modern and bright, even cheerful, and some of the subcontractor structures and quarters are on a par with counterparts in industrial parks in the Lower 48. But a considerable number of Deadhorse's buildings and lots are unkempt, junky, littered, and strewn with unused or abandoned pipe, equipment, and building material. No one really seems to care, since almost no one lives here year-round. Virtually the entire population consists of crews and individuals who arrive or depart on periodic shift assignments. There are no church buildings, schools, movie theaters, or any of the other trappings of a bona fide community. Few, if any, of the workers bring spouses or family. They claim residence in Anchorage, Fairbanks, and even far-flung points like Dallas and Fort Worth.

So what's the attraction? Well, it may be drab, dreary, and desolate, but in a strange sort of way, it's dramatic and absorbing. There's a lot of coming-going-moving-shaking activity, and if you take one of the organized tours available, you'll learn a lot about the place and the process by which the United States at one time got a whopping 2 million barrels of crude oil a day. You can have your picture taken at *Pipeline Mile Zero.* You'll likely see wild caribou grazing virtually in the shadow of oil rigs and pipelines just outside of town, and any number of waterfowl species resting or nesting on the tundra. And if you don't happen to have Point Barrow on your itinerary, where else will you be able to skip a stone on the Arctic Ocean? (Or, if you're a winter or very early summer visitor, actually take a few steps out onto the Arctic ice pack.)

You can't, by the way, just mosey around Deadhorse in your car on your own as you would back home. Much of this community, including roads, is private property, and you need permission to visit many sites, including the shores of the Arctic Ocean. This is the reason many visitors choose all-inclusive van or motor coach drive/fly tours from Fairbanks or Anchorage. If you plan to drive here in your own vehicle, you should definitely make housing reservations ahead of time.

Your two best options in town are the *Aurora Hotel* (907-670-0600; theaurorahotel.net), which offers the most hotel-like experience you'll get in town, starting from $200 for a "Jack and Jill" room with a twin bunk and shared bathroom, or $275 for a mini room with a twin bed and a private bathroom; and *Deadhorse Camp* (907-474-3565; deadhorsecamp.com), which has spartan, industrial rooms with twin beds, a table and chair, and that's about it. Prices start from $229 per night, single or double occupancy, and all restroom and shower facilities are shared. That sort of thing is all part of the adventure when traveling in remote Alaska. If they say no rooms are available, try calling back a couple of weeks before your planned stay. Often, the lodgings will hold rooms for workers until then, but if those rooms don't get booked up they'll be released for use by the public.

If you'd like to get a bird's-eye view of the area, consider traveling with *Alaska Tours* (907-277-3000; alaskatours.com). They offer several tours that journey north of the Arctic Circle, with their *Arctic Ocean and Prudhoe Bay* tour going farthest afield. You'll take ground transport all the way up the Dalton Highway to Prudhoe Bay, then fly back south after an overnight stay. Prices for the 3-day, 2-night package start at $1,399 per person.

There are a couple of gas stations in Prudhoe Bay, and if you have vehicle problems, just ask around—one of the shops will be able to help you.

Incidentally, no one uses street addresses here. To find something, just look for signs or ask someone.

The Dalton Highway, of course, is a north–south, single-direction road. There are no loops or alternate routes back. If you're driving, when your visit ends, you simply retrace your path to the Elliott Highway and on to Fairbanks to begin your next adventure.

Places to Stay in the Far North

COLDFOOT

Coldfoot Camp
907-474-3400,
coldfootcamp.com.
Modular housing in a true work camp: spartan but clean with private bathrooms.

DEADHORSE

Aurora Hotel
907-670-0600;
theaurorahotel.net.
Private bathrooms and a few hotel amenities.

Deadhorse Camp
907-474-3565;
deadhorsecamp.com.
Spartan work camp accommodations and shared bathrooms.

KOTZEBUE

Nullagvik Hotel
306 Shore Avenue;
907-442-3331;
nullagvikhotel.com.
A modern hotel in a remote location; the name is Inupiaq for "a place to sleep."

NOME

Aurora Inn and Suites
Front Street;
907-443-3838;
aurorainnome.com.
Spacious, with a sauna and vehicle rentals.

Dredge No. 7 Inn
907-304-1270;
dredge7inn.com.
A collection of clean, comfortable, and homey rooms.

Nome Nugget Inn
Front Street;
907-434-6474;
nomenuggetinn.com.
A historic lodging, famous for its location near the Iditarod arch.

SELBY/NARVAK LAKE

Peace of Selby
Within Gates of the Arctic National Park and Noatak National Preserve;
907-672-3206;
alaskawilderness.net.
It's out there, but certainly peaceful.

UTQIAĠVIK

King Eider Inn
Across the street from the airport;
907-852-4700;
kingeider.net.

Clean, comfortable rooms and kitchenettes.

Top of the World Hotel
1204 Agvik;
907-852-3900;
tundratours.inc.
The newest, nicest hotel in town.

WISEMAN

Arctic Getaway Bed and Breakfast
Mile 189, Dalton Highway;
907-799-4455;
arcticgetaway.com.
The hosts make you feel at home.

Boreal Lodging
In Wiseman Village,
907-888-9785;
boreallodge.com.
Four rooms and a private cabin in a village too small for addresses.

Places to Eat in the Far North

KOTZEBUE

Nullagvik Restaurant
907-442-3331;
nullagvikhotel.com.

Reindeer stew and sausage, fresh local fish, and other tasty fare.

NOME

Milano's Pizzeria
2824 Front Street;
907-443-2924.

Japanese and Italian fare, plus seafood.

Pingo Bakery and Seafood House
308 Bering Street;
907-397-0654;
pingobakery-seafoodhouse
.com;

Great for breakfast and lunch.

UTQIAĠVIK

Sam & Lee's
1052 Kogiak Street;
907-852-5556.
Chinese and American food with great views.

Southwest Alaska

Strange opportunity you have in Southwest Alaska: If you really want to, you can travel farther off the beaten path in this region than in any other in the nation. Farther west and—here's the strange part—farther east.

The Aleutian Islands, as you probably know, stretch from the end of the Alaska Peninsula almost to Japan. The westernmost point in the United States lies on one of those islands, Amatignak, at longitude 179°10' west.

Now about the easternmost point. Just across the 180th meridian that separates the earth's Western Hemisphere from the Eastern Hemisphere (and exactly halfway around the world from the prime meridian at Greenwich, England) is Semisopochnoi Island's Pochnoi Point, at longitude 179°46' east. Thus the nation's most northern (at Point Barrow), western, and eastern real estate is located in Alaska. (The most southern, if you're curious, is on the southern side of the Big Island of Hawaii.)

Here are some other Alaska-size statistics about this region: You can visit Alaska's largest island, Kodiak, and in the process see the nation's biggest land omnivore, the Kodiak brown bear. You can photograph the biggest moose in Alaska on the

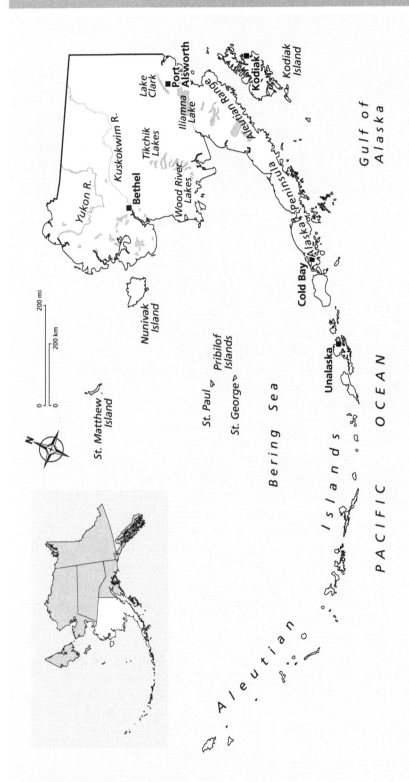

TOP 10 PLACES IN SOUTHWEST ALASKA

Beaches of Kodiak	Lake Clark
Cliff House	Margaret Bay
Fort Abercrombie	Raspberry Island
Katmai NP	Shuyak Island
Kodiak Island Winery	Unalaska

Alaska Peninsula. Some of North America's most volatile volcanoes have blown their tops in this area—one of the most awesome, Novarupta, is part of Katmai National Park and Preserve. Through the region flow some of the nation's wildest rivers. And way, way, *way* out in the Bering Sea you'll find two tiny islands on which you'll see more birds of more species than you ever thought possible. Every visitor comes home from the Pribilof Islands a confirmed bird-watcher.

Among Native residents in the region, to sketch historical residences in overly broad terms Yup'ik people lived on the western mainland, Aleuts on the Aleutian Islands, and the Alutiiq on Kodiak Island.

Kodiak Island, in fact, is a good place to start an exploration of the region. The island ranks not only as the largest in Alaska, with a population of about 14,100; it also contains Alaska's earliest continuing European settlement, the city of **Kodiak.**

No roads or bridges connect Kodiak Island to the Alaska mainland, but the Alaska Marine Highway System (800–642–0066; ferryalaska.com) offers regular, dependable passenger and vehicle ferry service from Homer and Whittier on the Kenai Peninsula several times each week. Alaska Airlines provides daily flights from Anchorage. There are visitor accommodations and services aplenty in the community. For information contact the **Kodiak Island Convention and Visitors Bureau** at 100 East Marine Way (907-486-4782; kodiak.org) or explore the helpful visitor guide on their website.

Although cruise ships do sometimes stop in Kodiak, it still feels very much off the beaten path; you can come away from a visit with a genuine feel for the way Alaskans live and work and play in this part of the Last Frontier. It's fun simply to wander along the boat docks and cannery sites, watching the frantic, frenzied busyness of salmon, crab, halibut, shrimp, and other fisheries landings. More than 3,000 commercial vessels—some quite large—use Kodiak's two harbors, St. Paul and St. Herman, each year, making the area one of the busiest in the world. While you're at St. Paul harbor downtown checking out the fleet, make sure to stop in at **Harborside Coffee and Goods** (210 Shelikof

Avenue; 907-486-5862; harborsidecoffeekodiak.com), a friendly, comfortable coffeehouse with a view of boats coming and going and fishermen tending to their chores. If you're going hiking, this coffee shop often has cans of bear spray to loan; just bring the can back when you're done.

A great deal of Alaska's early European history resides in Kodiak. The first Russian settlement, established in 1784, was at Three Saints Bay, but the Russian trader and manager Alexander Baranov relocated his headquarters to present-day Kodiak in 1792. Originally Baranov's warehouse for precious sea otter pelts, and now the **Kodiak History Museum** (907-486-5920; kodiak historymuseum.org), it was constructed about 1808 and is the oldest Russian building in Alaska. It's at 101 East Marine Way and was once named the Baranov Museum, with a focus on antiques and artifacts of the Russian and pre-Russian era. It still commemorates that history, but since its renaming, the collection and displays reflect a more holistic, inclusive look at Kodiak's peoples, both past and present-day. Admission is $10 for adults, free for children 12 and younger.

Kodiak's **Holy Resurrection Russian Orthodox Church** (907-486-3854; oca.org/parishes/oca-ak-kodhrc), the oldest parish in North America, stands in the city's downtown district at Kashaveroff Street and Mission Avenue. It's best to call for current information on tours. Inside the church you'll see colorful religious trappings of the Orthodox faith, including icons that date from Russia's czarist period. At **Saint Herman Theological Seminary** (907-486-3524; sthermanseminary.org) on Mission Road north of the church, you can visit a replica of the first Russian Orthodox church on the island; the original was built in 1796. Father Herman was one of the early Orthodox monks who arrived to evangelize, educate, and provide medical attention to Alaska Natives. On August 9, 1970, he became the first North American religious figure to be canonized by the Russian Orthodox Church.

southwestalaskatrivia

Mishap Creek, also known as Big Loss Creek, on Unimak Island in the Aleutians, derived its name from an unfortunate incident. A light-keeper, attempting to cross the creek after finding the bridge washed out, bundled up his clothes and tried to throw them across. Misjudging the distance, his clothes fell short of the far bank and were washed away.

—*Source:* U.S. Coast and Geodetic Survey

Of course, before the Americans and before the Russians, there were the Native residents of Kodiak, the Alutiiq (pronounced Al-LOO-tig) people. In Kodiak you can learn a lot of Indigenous history simply by attending the dances performed by a talented group called the **Kodiak Alutiiq Dancers.**

And these Alutiiq performers are truly one of a kind in their stories and music and in their unique "snow falling" attire, with tassels of brilliant white arctic fox descending over darker garments. Three dozen or so dancers perform regularly in the afternoons when cruise ships are docked. Performers range from small children to elders, and their dances run the gamut from an ancestral kayaking dance to more contemporary, enacted stories of rich humor, such as the tale of a little boy who eats pudding as fast as his frantic parents can make it.

The **Alutiiq Museum and Archaeological Repository** (844-425-8844; alutiiqmuseum.org) at 215 Mission Road, houses artifacts from numerous archaeological sites around the Kodiak Island Archipelago. The facility features a display gallery, state-of-the-art storage for sensitive artifacts, and a research laboratory. There's also a museum store that showcases the work of local artists. Admission is $7.

For some close-to-town hiking or exploring, walk across the bridge to **Near Island.** An easy walking path that circles the north end of the island starts on the north side of the road, just beyond the end of the bridge. Continue down the hill and you'll find **St. Herman's Harbor,** where during the summer you'll see the island's salmon fleet, if they aren't out fishing.

To view recent history, visitors can take a 4-mile drive out the Rezanof–Monashka Road to **Fort Abercrombie State Historical Park** (907-486-6339; dnr.alaska.gov) to see the remains of World War II gun emplacements, restored bunkers, and other such artifacts. It's a toss-up what you'll find more interesting—the massive concrete bunkers and fortifications that once protected Kodiak from a Japanese invasion or the breathtaking, panoramic view from rugged cliffsides and gentle shores. The area is thickly forested with Sitka spruce, berry plants, and wildflowers. Included in this 183-acre park are thirteen campsites for tenters and RVers, hiking trails, picnicking facilities, and good fishing and swimming spots.

Several roads are worth exploring, including the **Chiniak Highway** that runs southwest from town then southeast. Particularly scenic points and beaches can be found from about mile 35 to the end of the 42-mile road. It's great for picnics, photography, and viewing more World War II gun battery emplacements. If you do your beach exploring at low tide, you'll be amazed at the sealife left behind in small pools after the tide has receded—tiny crabs, anemones, starfish, sea dollars, snails, itty-bitty fish, seaweeds, and all manner of other creepy-crawlies.

The Anton Larsen Bay Road, which begins about 5 miles from downtown at a junction with the Chiniak Highway, leads to Anton Larsen Bay. Along the way you just may spot a brown bear. They don't call the golf course at mile 3 (from the junction) Bear Valley Golf Course for nothing.

Celebrating a Saint's Life

If you're in Kodiak in early August, you can take part in a unique celebration of a unique man. On August 9, pilgrims from around the world gather in Kodiak to celebrate the canonization of Saint Herman by the Russian Orthodox Church.

Father Herman came to Kodiak in 1794 to convert the Natives of Alaska to Christianity and protect them from abuse by the fur traders of the Russian American Company. He helped build the first church in Kodiak and eventually moved to a nearby island, which he named New Valaam, now called Spruce Island.

There, at Monk's Lagoon, he started an orphanage and school for Native children and developed what was probably the first experimental agriculture station. Father Herman is credited with miraculous powers, including healings, averting a tsunami, and befriending Kodiak brown bears. He died on the island in 1837.

Father Herman was canonized Saint Herman on August 9, 1970, and each year on that date a flotilla of boats, all volunteer, line up at St. Paul Harbor in Kodiak to ferry pilgrims to Monk's Lagoon for a short service commemorating Herman's elevation to sainthood. The trip takes most of the day, so bring a lunch. There is no charge, and all who want to visit this holy place are welcome.

For information on the pilgrimage, call the Holy Resurrection Russian Orthodox Church at 907-486-3854.

The road to **Pasagshak Bay** and Narrow Cape begins at mile 30.6 on the Chiniak Highway. The 16.5-mile road brings you through scenic Pasagshak Pass to **Pasagshak River State Recreation Site,** which has restroom facilities, a picnic area, and camping. Beyond the river's mouth, visit Pasagshak Beach, where die-hard, neoprene-clad surfers often can be seen catching the relentless waves. The road ends at **Fossil Beach.** Be careful when approaching the cliffs: They're unstable and falling rocks are a hazard.

If Kodiak has been, until recently, a lesser-known visitor destination, it has nonetheless been one of North America's best-known hunting and bear-watching areas for decades. The reason is *Ursus arctos middendorffi,* the Kodiak brown bear, which can weigh in at 1,500 pounds or more. Around 2,700 or more of the big bruins live on Kodiak Island, according to biologists. Most reside in the 2,491-square-mile **Kodiak National Wildlife Refuge** on Kodiak and nearby Uganik, Ban, and Afognak Islands. Visitors can dwell among these critters, if they like, by renting one of several backcountry recreation cabins constructed by the U.S. Fish and Wildlife Service. Access, incidentally, is only by float-equipped airplanes or boats. For information contact the Kodiak National Wildlife Refuge Headquarters, 1390 Buskin Road, Kodiak

99615 (907-487-2600), or stop by the *Visitor Center* (907-487-2626; fws.gov) at 402 Center Avenue.

If your budget allows, you can book a one-of-a-kind, truly off-the-beaten path experience with Kodiak's massive brown bears at the fly-in-only *Kodiak Brown Bear Center,* which blends rustic luxury and backcountry adventure on lands deep within the Kodiak National Wildlife Refuge. There are no more than about a half-dozen guests in residence at any given time, and the guides will (among other adventures) take you to the shores of fish-rich Karluk Lake, which has been a feeding ground for many generations of Kodiak brown bears. The lake was also of great importance to the early Alutiiq people, and this site remains of great archaeological significance; if you're very lucky, you might get to witness archaeological digs happening near the lodge, or attend presentations made by archaeologists in residence.

Another place to bask in Kodiak's unforgettable beauty is *Shuyak Island State Park.* The 47,000-acre park, incidentally, encompasses part of a coastal forest system unique to the Kodiak Archipelago that contains only one tree species: the Sitka spruce. The 12-mile-long, 11-mile-wide island is 54 air miles north of Kodiak and has more sheltered interior waterways than anywhere in the Kodiak Archipelago. That's what makes it a great kayaking destination. Access to Shuyak Island is via water or air, and camping is by tent or public use cabins, four of which are available for $75 a night. Contact the Alaska State Parks Kodiak District Office for current information (1400 Abercrombie Drive in Kodiak; 907-486-6339; dnr.alaska.gov).

Annual Events in Southwest Alaska

Cama-i Native Dance Festival
Held in Bethel each spring to celebrate, well, just to celebrate. Features Native crafts, dance, food, and other activities (907-543-4585; swaagak.org).

Kodiak Crab Festival
Held each May in Kodiak to celebrate spring. Lots of rides, crafts, entertainment, and a survival-suit race challenging those brave enough to swim in the cold (907-486–5557; kodiakcrabfest.com).

If you don't want to arrange your own sightseeing, fishing, or hiking expeditions, there are several Kodiak outfitters that can get you set up. *South Kodiak Adventures* (907-727-6331; kodiakadventures.com) offers sportfishing packages for halibut, lingcod, and several species of salmon as well as wildlife viewing and photography tours. They offer years of experience with local wildlife, particularly the famous Kodiak brown bears. In addition to bears,

Road-Tripping Kodiak

If you rent a car to explore Kodiak's more remote parks and beaches—and I certainly hope you will!—you'll be presented with a slip of paper explaining that local conditions may be rougher than you expected and be encouraged to purchase additional insurance coverage for the vehicle. Normally I pass on that additional coverage, but in this case I took it: And while I didn't end up needing to use that extra coverage, there were enough tire-busting potholes along the paved roads that I was glad to have that extra insurance riding along, just in case.

If you're going beachcombing on Kodiak, sometimes the real fun starts as you depart the pavement. In this case I'd set my sights on visiting Fossil Beach, almost 50 road miles south of Kodiak—but the rental I'd ended up with was a small, two-wheel-drive sedan. Not necessarily the best vehicle for what my online sources described as a rugged, sandy approach road.

Like most things in more remote areas of Alaska, you can't often predict what conditions will be like: You just have to show up and see how it goes. In this case, I decided I would see whether the car could get me at least within walking distance of the beach. Much to my pleasant surprise, it got me all the way there—even if there were a couple spots where I had to get a running start to build enough moment to go up a steep hill, or hop out and walk the road to spot which line of attack would work for my very limited ground clearance.

But it was all worth it when I reached the beach. There was nobody in sight—no people, no vehicles, no boats—and none appeared during the time I stood there, wearing every layer of clothing I'd brought as protection against the chill wind that whipped across the sand, whipping the waves into gray, white-capped hammers on the shore.

It's tempting to describe a setting like that as "lonely," and it's certainly true that I was alone, at least in the human sense. But moments like that tend to leave me feeling more connected, not less. I appreciate such reminders that, just like every other grain of sand on the beach, I am a small part of something very big.

you'll see all sorts of other land and marine mammals plus ancient petroglyphs while cruising in their 33-foot boat.

For a really "out-there" experience, try a guided float-and-fish trip on the Uganik River with *Quartz Creek Lodge* (907-654-5449; quartzcreeklodge. com). You'll be flown to Uganik Lake by float plane, then float and fish your way down to the river mouth, where you'll be met by a skiff to ferry you back to the lodge. The lodge rates start at $1,000 per person per day, including airfare from Kodiak city, lodging, meals, use of their equipment, and guide services.

Saltery Lake Lodge (907-350-2646; salterylakelodge.com) offers fishing and photography adventures on Saltery Lake, near Ugak Bay on the eastern side of Kodiak Island. The lodge operates a floatplane and fishing vessel to aid guests in their quests for sockeye, pink, chum, and silver salmon as well as Dolly Varden, rainbow, and steelhead. A canoe is available for exploring the lake. Prices start from $5,200 for a week, with the possibility of staying on additional nights (from $850) *if* availability allows.

No trip to Kodiak is complete without exploring the many bays, inlets, and coves that are home to Alaska's diverse wildlife. And what a safe place from which to view an occasional Kodiak brown bear! In town try *Kayak Kodiak* (907-515-5122; kayakingkodiak.com). They offer group tours of 2 ½ to 3 hours, or a private "guide's choice" option if you have a rental car. If you're heading to Shuyak Island, *Sea Hawk Air* (907-486-8282; seahawkair.com) can get you there and rent you a sea kayak, too.

southwest alaska trivia

The Aleut people are known for producing beautiful handwoven baskets. The baskets come in all shapes but are most often cylindrical with a small knob as a handle. They are made from rye grass and can be ornately woven. The three most common styles of Aleut baskets are named after their islands of origin: Atka, Unalaska, and Attu.

A little farther out is *Spirit of Alaska Wilderness Adventures* (866-910-2327; spiritofalaska.com) a business located on the south end of the already remote Amook Island in Uyak Bay. This company is designed with the independent traveler in mind. Getting there—usually by floatplane, then by boat—will cost the most, and it'll cost you $4,550 for one person to stay for 3 days and enjoy all the kayaking, wildlife viewing, fishing, beachcombing, or whatever else you choose to do, as well as lodging in their bunkhouse. Bring your own food. The price goes down as you stay longer or add people to your party: For example, two guests together costs $3,150 each for 3 days.

For charter fishing try *Kodiak Island Charters* (907-539-8430 or 907-654-9635; kodiakislandcharters.com). They offer full-day, mixed-species charters from $450 plus tax. You may catch halibut, salmon, sea bass, lingcod, and sometimes Pacific cod.

You can also explore by bike. Kodiak is a great place for cycling. Bike rentals are available at *58 Degrees North* (907-486-6249; no website), located at 1231 Mill Bay Road. You can rent bikes by the hour or the day.

For a unique lodging alternative, try the *Cliff House B&B* (907-539-5009; kodiak-wildlife-viewing-kodiak-bnb.com). This B&B looks down on the entrance channel to one of Kodiak's harbors, so you can expect to see all sorts of boats parading by along with a lot of wildlife. The location is close enough to reach downtown by walking along the waterfront, but the seemingly endless views over the water make it feel like you're sitting on the edge of nowhere. They offer a suite and three rooms, starting from $190.

A unique stay is offered at the remote **Zachar Bay Lodge** (907-486-4120; zacharbaylodge.com), a cannery-turned-vacation destination 50 air miles southwest of Kodiak. This family-run business offers fishing and wildlife viewing, modern accommodations, and great meals. Package rates include round-trip airfare from Kodiak, lodging and daily activities, and start from $4,950 per person (double occupancy) for wildlife- and bear-watching, or $5,000 per person (again, assuming double occupancy) for fishing.

A truly remote destination is **Raspberry Island Remote Lodge** (701-526-1677; raspberryisland.com) operated by Birch and Tiffany Robbins. The camp is situated amid an ancient spruce forest that prompts wide-eyed gawking. At the lodge, you'll enjoy fishing, sightseeing, hiking, boating—you name it. Then, at the end of the day, you're on your own to lounge in the camp's hot spa or sauna, relax on the sundeck, or just retreat to your room to relax.

Southwest Alaska facts

Wood-Tikchik State Park is the largest park in Alaska. It encompasses 1.6 million acres of wilderness in Southwest Alaska, near Dillingham.

The Aleutian Chain extends more than 1,100 miles and consists of more than one hundred islands.

Lake Iliamna, on the Alaska Peninsula in Southwest Alaska, is the state's largest lake. It covers 1,000 square miles and is 70 miles long, 20 miles wide, and 1,000 feet deep.

Kodiak became the first capital of Russian America in the late 1700s and was a major fur-trading center for many years.

Kayak Island in the Gulf of Alaska was the site of the first landing of Europeans in Alaska, on July 20, 1741.

Katmai National Park

During the morning of June 1, 1912, a volcanic mountain in what is now **Katmai National Park and Preserve** began a series of violent quakes and eruptions, the likes of which had seldom been recorded in earth's history. A full foot of volcanic ash fell on Kodiak, 100 miles distant, and darkened the sky to inky blackness. When the eruptions subsided, a valley at the site lay buried under 700 feet of ash. In 1916, when the first expedition entered the area, thousands of still-steaming fumeroles inspired the name Valley of 10,000 Smokes. That valley, curiously, remains stark and desolate to this day, though the surrounding area now thrives with lush growth and beautiful lakes and rivers teeming with salmon and other fish. You can visit the park easily, though no roads lead to it. Propeller-equipped aircraft offer daily access from King Salmon (accessible by jet from Anchorage) and less frequent flights are also available from Kodiak.

If you're a photographer, you may want to join an *Expeditions Alaska* (770-952-4549; expeditionsalaska.com) photo tour. With tours that typically allow 4 to 8 days in the area, and groups no larger than eight guests, you'll have time to photograph not only lots of massive brown bears but also other wildlife including seals, sea otters and eagles—and spectacular landscapes, of course. Prices typically range around $8,900 per person for a six-night trip, including all your food, accommodations aboard the 107-foot yacht that will serve as your base camp, as well as guide services and emergency equipment.

Incidentally, if you want to bring a tent and camp in the National Park Service *Brooks Camp* (907-246-3305; nps.gov/katm) near the Brooks Lodge, be advised that reservations are required, as space is limited to sixty campers. Make your reservations online at recreation.gov, or call 877-444-6777.

Katmai Wilderness Lodge (866-938-4560; katmai-wilderness.com), head-quartered in Kodiak and located on Kukak Bay on the eastern coast of Katmai National Park, limits its guest list to twelve visitors a day. The company offers abundant wildlife viewing both ashore and from the water, including brown bears, whales, fox, eagles, seals, sea lions, and sea otters. There are also glacier treks, nature hikes, and kayak trips. The area is especially rich in archaeological resources. A 4-day bear-viewing package from Kodiak costs $5,150; 5 days and 4 nights in a comfortable log cabin, with cook and guide, cost $5,800. Prices include a floatplane trip from Kodiak. For details call (800) 488–8767 or visit www.katmai-wilderness.com.

Unalaska and Dutch Harbor

If you look just at location, *Unalaska* and its adjacent neighbor, *Dutch Harbor,* would seem the most unlikely of tourist destinations, situated as they are out on the Aleutian Chain. The two towns (functionally they're really just one; only a small bridge separates them) lie 800 air miles from Anchorage, about midway along the 1,000-mile Aleutian Islands chain that extends westerly from the Alaska Peninsula almost to Japan.

If you're a true fan of out-of-the-way travel, don't overlook this destination. Unalaska and Dutch Harbor offer a surprising number of pleasurable places to see, lots of things to do, and an amazing comfort level. Although no roads or surface highways lead there, the towns enjoy excellent daily air service from Anchorage (via Aleutian Airways) as well as a monthly schedule of summer calls by the Alaska Marine Highway System's passenger and auto ferry **Tustumena,** although the time is coming when the so-called "Rusty Tusty," which is showing its age, will need to be retired or replaced. Traveling aboard the stateroom-equipped ferry is a terrific way to see this part of Alaska. The vessel leaves Homer twice a month, April through September, en route to Kodiak, Chignik, Sand Point, King Cove, Cold Bay, False Pass, and Unalaska. She leaves Unalaska twice monthly, arriving back in Homer 2 days later. One-way fares start at $406 from Homer, meals not included (800-642-0066; ferryalaska.com).

Now for some geography: Unalaska is located on Unalaska Island and Dutch Harbor is situated on Amaknak Island. The bridge that connects them is called the Bridge to the Other Side.

Rich in Aleut, early Russian, and World War II history, Unalaska and Dutch Harbor have become a major bustling seafood landing and processing center in recent years. Together the two towns are in effect the top port in the United States in terms of pounds and value of fish and crab landed. The year-round population totals more than 4,300 residents, and there are thousands of additional commercial fishermen coming and going at all times. Recently the community has enjoyed a small but growing visitor influx, particularly World War II veterans who served in this theater in the 1940s. Many return to see the site of Japanese bombing attacks and the defensive fortifications the U.S. troops built and manned along shorelines and on mountainsides.

Birders come from around the world to see the rare whiskered auklet and other species, and anglers journey here to land world-class halibut and three kinds of salmon.

Accommodations here are more plush than you might imagine for such a remote location. The wonderfully named **Grand Aleutian Hotel** (498 Salmon

Margaret Bay, a Land Rich in History

There's a place in Unalaska that tells much of the story of life in the Aleutians before the white man arrived. The site, in Margaret Bay, is being studied by scientists from around the country. Excavation of the site has revealed the tools and implements used by the Unangan people who inhabited this village more than 6,000 years ago.

Excavations at the site began in May 1996. It revealed remains of several stone-walled semisubterranean houses, as well as tools made of chipped stone, blades, stone lamps, bowls, lebrets, grinders, and pendants. The researchers even uncovered miniature carved masks.

If you're interested in archaeology yourself, you'll probably enjoy the exhibits and impressive archaeological collections of *The Museum of the Aleutians* (907-581-5150; aleutians .org) at 314 Salmon Way in Unalaska.

Way; 907-581-3844; grandaleutian.com), in fact, offers a surprising degree of luxury in its 112 rooms, public areas, and gourmet restaurant, the **Chart Room,** where the chefs make innovative use of locally abundant seafood. The hotel offers rooms starting at $215 for doubles as well as tour packages for sightseers, birders, and sportfishers.

With such excellent commercial fishing in this region, it goes without saying that those who enjoy recreational fishing will have a fine time here. **Keepin It Reel Charters** (907-359-2466; keepinitreelchartersunlimited.com) is one of several outfits offering halibut fishing and sightseeing excursions out of Dutch Harbor.

The **Unalaska Visitors Bureau** can help with other activities in the area (907-581-2616; visit unalaska.org).

Surely the most compelling cultural and historical site is **Holy Ascension Russian Orthodox Cathedral,** constructed 1894–1896. It contains an astonishing 697 documented icons, artifacts, and significant works of art, one of the largest and richest such collections in Alaska. Within the structure, too, are remnants of earlier churches and chapels used in 1808, 1826, and 1853. Most ground tours offer a visit to this historic landmark. Call the visitor bureau at 907-581–2612 for details, or visit unalaska.org.

Other possibilities in Unalaska and Dutch Harbor include nature excursions that focus on wildlife and geological features, marine adventures including World War II shipwrecks, gold-mining claims, sportfishing aboard charter vessels, and visits to a state-of-the-art processing plant. Again, contact the visitor bureau.

Lastly, you'll also want to touch base with the visitor bureau to see who is offering birding tours during your visit. Unalaska is truly a "life list" destination for birders, who come in search of the roughly forty million seabirds who nest in the Aleutians, and the many more millions who migrate through in spring and fall.

southwest alaska trivia

Lake Iliamna, the state's largest lake, is reported to be inhabited by a sea monster. There's speculation that it is either a whale that somehow made its way into the lake in pursuit of salmon (the lake, by the way, supports the world's largest sockeye salmon run) or an oversized sturgeon.

Much of the land on Unalaska, Amaknak, and Sedanka Islands is privately owned by the **Ounalashka Corporation** (907-581-1276; ounalashka.com), an Alaska Native corporation. It asks visitors who want to hike, ski, bike, or camp on this land to first obtain a permit from the corporate office. Permits may be requested by phone, or from the office between 8:00 a.m. and 5:00 p.m., Monday through Friday. The office is located at 400 Salmon Way.

The Pribilof Islands

If you think the Aleutians are "far out," wait until you hear about *St. Paul* and *St. George* Islands in the lonesome middle of the Bering Sea. Located about 800 air miles west-southwest of Anchorage and more than 200 miles north of the Aleutian Chain, the Pribilof Islands are home to fewer than 1,000 people, but—in the summer at least—the islands provide a hauling-out place for an estimated one and a quarter million howling, barking, fighting, breeding, birthing fur seals. In addition, the islands' craggy sea cliffs provide a summer nesting sanctuary for more than two million seabirds (with more than two hundred species represented), some of which you'll see nowhere else in this hemisphere. Add domestic reindeer and fascinating Native Aleut cultures and history, and you have a superb, offbeat travel destination.

It's surprisingly easy to visit the Pribilofs with the help of *St. Paul Island Tour* (888-408-1685; stpaulislandtour.com), which is owned by the local Alaska Native corporation, TDX, and offers 3- to 8-day all-inclusive guided tours. You pay your own airfare, but everything else is handled for you, including meals, accommodations at the King Eider Inn (the island's only hotel), transportation, and daily forays to beaches and cliffs. These trips tend to focus on birding, but you may also have opportunities to sit behind protective blinds at various beaches and view thousands of northern fur seals that congregate here to breed, including bellowing "beachmasters," their "harems," and pups. A 3-day, 2-night tour starts from $2,495 per person, double occupancy. There is a single supplement of $125 per night, and an "en suite" supplement of $75 per night if you don't want to share a bathroom. The 8-day option goes for $3,745.

Nowadays there isn't really a way for casual adventurers to visit St. George, an even smaller island that sits about 40 air miles south of St. Paul. This is the sort of place where you must make arrangements in advance before arriving—otherwise, you literally won't have a place to sleep or eat, because the tourism infrastructure simply does not exist. If tourism to St. George does again get easier in the future, the staff at St. Paul Island Tour are the perfect folks to ask about it.

Ravn Alaska (907-266-8394; ravnalaska.com) operates regular service between Anchorage and St. Paul Island via DeHavilland Dash 8 twin-engine turboprop aircraft; you can expect to share the cabin with about two dozen other passengers. Sticker shock is a common reaction when pricing airfares to and from a location so remote: For example, a round-trip currently costs about $1,500. Weather delays are also common as St. Paul Island is frequently fogged in, so it's a good idea to consult the staff at St. Paul Island Tour about which days you should book your arrival flight for, then budget for extra hotel nights in case you get weathered *in* at the island.

If you already have plans to visit Unalaska, there's one other convenient flight link to St. Paul Island: *Grant Aviation* (flygrant.com) offers three-times-a-week scheduled flights from Dutch Harbor (so basically, Unalaska) to St. Paul. Those flights start at about $250 one way, so they're a lot cheaper than flying back to a hub city like Anchorage, then heading out to the Pribilofs.

Lake Clark National Park

It's probably one of the National Park System's least known and visited parks— but that's one of the things that makes *Lake Clark National Park and Preserve,* across Cook Inlet from the Kenai Peninsula, special. Access is only by air (or water, on the shores of Cook Inlet); you certainly won't find Yellowstone- or Yosemite-type roads and trails within the park boundaries. This is some of the wildest and most breathtakingly beautiful country on earth, with saltwater shores, turquoise blue lakes, steaming volcanoes, and cascading waterfalls that drop from towering mountainsides. Three rivers in the park have been designated National Wild Rivers. You travel in this country by foot, by boat, or by air. Accommodations in the backcountry are tents; either you bring your own or book with an outdoor guiding service that provides everything from fly-in charters to shelter, food, and expertise.

To access Lake Clark you can hop a 1- to 2-hour charter flight from either Anchorage or Homer. Check with *Rust's Flying Service* out of Anchorage (907-243-1595; flyrusts.com), which focuses on guided bear-viewing trips, or *Beryl Air* (907-299-5494; berylair.com) out of Homer, which offers the broadest range of flightseeing and ground exploration tours, starting from about $525 per person for a flight and ground tour of the park. Expect to pay about $1,200 per person for a guided bear-viewing trip from Anchorage, or between $525 and $1,000 per person (depending on the trip) for flightseeing out of Homer. Both of these air services also offer charter flights if you need them to air-taxi you into the park for a backcountry adventure,.

If you're a photographer you may want to join an annual *Van Os Photo Safari* (206-463-5383; photosafaris.com) in Lake Clark National Park. Air transportation from Anchorage, hotel accommodations, meals, tours, and the expertise of a professional wildlife photographer are included in the weeklong tour. Trips are in the $9,000 range and limited to eight guests.

If you want to actually spend some time with your boots on the ground (or paddles in the water), **Port Alsworth** is the primary jumping-off point for exploring the park. There you'll find the **Lake Clark National Park Visitor Center** (907-644-3660; nps.gov/lacl) and the **Tanalian Falls Trail Head,** along with a number of lodges and private airstrips. You can always find air taxis from here to the park, too, At **The Farm Lodge** (907-781-2211; thefarm-lodge.com), the guest cabins all have private bathrooms and running water. They offer day trips (starting from $650 per person for a party of two), and overnight trips (starting from $1,250 per person in a party of two for a 3-day, 2-night stay that includes day tours in the park). Both packages include airfare from Anchorage.

If a lodge stay sounds too cushy, **Alaska's Backcountry Inn** (907-982-3007; alaskasbackcountryinn.com) rents two cabins: one of them easily sleeps four in one queen bed and two loft beds (from $395 plus tax). The other has two queen beds and beautiful views of Lake Clark (from $500 plus tax). The **Wilder B&B** (no phone; wilderbb.wordpress.com; email wilderbnb@gmail.com) sits right on the edge of the woods in Port Alsworth itself and can sleep five to six people per cabin, although the costs (from $350 for one person, $75 each additional person) do add up.

southwestalaskatrivia

Unimak, the first island in the Aleutian Chain, is home to Shishaldin Volcano. Shishaldin has erupted several times over the last two centuries, earning the local name of Smoking Moses and, before that, Pogromni, Russian for "desolation."

Originally established by Carl and Kirsten Dixon of the exceptional **Within the Wild Adventure Company**, the **Redoubt Bay Lodge** (907-776-3340; redoubtbaylodge.com) is under new ownership, but still offers a blend of the rustic, beautiful and exceptional wilderness, located only 50 air miles southwest of Anchorage. This lodge is home to one of the densest bear populations in the state, but bear-viewing is just one of the attractions here. It also excels for fishing, hiking, kayaking, and overall sightseeing. During the season June through August, all-inclusive rates start from $1,950 per person; 2 nights from $3,075; and 3 nights from $3,950. The rate includes float plane transport from Anchorage, gourmet meals, accommodations, and guided trips. You can save about $250 per night if you're coming from North Kenai instead, or you can fly out for a simple day trip of fishing or bear-viewing.

Bethel

The city of **Bethel** and the surrounding Yukon-Kuskokwim Delta country really don't come readily to mind when one compiles a list of Alaska's better known visitor destinations. Located 400 air miles from Anchorage on the banks of the mighty Kuskokwim River, this city of 5,500 mostly Yup'ik residents is primarily a commercial fishing, trading, and government center. None of the Goliaths of the travel industry have offices here. Fact is, there aren't many Davids, either.

But of course that's what attracts a good number of us. That and the community's location about 90 miles inland from the Bering Sea and the mouth of the Kuskokwim River. Bethel sits in the midst of the United States' largest game refuge, the 20-million-acre **Yukon Delta National Wildlife Range.**

The range, incidentally, is one of those places where you really ought not to venture on your own—not, at least, without knowledgeable local advice. Fortunately, such information is readily available. **Papa Bear Adventures** (907-545-1155; pbadventures.com) offers outfitting and transportation services in the Bethel Area and can get you set up for unguided fishing, floating, and just about any other adventure you might tackle.

Kuskokwim Wilderness Adventures (907-545-4092; kuskocharter.com), owned by lifelong Bethel residents Pete and Bethany Kaiser, is another good resource if you're looking for river travel. They offer custom charters and river tours, and rafting pickups.

Make sure you include the **Yupiit Piciryarait Cultural Center** and its **museum** (401 Chief Eddie Homan Highway; 907-543-8561) and **gift shop** in your itinerary. The center celebrates Yup'ik culture and is an important gathering place for cultural events, while the museum is chock full of art, artifacts, tools, and household items from the past and present. There's a full-size kayak, complete with a realistic paddler in it, paddle, grass mat, ice pick, and other accessories. You also will find a mounted musk ox head and cape on the wall, mounted birds of the region, dolls, grass baskets, ivory work, and beaded items. The gift shop is well-stocked with beautiful craft items.

There are several hotel and B&B accommodations in Bethel, among them the **Sleepy Salmon Bed & Breakfast** (907-543-2519; sleepysalmon.net), which offers three rooms. Prices for one person start from $200 with a shared bath and full bed, $210 for a shared bath and queen bed, or $225 for the Kuskokwim Room with a private bath and full bed. The fee for additional people is $75 each. Your stay includes a continental breakfast and free WiFi, although travelers are sometimes disappointed to find that rural Alaskan WiFi usually isn't anywhere as fast as what you'd expect in a city. A second, if less-homey, option is the **River House Hotel** (907-543-3552; riverhousehotelbethel.com), whose rooms start at $220 for a full or twin bed and private bathroom, single occupancy. Your stay includes access to a self-catering–style community kitchen.

When it comes to food, it's important to adjust your expectations to match the possibilities in a rural area like this. Ingredients are expensive, which reflects in the food prices, and it's very common to see a mix of cuisines at the same place. With that said, some of the best places to look for a meal include the long-standing local institution *Snack Shack* (520 Third Avenue; 907-543-2218; no website), which offers good Chinese food and a selection of burgers; *UnCommon Pizza* (401 Chief Eddie Hoffman Highway; 907-543-1307; uncommonpizza.com), which feels like a chill sports bar with wings, pizza, sandwiches, and burgers to match; and *The Three Tortillas* (401 Ridgecrest Drive; 907-545-1917; no website), which is the only dedicated Mexican restaurant in the area.

southwest alaska trivia

Bethel is one of the westernmost communities in Alaska. It began as a mission in 1889 when Moravian missionaries came to "tame" the people. In keeping with its Godly ambitions, the community became known as "Bethel," which comes from the biblical passage Genesis 35:1, "Arise, go up to Bethel, and dwell there."

Places to Stay in Southwest Alaska

BETHEL

River House Hotel
600 First Avenue;
907-543-3552;
riverhousehotelbethel.com.
Practical rooms with a community kitchen.

Sleepy Salmon Bed & Breakfast
214 Akiak Drive;
907-543-2519;
sleepysalmon.net.
Three homey rooms, one with a private bath.

KATMAI NATIONAL PARK AND PRESERVE

Brooks Camp
Near Brooks Lodge;
907-246-3305;
nps.gov/katm.
Reservations required.

Katmai Wilderness Lodge
Eastern coast of Katmai
National Park;
866-938-4560;
katmai-wilderness.com.
Remote, all-inclusive adventuring.

KODIAK

Best Western Kodiak Inn
236 Rezanof Drive;
907-486-5712;
bestwestern.com.
Chain hotel but with quirky personality.

Cliff House B&B
1223 Kouskov;
907-539-5009;
kodiak-wildlife-viewing
-kodiak-bnb.com.
Great views of a busy harbor.

Quartz Creek Lodge
907-654-5449;
quartzcreeklodge.com.
Central location in Kodiak Island.

**Raspberry Island
Remote Lodge**
On Raspberry Island outside
Kodiak;
701-526-1677;
raspberryisland.com.
Rustic luxury, with
unexpected amenities like
hydroelectric power and hot
tubs.

Saltery Lake Lodge
1516 Larch Street;
907-350-2646;
salterylakelodge.com.
Fishing and hunting
adventures in a remote
location.

Zachar Bay Lodge
50 miles southwest of
Kodiak;
907-486-4120,
zacharbaylodge.com.
A cannery-turned-vacation
destination.

LAKE CLARK AREA

Redoubt Bay Lodge
907-776-3340,
redoubtbaylodge.com.
Handcrafted lodge and
cabins near the eastern end
of the park. Great bear-
viewing opportunities.

PORT ALSWORTH

**Alaska's
Backcountry Inn**
907-982-3007;
alaskasbackcountryinn.com.

Two cabins; one has views
of Lake Clark.

The Farm Lodge
907-781-2211;
thefarmlodge.com.
Cozy guest cabins with
running water.

Wilder B&B
no phone,
wilderbb.wordpress.com.
Perfectly poised right on the
edge of the woods.

UNALASKA

**Grand Aleutian
Hotel**
498 Salmon Way;
907-581-3844;
grandaleutian.com.
Upscale accommodations.

Places to Eat in
Southwest Alaska

BETHEL

Snack Shack
520 Third Avenue;
907-543-2218.
Good Chinese food and a
selection of burgers.

The Three Tortillas
401 Ridgecrest Drive;
907-545-1917.
The only dedicated Mexican
restaurant in the area.

UnCommon Pizza
401 Chief Eddie Hoffman
Highway;
907-543-1307;
uncommonpizza.com.
A chill sports bar vibe with
pizza, wings, burgers, and
sandwiches.

KODIAK

El Chicano
202 Rezanof Drive West;
907-486-6116.
Tasty Mexican food.

**Harborside Coffee
and Goods**
210 Shelikof Avenue;
907-486-5862;
harborsidecoffeekodiak
.com.
Friendly, comfortable
coffeehouse.

Java Flats
11206 Rezanof Drive West;
907-487-2622;
javaflats.com.
Great breakfast and lunch
options plus baked goods.

UNALASKA

**Chart Room
at the Grand
Aleutian Hotel**
498 Salmon Way;
907-581-3844;
grandaleutian.com.
Freshly caught, local
seafood.

Indexes

General Index

Museums Index

National and State Parks Index

Explore More

GLOBE PEQUOT IS YOUR GUIDE to special places, focusing on local pride close to home and helping you discover new destinations to explore from coast to coast. We publish books about iconic people and places, tapping into regional interest, history, cooking and food culture, folklore and the paranormal – all the things that make each region unique. With more than 75 years in publishing, we strive to give you the most up-to-date, regional information by local experts.

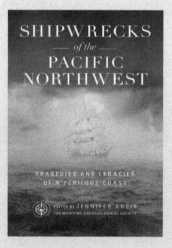

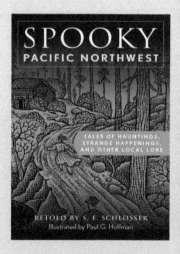

Globe Pequot

Available wherever books are sold.
Orders can also be placed at www.GlobePequot.com,
ne from 8:00 A.M. to 5:00 P.M. EST at 1-800-462-6420 ext. 3024,
or by email at orders@nbnbooks.com.